Rising

FROM THE

DEAD

Suzanne Humphries, MD

Rising From the Dead

ISBN-10: 0692648186

ISBN-13: 978-0692648186

Dedication

You have turned for me my mourning into dancing;
You have put off my sackcloth and clothed me with gladness,
To the end that my glory may sing praise to You and not be silent.
O LORD my God, I will give thanks to You forever.

~ Ps 30:11-12

Contents

Introduction
The Walking Dead?

I was among the 'walking dead' for many years. Fortunately the homing device that every human has, never stopped sending out signals and waiting for a response. After many course corrections, I finally reached my destination—to start a new journey. It's been an interesting and adventurous ride.

Certain types of dissatisfaction can be helpful and in some ways, so can unhappiness. Why? Because those sentiments have the capacity to usher in change in a person's life. In the midst of my dispiritedness, others were traveling the same path. Surveys today reveal that around 50% of doctors would like to leave the profession and nearly half would not recommend it to their children or friends. Doctors want more time to spend with each patient to be able to practice rational, individually tailored medicine, rather than being forced to order a pre-selected set of tests expected of them. They are tired of the demands placed on them by the conveyor-belt type of 'best practice' protocols dictated by insurance companies and so-called health experts. Despite their despondency, most doctors will not leave. They will be medically manacled by huge debt, or if they have paid that off, will bide their time, riding the cash wave as indemnity for the lack of gratification. I surfed the cash wave for a few years, but it was not sufficient propitiation for my soul.

This book was written to show how the medical system takes the brightest of students, the cream of the crop—and turns them into trained technicians, slowly killing commonsense and their hopes of seeing lasting cures. The training dampens their initiative and traps them in blinkered thinking patterns, beneath a dangling guillotine of huge student loans, which hang over their necks indefinitely.

Medical training leads doctors into one of two factions. The first one contains the happy automatons, content to ride the money wave. The other group is a well-kept secret; a clan of empty shells harboring the frustrated walking dead. At such an inference, most of them will not thank you because they don't even know they are dead. If you try to revive them, they might punch you in the face.

Just maybe this book will help people understand why patients feel unheard, and how difficult, but rewarding, it is for a doctor to come alive.

I came into the world on the 31st of May, 1964 just one year after the measles vaccine was released for mass injection. The public lauded the new vaccine and accepted it without question. In 1967, when I was three, there were numerous announcements from the highest levels of the Department of Public Health of the United States Government, that measles was going to be eradicated that year.[1] I had the vaccine two years later because measles was still not eradicated.

In the year I started medical school, 1989, there were 18,193[2] cases of measles in the USA. My second year, there were 27,786 cases prompting an additional MMR dose to be added to the childhood vaccine schedule. In 1993, I became a medical doctor.

Because I was vaccinated at age five, instead of having natural measles, a nurse at every medical center I've ever worked at, has pursued me to get another MMR jab. Why? Because measles was never eradicated from the USA in the most highly vaccinated population the earth has ever seen . . . even 49 years after it was supposed to be.

---

[1] Sencer, D. J., et al., 1967 "Epidemiologic basis for eradication of measles in 1967," *Public Health Reports*, Mar;82(3):253-256. PMID: 4960501

[2] MMWR, Centers For Disease Control, *Current trends in measles*, June 07, 1991/40(22);369-372

1

December 2000
Desolation

Tears rolled down my father's cheeks. What a shock. My father—
'John Wayne'—the tough guy who never cried, lay there, and
suddenly his face creased up. Out of the blue, this staunch cowboy
of a man repeated again and again, with closed eyes, "I don't want
to die, I don't want to die." So we did what most people do to
terminally ill people whose bodies are totally riddled with cancer,
and told him he would be in heaven; which people would meet him,
and watched as he calmed down, then bang.

The truck stopped and the driver got out and walked on.

Agonal breathing started immediately, as his body wound down
reacting to 'central control' having left. The one person I most loved
in my whole life—who had supported me through thick and
thin, whose joking warmth could make the worst situation turn
out okay—was gone. What was left there was the empty wrapper. I
lay across his bed weeping and sobbing until everything inside me
was empty.

At the funeral home, my colleagues from Cooper Hospital tried
to support me, but nothing could help at that time. I couldn't
bear to do the eulogy, and only found the strength to read a
poem written by Khalil Gibran. The next week off work was a
total fog of nothingness, and the first week back at work was
spent on autopilot.

Everything sucked. Looking back, so many events had culminated to this point of grayness.

Two years as an assistant professor in the Philadelphia area had been intellectually satisfying. The daily meetings with other professors who were more experienced, and teaching postgraduate fellows who were just beginning a nephrology career, was a treasure trove of challenging and interesting cases. The weekly meetings with the pathologist to review biopsy findings, weekly grand rounds, and daily morning reports with the nephrology team, had given me a few years to really hone my skills rather than feel that I would be treating patients in the dark. There was always someone to brainstorm with.

These two years had shown me some very harsh truths. Costs of living in Philadelphia were too high to do all the things I hoped to do after being a practicing physician. In 1998, the half-million dollars of student loans were now due for monthly payments of 2,700 USD per month. My salary was such that it wasn't possible to either make ends meet financially, or even enter the housing market from the bottom. Part of that was my fault, because out of naïvety I had accepted the job, not realizing that, salary-wise, I was being shafted.

This only dawned on me in 1999, when I scrolled through available jobs, and saw what the rest of the nephrologists were earning. I was not upset because I had learned so much and now felt secure enough to fly solo. Before Dad died, I had lined up a possible job interview for a better paying job that still involved teaching opportunities.

Change was needed in more ways than one. Life was desolate and gray with Dad gone, and my huge student-loan debt was growing by the day. Now was the time to move on.

2 Getting Made

January 2001. Holding onto the contents of my stomach as we lurched from turbulence to turbulence, breaking through the clouds, an amazing sight greeted me. Snow, coastline, marching forests of green trees in all directions, small towns . . . the middle part of the state of Maine, which was the complete opposite to Philadelphia. Step onto the tarmac and into a tiny airport with two conveyor belts. No chance of getting lost here! By my second trip, the desk attendant knew me by name.

"Dr. Humphries?" a voice boomed out. The cab driver signaled me over and put my luggage in the trunk, then crossed the boring flatlands of Bangor's strip mall district, to a hotel where I spent the night.

Stepping into the building of Northeast Nephrology the next morning, was wonderful; nice, clean, modern architecture, with a fantastic view overlooking a freight train track, and an iced-over Penobscot river.

Dr. P., the founder of the practice 30 years before, introduced himself. "One thing you'll learn about me," said Dr. P. . . . very . . . slowly, "is that I do everything slow. I talk slow, I write slow, I think slow, and I walk slow." Yet it quickly became clear that this highly intelligent man was very precise and absolutely meticulous in his clinical analysis. He is one of those people that everyone automatically loves and probably doesn't have an enemy in the world. He exemplifies 'salt of the earth'.

His slow approach was the mark of careful thought processes. Dr. P. had once been a dentist on a cutter in the Southern Hemisphere; extracting teeth out of sailors strapped to the operating table. He had paid for his medical school tuition from his previous earnings as a farmer.

On the other hand, the next doctor down the time line hierarchy was best described as Dr. Mediumspeed; very sincere, thoughtful, and thorough in everything he did. Dr. Mediumspeed's education was at top medical schools, and he was a very lovely man. With both of them, their word was as good as gold.

Northeast Nephrology was in need of a high-quality associate. It was clear they wouldn't settle for less than their goal. I was interviewed by the nurses, and pretty much everyone except the local flora and fauna. They made it plain that they wanted to check me out thoroughly to make sure I was as good as I seemed.

In March, some paperwork arrived requesting a return visit in April for a contract settlement, and to start the licensing applications and find lodgings.

April is what Mainers call mud season. Slushy snow everywhere, and rain from every direction turns the ground to muck. Everyone wears rubber shoes so as not to wreck footwear. Northern Maine offered an excellent salary to cost-of-living ratio. I was handed a signing bonus check for 20,000 USD for use towards a new mortgage on my first house. The real estate agent picked me up in her Jeep Grand Cherokee, which sat high over the muddy ground.

The owners of the third house we went to see were not around that weekend. I stepped out of the Cherokee, walked around the property, and just knew. The feel; the look from outside; its location next to the river bank—everything had my name written on it. I didn't even get to see inside. As soon as the house was on the market, for 220,000 USD, I obtained the mortgage, and became the occupant of a house that would have cost millions in any major USA city.

My large modern 'castle' had a huge wall of windows and 2,200 square feet of inside footage, surrounded by multi-tiered outside decking the size of a large suburban backyard. The rock gardens required almost no maintenance, and a hiking/skiing trail starting at my back door, led to the city four miles away. With a long winding driveway leading off the street, my parcel of land was 2.2 acres and had no visible neighbors.

A path from the house led to a riverbank with nothing but wilderness on the other side. Some days, I would sit in the living room watching fox walk in the snow in winter and mother fox with fluffy babies in spring, or an eagle eating a whole snake on the branch of a tree. Gray herons, beavers, deer, and wild flowers thrived all around.

My nephrology partners had started the nephrology program based at the tertiary care teaching hospital. They were very kind gentlemen and more than happy to have me on board. Dr. P. was 'slow', Dr. Mediumspeed was 'medium', and I was 'fast', and we made a great team.

The practice covered the territory east of Bangor, Maine, out to the ocean, west to the New Hampshire border and northward to Canada. The kidney disease population rapidly increased over the next 10 years. By the time I left, we were covering five busy dialysis units, two hospitals, and a busy outpatient practice.

In the 10 years I spent there, I worked with six different nephrologists: all top-notch doctors who had high ethical, academic, and work standards. I got on great with my medical partners, and loved my staff and patients. We spent time with our patients: scheduling up to 90 minutes with a new patient and up to one hour with a follow-up if necessary. We chose a good lifestyle over greed, and as a result took nine weeks of vacation per year, Mondays off after being on call for the weekend, and all standard holidays were days off. My annual salary ranged from 160,000 to 300,000 USD over those years. That was a lot of money for Maine, and because there was always plenty of extra cash flowing, the huge student loans that had hung over me like a weight about to fall on my head, were paid off eight years into the job.

My trained therapy dog Henry was a daily part of the workday. He patrolled his permitted areas in the dialysis units, office, and hospital, giving both patients and staff his version of appreciation. Everyone adored him and he loved the stimulation and affection he received back from everyone.

Finally, I had it made. My dream job was so wonderful, that it was hard to believe. I used to have nightmares that I was no longer working there in the future, and was always so happy to wake up and realize it was not real. Never would I have thought that the day would come when of all things, the bad dream came true . . . by my own choosing.

In 2009, a series of events within the hospital turned my thinking and my world upside down. My primary passion from the very start of medical school, had always been the safety, welfare, and health of my patients, something I was now ordered to compromise. I sat back, looked at the choices and decided that my loyalties must lie with my patients, not policy. What sense did it make to turn my back on good medicine and patient wellbeing, or compromise my standards? In response, the policy makers isolated me, as well as putting me under helicopter observation for the next two years. I felt betrayed and duped. Even worse, patients were suffering and there was nothing I could do about it.

As I considered these circumstances, and reviewed many events in my training from the wisdom of hindsight, I saw very clearly that the medicine I was now being told to practice, was a far cry from the medicine I had envisaged the day I began medical school.

Every day, I was caring for people suffering from conditions they might not have endured if medical students had been taught a kind of medicine that heals, rather than methods which, at best, buys a person time and, at worst, kills them before their rightful end.

Pig In A Poke

Have you ever bought something, trusting that what was in the package was exactly what you paid for, only to later look more closely and realize that you had been duped? To me, that is a pig in a poke.

Before the winter of 2009, I never questioned the idea that vaccines were safe and the best way to prevent diseases. I gave vaccines, paid for the goods and never thought to look in the bag, until there was a reason to examine the contents thoroughly.

The H1N1 pandemic swine flu was supposedly going to kill millions in the year 2009 so, in addition to the seasonal flu vaccine, a separate swine flu vaccine was given. There was a shortage of the swine flu vaccine and so it was only given to those most at risk.

One Monday after picking up the weekend service, a hospital inpatient with kidney failure got very grumpy with me. Seeing him in the middle of his dialysis treatment, I'd asked the usual questions, like "And how long have you been on dialysis?" and the man exploded. "I've never been on dialysis! I never had anything wrong, until they gave me that shot." . . . Working up a lather he almost yelled . . . "I was fine until I had that vaccine!" Taken aback, I asked, "What vaccine did you get? When did you get it, and how do you know your kidneys were fine before?" Apparently he'd told his story to everyone, but had been blown off. Now, he was startled that anyone was even asking sensible questions. So he tumbled the whole story out. After a very thorough investigation and a fine-tooth-combed patient history analysis, which did indeed reveal that his kidney function was perfectly normal a month before, I decided that his words and beliefs had merit. That event is forever burned into my memory, because the words spoken marked the first of many similar stories to come. Or perhaps it would be more accurate to say that, for the first time, I was prepared to hear an unpalatable truth.

After the first man with kidney failure, I began asking other people, with unusual case presentations, whether or not they had been recently vaccinated. Some would become wide-eyed after the question, as if they too had never considered any connection, but in others, the light dawned and after picking up their jaws, they often replied, "YES, it was shortly after that!" Sure enough, the records would show the time relationship. Sometimes violent sickness began on the very day. This entire story has been recorded and is on YouTube in a video I called *Honesty vs. Policy* and it details several of these cases.

After three people came in with fulminant kidney failure, temporally related to vaccination, I thought it prudent to bring the cases to the attention of the hospital chief of medical staff. Upon passing him in the hallway, we stopped for the usual cordial robotic small talk: "Hello. How are you? How is the practice going? Are you happy here?" To which the answer for the previous seven years had been "Great. Great and yes!" But this time I had news! "We have a problem. I've seen three cases of kidney failure in adults shortly after they were vaccinated and two of the three told me they were fine until the vaccine. All of them had documented normal kidney function within two months of the vaccine. What do you think?"

After a short silence, I got to know a different side of this man. Perhaps he could also say he got to know a different side of me. His immediate response was, "It was not a vaccine reaction. They just got the flu and the vaccine didn't have time to work." The problem was that none of the three even had flu-like symptoms. Why did he automatically jump to that conclusion? It is true that even less than once in a blue moon, influenza infection all by itself can lead to interstitial nephritis and kidney shut down. I'd never treated a case of flu-related kidney failure in all my years of practice as a very busy nephrologist in large tertiary care centers. But I had seen many cases of kidney failure from all sorts of viral illnesses, which had been made worse from fever-reducing anti-inflammatory drugs and dehydration. None of that had happened with these three cases. What sort of a coincidence would it be, for three people to be admitted in a very short period of time with acute kidney failure after a flu vaccine—with no flu symptoms, and . . . be told that the problem was influenza? Ridiculous.

After these three outpatient cases, I began to ask all my patients, "When was your last vaccine?"

Around this time, I admitted a patient of mine for a kidney biopsy. I came to write the admitting order 45 minutes after she arrived, and saw that she had been given a flu shot before I got there, with an order that had my name on it. I hadn't ordered it, so I asked the nurse how this could be. Astonishingly she said that it was now policy for the pharmacist to put a doctor's signature on the order if the patient gave consent. They were very efficient that day. Usually it could take forever to get an IV infusion set up, yet suddenly vaccines were given immediately on arrival. While the first problem for me was that I didn't order the vaccine, the second was that the policy extended to ALL admissions, even if they had sepsis or worsening cancer, or were having a heart attack or stroke. A third problem was that there was no realization that a vaccine, or two, might make it more difficult for a clinician to subsequently work out what the problems were caused by, and correctly diagnose and treat the patient. Plainly, there was no consideration as to the utility, benefit, or detriment of a flu shot, to any seriously, acutely ill patient.

As time went on, inpatient consults became quite revealing because we could track the kidney function from normal or slightly impaired, to failed after a vaccine was given on admission. A revolution was now taking place in my thinking. Not just about orders being given using my unauthorized signature, but also, how medicine was taught to us, practiced, and the priorities of those higher up on the ladder, whom up until now, I had thought were interested in accurate diagnoses, and getting sick people well.

In the past when I was consulted on kidney failure cases and said, "Oh that was the statin/antibiotic/diuretic that did that!" instantly the drug would be stopped—no questions asked. Now, however, a new standard was applied to vaccines. It didn't matter that the internist's notes in the charts said, "No obvious etiology of kidney failure found after thorough evaluation." It didn't matter that I considered the vaccine a possible cause when all other potential culprits had been eliminated. It was never the vaccine. The collective mindset said, with glazed-over eyes, "Vaccines? Not possible or likely."

As for the average doctor, what reason would they have to consider that a vaccine could provoke an unintended consequence that might add another layer to whatever reason the person came to the hospital for? Most doctors haven't a clue what is in a vaccine. They don't understand the raging inflammatory storm that vaccines incite, how vaccines are made, or which part of the immune system is ramped up after flu vaccines. Because of what they are told, most doctors simply believe that if you are a good citizen you get vaccinated as a doctor, and you get as many flu shots into your patients as possible, for the sake of herd immunity. Doctors just do as they are told from on high. End of story. Up until 2009, so had I.

When I was discussing the issue one day on a cardiology ward, a cardiologist who knew me well, approached me with wide eyes. He was horrified, thinking he was behind on the latest recommendation. He said "Wait! Are we not supposed to be giving flu shots? I have been brow-beating my patients into flu shots whenever possible!" I explained the situation I witnessed and he listened. He also had never considered a vaccine to be a potential danger in any way. Whether or not he has since changed his thinking, or his practice at all, I don't know. What was telling to me, was that all he wanted to know was what he had missed. He was not interested in thinking it out on his own. He was far too busy for that. He just wanted to know if he missed anything of 'importance', so that he could be a good, correct doctor. Kind of like the student who only wants to know what will be on the exam, but not how to think about how that information might fit into the bigger picture.

Several months went by, and the medical executive committee met to discuss my concerns, without allowing me to be present at the meeting. I was informed in writing that the nursing staff were becoming confused by me discontinuing orders to vaccinate and that I should adhere to hospital policy. I thought this odd, given that nurses are not accustomed to giving the same treatment to every patient, and are fully capable of reading individualized orders.

The next time the medical chief of staff and I met in the corridor, an oncologist was present. At one point, I asked the chief, "Why doesn't anyone else see the problem here? Why is it just me? How can you think all this is okay? Why is it now considered normal to vaccinate very sick people on their first hospital day?" The oncologist gave an answer that surprised me. She said, "Medical religion!" and turned and walked away. That was a strange outburst from her because in the months that followed, I watched her continue marching down the aisle of medical religion—not only with her own health issues that she shared with me, but also with her cancer patients. It just goes to show how easy it was for good doctors to see some problems in the medical system, yet be blinded by what they were taught was best practice. She undoubtedly thought her only option for certain medical issues was the hammer and nail approach. I suffered similar blindness, and at times felt that I was looking through thick lace until I began to understand more and more of the bigger picture.

Getting back to the pig in the poke . . . I looked deeper into the poke, because I was forced to—but ONLY after I realized that what I thought I purchased with my medical education, was not complexity of thinking or even complete analysis of science, but rote training, and reactive responses.

A good doctor researches fact. My research turned up a mass of medical articles about kidney failure related to influenza and other vaccines, and reasons to suspect that vaccines could also be causing many of the other diseases commonly labeled as 'idiopathic'. I was shocked at the potential scope of the damage I had previously brushed off because of lack of education. Like my colleagues, I had considered many vaccine reactions to be coincidences. Auto-immune diseases and kidney diseases requiring harsh immune-suppressive drugs are not unheard of, after vaccines. Nowhere in medical school, internship, residency, or fellowship, had kidney failure after vaccines been discussed. Why not? Only between 1-10% of vaccine reactions are ever reported and far fewer will make it into medical journals as case reports, yet these case reports were easy to find. To this day, the case reports are mounting.

I wrote all the cases out and put together a comprehensive brief for the hospital administration, but to no avail. Not even science could get through as the snake-oil salesmen continued to deny my findings. It was obvious from their lack of research, automaton responses, and patch-protecting behavior, that this pig in the poke I had bought into, was actually a serpent. By this time, I wasn't listening to the snake-oil smooth talk. I could see with my own eyes now, that the threat from the snake's venom was no longer a matter of debate.

As time went on, it was interesting seeing the divide in the hospital staff. Nurses would bail me up in quiet corners and tell me stories that completely backed up what I was seeing. They would guardedly support me, when their superiors were out of eye- or ear-shot. A deeper respect was building between those who could see what I saw, while an icy wind roared from those on high.

I kept presenting the administration with facts they could not respond to, in the hope that they would get a blinding revelation of the obvious. Finally, they recruited the Northeast Healthcare Quality Foundation, the "quality improvement organization" for Maine, New Hampshire, and Vermont, to get me off their backs. Dr. Lawrence D. Ramunno sent a letter invoking the fallacy of authority, which adamantly informed me that hospital vaccination against influenza virus would become a global measure for all admissions in 2010, and **that my evidence of harm was not significant because 10 professional organizations endorse vaccination**.

This condescending, vapid letter was worse than the snake that I now saw, which had eaten the pig in the poke. It illustrated callous disregard of clinicians at the highest level, and the willful blindness prepared to ignore clearly documented cases, and their own medical literature. Not satisfied with demanding that I practice automaton obedience to dictates from on high, they initiated a shadow observation, where everything I did and wrote in the hospital, from then on, was observed and scrutinized.

This unscientific and unprofessional harassment only served to reinforce my decision to leave no policy unquestioned, ever again. It could be that people who conceal the full story in one poke may present equally vacuous information in other policies. For the first time in my career, I was belittled for presenting rational science-based arguments that questioned ignorance, while the administration arrogantly and irrationally defended the indefensible.

In 2009, I understood the limited efficacy of influenza vaccines. Any clinician with eyes could see that flu vaccines were a flawed, blunt weapon. Now today's pro-vaccine scientists publish articles revealing, in great detail, how flu vaccines are ineffective and why they limit the body's ability to fight infections by stopping CD8 activation.[3,4,5] Part of their rationale in detailing the flaws of today's vaccines, is to justify applying for grant money to develop a new generation of patented, 'better' flu vaccines.[6]

But vaccines that damage the body's ability to fight infections, by stopping CD8 activation, are a total violation of every sick person's potential recovery in the hospital. Any vaccine that interferes with a sick person's immune system during a serious medical event can create another crisis, which can cloud the diagnostic ability of the clinician and will usually just be brushed aside as bad luck.

Who, other than the owner of the goose that lays the vaccine golden eggs, could have convinced the hospital administration to agree to vaccinate a person in the middle of a heart attack, just as they are wheeled into the hospital? Why is it, that what I still consider to be medical malpractice, scientific nonsense, and potential murder, was allowed to become irrevocable hospital policy?

Ten years after signing my Maine contract, I left the practice in good standing, to study and later to try to bring to my patients the kind of medicine that could offer a potential lasting cure; the kind of medicine I thought I had signed into medical school to learn.

---

[3] Bodewes, R., et al., 2011 "Annual vaccination against influenza virus hampers development of virus-specific CD8[+] T cell immunity in children," *Journal of Virology*, Nov;85(22):11995-12000. PMID: 21880755

[4] Bodewes, R., et al., 2012 "Pediatric influenza vaccination: understanding the T-cell response," *Expert Reviews of Vaccines*, Aug;11(8):963-71. PMID: 23002977

[5] Hayward, A. C., et al., 2015 "Natural T Cell-mediated Protection against Seasonal and Pandemic Influenza. Results of the Flu Watch Cohort Study," *American Journal of Respiratory and Critical Care Medicine*, Jun 15;191(12):1422-31. PMID: 25844934

[6] Skibinski, D. A., 2013 "Enhanced neutralizing antibody titers and Th1 polarization from a novel Escherichia coli derived pandemic influenza vaccine," *PLoS One*, Oct 18;8(10). PMID: 24204639

The kind of medicine that ironically earns the doctor a label—quack.

The pages that follow, detail how a true medical skeptic is born.

Most of those who religiously believe in all that conventional medicine offers, look at me and think I have a screw missing, if not several. But the reality is that I am a product of extensive education from within the medical system. I was a shining star within the system, and I could have remained a shining star inside the system. But because my focus was always the welfare of my patients and making a real difference, I rejected any limit or policy placed on me that made no medical sense.

Too much of what we erroneously call 'medicine' is about using reductionist thinking to maintain a mirage of miraculous perfection. Inside this poke, if you dare to look—you will find overwhelming evidence that the medical system is not really about health, science, or truth.

Core to its survival is political policy, which puts payment, and profit, before the patient's best interests. I didn't know that the medical system operated this way in 1981 when I sat in high school thinking, "What am I going to do with my life?" Although I started out eager-eyed, and raring to go, I was as naïve as a tadpole in a pond.

Shattering The Crystal Ball

My parents decided to send me to a private Catholic high school about 30 minutes from our home. Knowing nothing about public schooling, I went without argument. There were two tracts in high school; one for those who wanted to have university as an option and one for those who didn't. I chose the college preparatory tract to keep my options open, because I didn't have a clue what I wanted to do for the rest of my life.

As a child, I prayed in earnest over my rosary and I loved God.

My belief waned through 12 years of Catholic school and weekly (sometimes daily) mass. Catholicism designates the power to priests, the pope, and the church. I'd seen too many Catholics do and say things that I knew the 'Jesus' they called their savior and prototype, would never have condoned; for instance the sexual activities of priests overlooked or even successfully shielded from the public eye—so long as they don't get married! I saw enough discrepancies and widespread hypocrisy to make me bitter and angry. The Bible started to look like nothing but a storybook of dubious patriarchal origins. It had the occasional helpful moral lesson about life with stories tossed in, illustrating humanity's ugly face and the tendencies people had when left to their own choosing.

Just looking at the saint whom my primary school was named after, St. Joan of Arc, told me as much as I wanted to know about the Roman Catholic Church. Eugenius IV condemned Joan of Arc to be burned as a witch and heretic, but she was beatified by Pius X in

1909 and canonized by Benedict XV in 1920. Today her image is one of a 'national heroine' inside France's Notre Dame Cathedral. Popes are supposed to be infallible, right? So how could an infallible pope condemn a saint to death and then another infallible pope beatify her? And worse, none of this was ever discussed in any of our lessons.

The early years of Catholic school indoctrination and later watching their walk not match the talk, led to dismay.

While as a child, I had once thought that God created everything and that Jesus was God incarnate, I didn't think I could fit into the rules that the church said God said I had to adhere to. So I became defiant, and rebellious. I took that a step further and reasoned that this ugliness, duplicity, and stupidity seen in Catholicism and humanity proved there was no God, because a loving God could not have possibly allowed ghastly things to happen. The fundamental concept and truth of 'freewill', of God handing over to man the right to make all his own choices with regard to God, himself, the world and all that is in it, never entered my thinking. I became an atheist as soon as I was allowed. By age 18, God was no longer much a part of my thinking.

I didn't have a drive for excellence until I hit university. School was just a matter of effortlessly doing what was expected and earning mostly Bs with the occasional A tossed in. High school sport was far more important to me than academia, so I just did my homework, took my tests, and played school softball, basketball, and field hockey all year long.

At the end of high school senior year, meeting with a guidance counselor was the ritual. Their words were considered the views of an oracle. I had never even met this priest, who apparently had pontifical power over the rest of my lifelong career. Father Phil and I met for about 30 minutes. He reviewed my records and noted that I thrived in sciences, but declared that I would never survive physics. "Nursing is the most suitable option for you Suzanne. It doesn't need physics."

With the snap of his fingers, I allowed him to choose my career. Why he said any of that is a mystery because I had got all Bs in high school physics, even though Mr. Vogel, the classic, emaciated, bachelor, soft-spoken, nerdy physics teacher, and I . . . were not exactly in sync, but we had enough respect for each other to ignore our differences. As a long-legged first baseman and lead hitter, I was offered a partial softball scholarship to the University of Connecticut, but my father thought I would get a better and cheaper education staying local and going to New Jersey's State University. So I took the SAT, applied, and started at Rutgers University in September of 1982.

High school graduation day came and went, and I don't even remember it. Nor do I remember the summer before starting university. But the beginning of university, and what followed, is etched in my brain. The first day. Does anyone forget that? Halfway down a huge tiered auditorium, which seated 200 students, I saw a wild-eyed biology professor frantically writing on all the sliding chalk-

High school graduation

boards, starting with "The Central Dogma" that has since been somewhat undermined by the developing understanding of epigenetics.

It is amazing how so many things in life can come full circle. There were a couple of fun young men in my class named Jake and Elliot. They were best friends since childhood and raised the level of humor in our study group. Because they thought it a good idea to get jobs as nurses' aides in a nursing home, I did too. I quit my two jobs—one as a lifeguard, and the other as a cashier in a Roy Rogers fast-food restaurant, wearing a cowgirl hat and boots, and twanging the obligatory "Howdy partner", "Happy trails", and "Round up your burger", and went and purchased the requisite hospital whites.

Little did I know, that those clothes would wind up coated in every color and smell of body fluid imaginable over the next two years. Aside from the ability to prove the good use of bleach, white never made much sense to me as a hospital uniform color.

Mrs. Peck was the first patient I was put in charge of. A lonely, semi-demented 80-year-old with desperately frightened eyes, she sat in a geri chair staring straight ahead. A massive stroke had resulted in total paralysis on half of her body. Her clothes were impregnated with unidentifiable muck glued into the fabric and she smelled like old food, urine, and feces. She was grateful for every act of gentleness and kindness I gave her. This was before the days when nurses' aides were trained in any formal or even informal way. Later, a more senior aide would come and show me the ropes. I was tossed onto the ward and told to go feed Mrs. Peck. I had fed many babies, so feeding Mrs. Peck was kind of second nature except for the mouth paralysis that meant that food had to be continuously rerouted. I sat patiently and fed her bite after bite, which I would later understand was not something any nursing home patient could count on. When I was finished, and wiped her mouth and neck, she said a slow and resonant "Thannnnk Yoouuuu" and put her head back down on the table. Mrs. Peck had long past given up on life. Such was life and death in Cooper River Convalescent Center.

Next, I looked after Mr. Reed who probably had very late stage multiple sclerosis. He was around 50 years of age, had no teeth, severely contracted limbs and, while his brain was totally fine, he was 100% bedbound. I was introduced to him while he lay naked, on one side getting his sponge bath and bed change. After he was cleaned, his wounds were packed. The smell of infected flesh was new to me, as was seeing full-thickness open bedsores down to the bone. Tendon and muscle were fully visible in at least six areas on the buttocks, sacrum, and arms. In my two years there, those wounds never healed. It wasn't until decades later that I could clearly see how pureed hospital food of dubious quality and lacking core nutrients such as vitamins C, D, and minerals would work against both healing and health restoration. For whatever reason, it didn't (and still doesn't) occur to most rest homes, or even hospitals, that what goes into a person's mouth might be important.

And finally, the incorrigible Mrs. Grimes, who would lie in her bed screaming and yelling. Most of us learned to resent her. Months later, on my shift, she had an epileptic fit and I found her lying unresponsive. Being certified in CPR, I did what I thought had to be done. There was no obvious reason for her unconsciousness, but when I shook her she groaned. Her pulse was rapid and thread-like and she was barely breathing. So I checked the airway, removed her carbohydrate-caked dentures, and gave her a first breath, upon which a trachea of pressurized vomit released, like whale spout, into my mouth. A certified RN came to the room, sighed, and joined me. Apparently, mouth guards had not yet been invented. Our attempts to resuscitate her failed, and that horrific and disgusting experience was all for naught.

I went home totally distraught, and my father was the only person home. He was watching TV when I burst in and interrupted, describing what had happened. He didn't really know what to say, but we sat together on the couch and I'm still glad he was there to tell. Feeling like I would never be clean again, I peeled off the white uniform stained in vomit, brushed my teeth for a very long time, and had a 30-minute shower. There would be many more such nights to come.

Part of being a nurses' aide involved washing and bathing the residents periodically. There was a young married couple who both had Down syndrome and numerous physical restrictions. It was my day to bathe the wife, who was quite a large lady. I rolled her wheelchair into the large disability bathroom but, while transferring her into the bath chair, she had a spastic episode, which threw me off balance and we both went to ground. My ankle was twisted badly. After finding that she was okay, I called for help and we were both scraped off the ground. A soft cast was placed on my ankle for two weeks and it eventually healed. But my lower back was still significantly painful. Logic dictated that I should see a doctor for that, so the osteopath on duty offered to have a look. After about a three-minute assessment, he prescribed a drug I had never heard of, but will never forget. Norgesic Forte: an antispasmodic. It made me so nauseated and sick that I forgot about my lower back. That was my introduction into the pharmaceutical dishing out of drugs that make you feel worse than the problem they are prescribed for.

There were many social and medical learning experiences in those years, matched only by the amount of laughing we all did on breaks and after hours on weekends when I, an RN named Roz, and some of the other aides, would do things together.

Generally speaking, there were two kinds of aides; the black aides who were mostly there as a job for life, and the young white college students who wanted to have a career in the medical field and to get our feet wet . . . literally. Kelly was a beautiful, voluptuous 18-year-old about to embark on a nursing career. Because her father was an oil-field engineer employed in Saudi Arabia, Kelly went to a Saudi school for Western kids. A lot of her stories started with "In Saudi Arabia . . . " and described designer fashions, Ferragamo, Bandolino, Gucci etc., along with prices of shoes I would have never dreamed of. The mystery was, why did this gorgeous woman, with such expensive tastes in clothes, want to become a nurse and work in a nursing home? She later said that she wanted to marry a doctor. My first *"House of God"*[7] experience came second hand via Kelly.

Mrs. S. was a small, elf-faced, high-maintenance patient who lived in her own private room at the end of the hall. We all grew to know her scream from the others, but we also learned that the screeching sounds coming from her room were of no importance. Some patients just naturally grab you by the heartstrings more than others. Mrs. S. didn't tug at any heart cockles. In the eyes of everyone at the home, including the other patients, she was just a demented nuisance whose body refused to die. Kelly found a reason to request Mrs. S. on her duty list after she met her son, James. He was a red-faced, ruddy Irish-looking man, about 55, tall, and gorgeous. Kelly was immediately smitten with him, and after a few days of relentless flirtation, she managed to exchange phone numbers with him and set up a date. Within a week, she described sex with him in positions I didn't know existed. Mrs. S. had acquired an aide who cared more than any other—at least for some hours in the day. I suspect that Kelly eventually found her doctor and married him.

As for *The House of God*, the Fat Man's logic[8] was sound but as I learned later, the male doctor experience is antithetical to the female one.

---

[7] *The House of God* is a satirical novel by Samuel Shem (a pseudonym used by psychiatrist Stephen Bergman), published in 1978. The novel follows a group of medical interns at a fictionalized version of Beth Israel Hospital over the course of a year in the early 1970s, focusing on the psychological harm and dehumanization caused by their residency training. The male interns spent much of their time in different positions with highly sexed nurses.

[8] In *The House of God*, the Fat Man was a senior resident who taught that most of the diagnostic procedures, treatments, and medications received by the elderly patients actually harm instead of helping them. His advice was to do as

After two years, I applied for and secured an evening and weekend front-desk secretarial job at the same nursing home. I'd had quite enough of long hours on my feet, heavy lifting, bizarre social encounters, and all I could take of blood, pus, vomit, urine, and stool. It turned out to be quite a wise move because there was a lot of time to study in the wee hours of the morning and weekends after the phones died down and all the work was done.

Humorous and bizarre experiences did not end at the corridor between the lobby and wards. The residents were allowed to come to the lobby and visit with me or sit in the sunroom. There was a 90-year-old named Mrs. DeFalco who liked to tell the same joke to everyone who entered. I heard the joke so many times I still remember it: "A boy rode his bike by a Catholic church and asked a bystander, "Is mass out?" The lady replied, "No, but your hat is on backwards."

Mrs. DeFalco used to stop each visitor willing to talk to her, sidelining them for as long as she could. When the visitor finally found a segue out, Mrs. DeFalco would turn to me and say, "Boy, what a load of hot air s/he was!"

Olive and Betsy were two elderly but child-like residents who had full-body capacity but extreme dementia. One day they gavotted out to model a new wardrobe invention for me. With gaping smiles and great alacrity, they said, "Hello honey, how are you today?" while spinning around 360 degrees. Perhaps the laundry was a tad behind that day or perhaps the ladies were just overheated, because they had put on their nylon stretch trousers pulled up to mid-trunk, and tucked their breasts inside the waistband, cleverly obscuring the nipples, and abiding by all decency rules even though

---

little touching, testing, and prescribing to them as possible. Sure enough, this tactic was vastly more successful than that of the aggressive female resident named Jo, who was responsible for several deaths upon directing the interns to touch, test, and treat anything possible.

they were completely topless. While suppressing a huge giggle, I informed them that I would call for a nurse to get a shawl for them in case they got a chill.

While the nights were always quiet, days could be either tranquil or animated with streakers bolting out the door towards the river, ambulances going back and forth, and family members visiting and often leaving in tears of anguish.

Even though the work was interesting and important, I could see how difficult a life of employment in such a facility could be. I became even more driven to do really well in university, and for the rest of my student years I wanted the easiest jobs possible in order to be able to study even while at work. There were various cushy jobs like lifeguarding a mostly empty pool and work-study here and there around campus where I managed to get plenty of reading done.

But sometimes money can be enticing. In 1984 when the minimum wage was 3.35 USD, United Parcel Service offered a whopping 8.00 USD per hour for early morning grunt work. I applied and was hired, but only because some friends vouched for me. It turned out that I was probably the smallest and physically weakest person to have ever unloaded UPS tractor-trailers in the middle of the night. The first day on the job started at 4:00 AM sharp with a loud buzzer and ended at 8:00 AM with the second buzzer. Those days were long, and staying awake in calculus class at 9:00 AM was a challenge. Getting up in time was a nightmare, but not as physically nightmarish as the parcel-tossing work. It was non-stop package movement from the trailers to the rolling metal slide, down to the moving belt where the packages were sorted by humans. Bets were placed as to how long I would last, but nobody won. In order to hoist the heavier packages, I had a technique that involved the whole body and created deepening bruises and colors on my thighs and forearms. Eventually I moved up to package sorter, which was a bit more humane, but was still too demanding on my thin frame. I lasted over a year until the pain and bruising was no longer worth it to me. I missed the money, but not the brutal work and early hours before starting school.

By my second year of university, I became more averse to the prospect of being a nurse and taking perfunctory barked orders from a doctor for the rest of my career. Don't get me wrong, as a doctor I gained more respect for nurses and the profession than I ever did in nursing school, because I learned that it was the older, seasoned nurses that would be my best teachers in the early years, and strongest allies later on, when the going got rough. As a doctor, I also treated nurses with the care and respect that I had rarely experienced as a nurse's aide. But the study was boring with little challenge, and I wanted more out of life. So I talked to the anatomy professor for nursing, Dr. Smith, and to my surprise, she said, "Yes you should get out of this."

However, not really knowing which way to go, I wound up in a physics laboratory talking to an older graduate student. He kept telling me enthusiastically that I should major in pure theoretical physics because microprocessor and microchip technology was going to be the big fantastic money-making wave of the future. "This," he said, "is going to be a revolutionary addition to medicine." That sounded interesting and progressive. Because the campus I attended was a relatively small one, the same physics classes were not offered every year, but sometimes once every two years. To hop into the physics major tract, meant taking mechanics and electronics before doing the preliminary course in entry-level physics. I was assured that I could do it; that there would be tutors to help, so I enrolled in the upcoming year's pure theoretical physics track.

A whole new amazing world opened up an appreciation for order, design, and how things work. Advanced biology and organic chemistry were part of the curriculum I chose, in order to keep all later options open. Those courses revealed the intricate inner workings of living things, which never gets boring to me, even today. Physics taught me how to think on something until I saw the answer; to keep delving deeper and go over and over a problem until I arrived at a solution. I've always loved puzzles of any sort, and the coursework for earning a physics degree was the ultimate in puzzle solving.

We had gone through the 'Big Bang' in year one of university, and that seemed rational and fine. I had accepted it blindly with no scientific scrutiny, just as so many atheists and scientists do. But in my fourth year, in electromagnetic theory class, we learnt Fourier analysis, which is a complex mathematical practice that defines periodic waveforms in terms of trigonometric functions.

Simply put, Fourier analysis is the mathematical painting out of invisible energy forms, like audio, radio, light, and seismic motions as they pass through the invisible ether. Looking at the chalkboard where the professor had drawn out a wave and the long mathematical equation that went with it, I was blown over by a deep unshakable knowing that I was totally wrong over my atheism. While many people become atheists as a result of studying science, I had the complete opposite result. It was as if I had heard God whispering "I am everywhere." And I knew that not only is there a creator God, but 'it' is everywhere.

With this in mind, and being what I would have called a feminist then, I decided to find my idea of God outside of any church. After reading Starhawk's *The Spiral Dance* and then *The Fifth Sacred Thing*, I decided to dabble in Wicca for a few years. It was women-centered and I wanted some form of spirituality or God that I could truly feel right about.

There were some intellectually challenging times, but there was never a time when I wanted to quit. If I came to a barrier, I would sit for hours looking at the same problem, until I could see the solution. Figuring out mechanical forces in bridges was really fun, but quantum mechanics stretched my brain just about as far as it could go. Fortunately it didn't need to stretch beyond that to earn my degree.

School wasn't all academia for me, but alongside the play came trouble.

5 Angels In The Dust

When I look back on my graduation photos, I can remember how happy I was to be finally done, after five years and switching majors, going to school all summer, holding at least two jobs all five years, and playing varsity sports. Yay!

Partying was not a big thing for me because I noticed early on that wherever alcohol was, trouble always seemed to follow. My final lesson on the dangers of alcohol came in the fourth year of university.

Our softball team, for which I was the first baseman, was doing well. After a long practice in the spring heat, a few members of the team headed for a bar. I went and ordered a strawberry daiquiri. About an hour into the evening, something changed. I became disoriented and, according to witnesses, I was not making sense. One of my so-called friends thought I was faking whatever was going on and in a stroke of genius decided to toss me out the front door. I fell down four steps. While whatever happened in the bar before that is a blur, I recall everything after falling down the steps as if it was yesterday.

Shock filled my body and I felt like I had to run because I thought something was chasing me. I was very physically fit and took off about a mile up the highway until I got to a racetrack, which was under a total overhaul renovation. Feeling that my pursuer was gaining on me, I decided to scale the surrounding six-foot brick wall with barbed wire at the top. The amount of adrenaline in me must have been astronomical because I had no trouble getting up and over. My skin was ripped all over my hands, arms, legs, and face, yet I felt no pain.

The on-duty patrolman spotted me and came towards me with a flashlight. Thinking he was the pursuer, I again took off and found a place to hide near the bleachers.

Probably because the guard alerted them at first sighting of me, I was quickly surrounded by four police cars with sirens and lights then commanded to give myself up. Because I felt so desperate not to be captured, I had to conjure up an escape plan while being loosely held. I was taking karate lessons in those days so decided to use a back kick into the groin of the officer who had taken hold of me, and took off running again.

Within a few strides, I was toppled by several police who swung their nightsticks at the back of my legs, which crippled me and left me helpless. From here on in, and rightly so, there was no mercy on me. My hands and ankles were cuffed behind my back. I was carried belly down by my elbows and ankles, roughly put into the back of a police car, taken to the local jail, booked, fingerprinted, and my mug shot was taken.

A very calm and polite woman was called in to do the pat down from head to toe and she asked to have my shoelaces. I was then placed into a holding cell until someone came and posted bail, several hours later.

It must have been a relief for the guards to see me go because while in the jail cell I was in a delusional mental film, thinking that I was a freedom fighter, and singing the Steven Biko song over and over. Apart from the ludicrousness of the situation, I'm tone deaf, so what came out of my mouth probably sounded like cats fighting.

The following morning I woke up and felt the full throbbing force of all my injuries. My shoulders had been badly stretched beyond their capacity and my arms were stiff and useless for several days. The cuts over my legs and hands from the barbed wire were inflamed and tender and still had dried blood caked around the punctures and tears. Dirt and little rocks were embedded into my lips and chin—and a hangover pounded in my head the likes of nothing I'd ever known before or since.

The physical was nothing in comparison to the mental. What had I done? I felt like my life was over and just wanted to melt into the earth and disappear. Owing hundreds of dollars in bail money that I didn't have, really hurt. Knowing that my parents could find out should this ever hit the newspapers, more than mortified me.

Worst of all, I was due in court to defend myself in two weeks.

Most of the time when the police arrest someone, they don't feel the need to show up to the hearing. But every last one showed to this one. They were upset. The fellow I kicked spent the night in the hospital and was none too happy where I had bruised him.

The judge looked at me in disbelief after reciting the charges: drunk and disorderly, resisting arrest, trespassing and . . . aggravated assault on an officer of the law. Apparently when you kick a police officer in the family jewels, it is no longer simple assault but gets automatically upgraded.

When the judge asked me what happened, I had no defense. I had one, maybe two drinks. It made no sense to me, so I just told him I had a really bad night and the alcohol went to my head.

The public defender told the judge that I was an A student in physics and a varsity athlete and asked that because it was my first offense and so atypical, and because I was repentant, would he downgrade the assault to simple assault. He did.

I left that day with four charges on a criminal record and a mountain of embarrassment, which I thought I would never overcome. After paying the fines, I tried to put it behind me. I hoped it would just go to sleep and never come back to haunt me, but it did.

What Now?

In my fourth year at university, after turning 21, I went to bartender school. Mixing colored liquids and memorizing the different drink recipes was a creative challenge and great fun. The instructor took it upon himself to fast track me in two weeks. After I passed my bartending exam, I took a job at a fancy restaurant with a busy bar, working weekends for a lot more money than United Parcel Service or any waitressing job paid.

During those two years, I got to see more of alcohol's effects upon different people, but never saw anything happen that resembled my strawberry daiquiri adventure. It would be years before I put the pieces together.

In May 1987, I left Rutgers University with a bachelor's degree in physics in hand.

Then came the anti-climactic thud. What now??

A friend from university wanted to go to medical school so took a job in an anatomy lab at Temple University in Philadelphia. She told me of another vacancy elsewhere in the department, so I applied and was given the job.

7 Naked Emperors

The bartending work continued for another few months after university graduation for extra cash, but the bar culture was too depressing. Always being the outsider there, I was happy to leave and take part-time weekend work for a few more months, working weddings and special events with a caterer. This seemed like something I could do simultaneously with labwork, but in December of 1987, I retired the bartending hat.

Being the head technician in a biochemistry lab was not how I thought life would be. However, that's how post-university life began.

The first six months in the lab included following the retiring technician around and getting tutorials on every procedure and maintenance aspect of the lab. Back then, I never thought that the superior cervical ganglia nerves of newborn rat pups, that I dissected, processed and grew artificially in petri dishes, would be of any future use in my life. But those years in the lab turned out to be invaluable to my research and understanding of vaccine literature today. Just about all the techniques that I understood and used in experiments back then, such as gel electrophoresis, column chromatography, radiolabeled amino acid tracing, and more, are often mentioned in today's scientific publications. Near the end of my two-year employment, a paper was published on the experiments I conducted in that lab and Dr. Black gave me authorship[9]. It was an honor to work with the postgraduate doctor and the other researchers in that lab.

While I don't see those years as wasted, experimenting on helpless animals, killing them, and doing all sorts of tests on their nerves and brains, was a job that was hard to get passionate about. One day I had to kill over 200 live mice by breaking their necks. Looking at the pile of bodies while hearing howling from the caged beagle colony all day, cemented my resolve to move on. I was bored and sickened by the whole thing. I really wanted to 'fix' things for people who needed immediate solutions.

As an intellectual late bloomer from a non-intellectual family, it had taken me a while to realize the potential of my own mind. At home there had been very little outside reading or curiosity beyond assigned schoolwork. Discussions were totally humdrum and a bit of a yawn. All I did until university was slightly more than was expected of me. University was gruelingly difficult but I assumed that was because I wasn't that smart and that it was all much easier for the men in my classes. So I credited my success to perspiration and inspiration, rather than being even above average in intelligence. Even though I had earned a BA in physics, I had had this idea that those accepted into medical school had to be so much smarter than me. My impression of medical doctors and students until then, was that they were the lofty gifted ones, capable of cognitive complexity and deep-thinking patterns beyond my ability. I had never considered applying to medical school . . . until I was assigned to teach six medical students who took a laboratory elective in my lab.

It was astounding how slow they were to pick up the concepts, basic chemistry calculations, or the laboratory methods. After a few

---

[9] Black, M. M., Baas, P. W., and Humphries, S., 1989 "Dynamics of alpha-tubulin deacetylation in intact neurons," *Journal of Neuroscience*, Jan;9(1):358-68. PMID: 2563279

weeks, it became clear to me that the emperor in my mind, was totally nude, and these students were not gifted at all. Most of them had come from medical royalty and were loaded with assured self-belief, but when the rubber met the road in the lab, they skidded to a halt with a painful screech.

I knew that if they had been accepted into medical school, then I could be too. This gave me the confidence I needed to consider applying to medical school for the fall of 1989.

Because I did my laboratory jobs well, several of the medical school professors were very enthusiastic and supportive when I mentioned my new inspiration to attend medical school. My boss, Dr. Black, was struck with a moment of indecision. He wrote a glowing letter of support but submitted it reluctantly, knowing he was losing a laboratory asset he would rather have kept around forever. But being a man of the highest moral and ethical standards, he gave me his blessing to move on. We hired a new person and I trained her before leaving.

With slight trepidation, I took the MCAT exam, applied to several medical schools, got into three of them, and chose Temple University School of Medicine.

Medical school began in August of 1989, the year that 18,193 people were infected with measles in the USA. By 1990, the USA saw 27,672 reported cases of measles. In 1991, measles continued its course in a heavily vaccinated population. The city of Philadelphia, where I was in medical school saw nine deaths from the disease and a total of 9,643 cases reported.

I never heard a word about it until 2015 when Paul Offit went ballistic over 600 countrywide cases in 2014, suggesting that all rights for vaccine choice be removed from parents and that reporters who publicize any debate could go to "journalism jail"[10]. The blitz continued with attorney Arthur Kaplan stating that vaccine hesitant doctors should have their medical licenses removed.[11]

[10] Kroll, D., "Journalism Jail for Faulty Medical Reporting," March 29, 2014, *Forbes Magazine*.

[11] Kaplan, A., "Revoke the license of any doctor who opposes vaccination," Feb 6, 2015, *The Washington Post*.

8

You're Joking, Right?

My parents were shocked at my new nutty idea of going to medical school. My mother was a stay-at-home mom, and Dad was a mechanic turned traveling car-parts salesman for a company called AP, selling mufflers and tail pipes to garages. I was greeted with, "Right, so how are you going to afford that?" "Why medical school? What was wrong with nursing?" They were not exactly jumping for joy, yet they didn't discourage me either. I think they were fearful that they would somehow lose me. But that didn't happen. I had undying loyalty towards both of them until their last breaths. No matter what, they were always my parents and my unconditional love and gratitude continued on, looking past all of our sometimes-passionate disagreements. My biggest regret today, regarding my parents, is that all I knew was conventional medicine when both of them were diagnosed with cancer.

Medical school is expensive, even at a state school, so my starting student loan was nearly 200,000 USD for tuition and living costs. In 1989, that was a lot of money, but I was constantly reassured that paying it back would be a breeze because, as a medical doctor, my income would be so high. It is definitely easier to practice medicine after graduation if you had wealthy parents footing the medical school bills.

At a luncheon, where the second-year students welcomed the first year, I met a gentleman named Larry. He asked me where I would be living and I said I didn't know. He said that about six blocks from the medical school, there was a double four-story brownstone, with some empty rooms if I wanted to live there. The rate was 45 USD per month and that included everything! There were two full kitchens, lots of storage, a billiards table, and more. I thought it was too good to be true, but went and saw the houses, the rooms available, and met some of the medical students residing there. All four years of students were represented. There were obvious fringe benefits like always having someone to study with, ask questions of, get old notes from, and hear what would be expected of me in the future. Perfect. I took the room and brought my four-year-old Brittany spaniel-golden retriever, Jazz, who was also welcome.

A hollowed out area beneath the staircases connected the two houses inside so we could even move between the houses without going outside. This was important because the only drawback to the living situation was that it was in an impoverished, crime-ridden neighborhood in North Philadelphia around 12th and Allegheny Ave. The houses were from a defunct medical fraternity, and belonged to an elderly infectious-disease professor who only owed taxes, which he paid. So our monthly rates just included upkeep on the houses and utilities. We thought we could live in a bubble amid crime, drugs, colored plastic crack vials in the crevices of the sidewalks, and habitual vandalism. Ironically, I noticed a 'No Drug Zone' sign on my way home with several empty crack vials lying at the base.

Due to constant break-ins, an eight-foot fence topped with razor wire encircling barbed wire was added and Larry adopted a German shepherd-Doberman mix, with a daunting bark, and named him Butch. Those additions did keep us safe from intruders the whole time I lived there, but intruders were not the only risk . . .

Medical school was totally exciting to begin with. I was going to be a doctor! I was in class with the best and brightest, and being taught the world's best medicine! Compared to studying physics in university, medical school was much easier. There wasn't too much to figure out—only much more to memorize—which was just a matter of putting in the hours.

The first day of medical school was the easiest one ever. It was mostly a feel-good schmooze session with all of the professors and staff. We were given a Meyers-Briggs personality test, just for fun, so we could better understand our own traits.

There are 16 types you can be. I can remember thinking, "So what? This is me. What was the point of this? You are who you are, and if you don't know who you are by now, why are you even here?" I'd been living with myself all those years, so I wasn't surprised. Other than chuckling and comparing, that was a total waste of effort. Perhaps they thought it would be an icebreaker? Some third- and fourth-year students took the stage and gave us their experiential viewpoint of what medical school was like for them. We were then briefed on what was going to be expected of us, given our assignment for the following day, and told to report to the gross anatomy lab dressed in scrubs.

Fearfully And Wonderfully Made

Our class of 200 was divided into groups of four, assigned by the letters of their surnames, and spread between two large laboratories. On the tables were 50 cadavers—people who had donated their bodies to science. Four students were assigned to study each cadaver. Yellow cotton gowns were put on over top of our scrubs, and a plastic apron on top of that. The idea was to shield us as much as possible from the high concentration of the formaldehyde embalming mix that soaked into every cell and space of the cadavers. The only problem with that theory was that the lungs could not really be shielded, aside from wearing a respirator and nobody did that. We learned to breathe very shallowly and live on as few breaths as possible throughout the day. Formaldehyde became impregnated in our clothes and our senses, and even long showers never totally removed the smell. The shoes we wore would never be of use anywhere else, so were tossed out at the end of the course.

For a lot of students, gross anatomy is the first time seeing a dead body that has not been made to look nice. For some it is the first time cutting into human flesh, without the pressure that would come later to a surgeon on a live body.

That first gross-anatomy day is as clear to me as today. After opening the metal casket, letting the panels creak on their hinges while swinging down to a drop at the sides, we all took a step back and stared at the clear-plastic tarp and the person inside it. With trepidation, we carefully pulled back the tarp from the cadaver. She was a tall, thin woman around 70 years old and still wearing pink nail polish. Her skin was wrinkled, pickled, and darkened somewhat by the embalming preservative, which also pooled beneath her. Every artery was infused with red dye, and every vein with blue, just to make it easier for us to find our way around. Beneath each table was a biohazard bucket where the little pieces of sinew or skin that were removed would be placed and kept with the cadaver until we were done with the full dissection.

The feeling that day was best characterized as 'chemical suffocation', which is still etched into both my brain, and my body, memory. Breathing very shallowly, and feeling faint and sick, we carried on, knowing that thousands had done it before us, and survived. I had seen these smelly lofty medical students in the elevators, reeking of formaldehyde, and had excitedly anticipated being in their shoes. Here I was now, gagging, being assaulted with formaldehyde, which soaked into my senses like nothing I've ever known, up to, or since then—and I was happy for it.

When it came time for the intricate genital and gonadal dissections, because our cadaver was female, we shared a body with a group who had been assigned to a male. Aside from that, our cadaver was there for us to methodically explore and disassemble, for the entire fall term. Every large- and medium-sized nerve, artery, and vein, the lymphatics, all muscles, and organs were carefully dissected, with everything gently teased apart using blunt instruments. It was a technique we had to learn to ensure that everything was kept as identifiable as possible.

In 1998, Dr. Carson Schneck was a middle-aged, energetic, bright-eyed MD, PhD professor. He loved his job and seemed to have an uncanny knack to be in several places at the same time. Whenever we needed his help finding something, he was there, spreading back the seemingly endless connective tissue to find the minutest hidden parts. According to Temple Medical School's website, he still worked in the anatomy lab in 2016.

There were four sets of instruments, one set for each of us: a scalpel for skin cutting, and forceps and hemostats to separate whatever pieces we were hunting down, away from all of the connective tissue, without damaging any surrounding tissues that could be of value later. While I had seen connective tissue in my lab animals, I had no idea just how much of it existed in the human body. It literally coats everything. An organized sticky web holds every tube, organ, and muscle in place.

Day one's assignment was to begin to dissect out the brachial plexus. One student would read the manual and the others would take turns finding the landmarks and splitting apart the tissues. I have no idea why the brachial plexus was the place to start but it was amazing. A series of six nerves exit out of the spine in the neck and shoulder region on each side and fuse and split apart like a superhighway in Los Angeles. Nerves branch out in different ways, merging and exiting where they are needed, supplying impulses to all the arm structures that humans move with coordination and ease, using only the slightest thought. Those nerves supply the shoulder and entire arm down to the fingertips. As time went on, the rest of the arm, hands, neck, head, chest, abdomen, pelvis, genitalia, legs, and feet were taken apart bit by bit.

When it came time for the leg, hip joint, or head to be dissected more deeply, Dr. Carson Schneck and another professor would come around with an orthopedic saw to dismember the area. I remember seeing people walking around holding legs, or pieces of skull. It felt morbidly surreal.

My awe for the human body grew with each day, realizing just how wonderfully made we are. The amazement continued on as I dissected the deeper, more micro and macroscopic organization, and the electrical hook-up of every layer inside and outside. We grew to have immense reverence and respect for these people who were expanding our understanding. It was like living in another world.

By the end, each medical student could name every nerve, artery, vein, lymphatic, taste bud, brain part, and anything else in the human body that had a name. A few times during the four months, two or three bodies would be tagged with numbers and we would be examined to test whether we could identify what had been tagged. CT scans and x-rays were also used for teaching the various positions and levels of different bones and organs. Several skeletons of human bodies were used to teach the bones and the insertion sites for tendons.

At the end of the year, there was a written final exam and a practical exam where any part of the body could be tagged for identification. After that, there was a really nice memorial service for the students and families of the people who donated their bodies. Dr. Schneck gave a moving speech and the students mingled and talked afterwards, as a thank you to the families, to show our appreciation and how much this experience meant to us.

10 Medical Mysteries

Back at the big student house, intruders were not the only threat. The house next door, which wasn't attached to us, was occupied by two flagrantly schizophrenic women who were perfectly lovely when they were medicated. But when they stopped their drugs, the delusions began. Usually they manifested their schizophrenia by talking out loud to voices in their heads, while standing outside the house. But one evening, when most of us were in the house studying, the delusions involved us in a big way. We heard a window break. It was someone driving by wanting us to know the house next door was on fire and for us to get out because the flames were coming close to one side of our building. After a few hours, the firemen said we could go back into the house. There was not much sleep that night, listening to the next-door sounds from everything being tossed out the windows and hosed down. On my way to med school in the morning, all that remained was a burned shell of a house and a lot of charred items on the front and side yards. The women who lived there matter-of-factly told the police that they had intentionally set fire to the house, because they thought their electricity and gas lines were going through our house, and they didn't want to pay our bills anymore. They were both pink papered into the psychiatric unit that night. We never heard from them or saw them again.

After shaking off the stress, we carried on as if nothing had happened. However, about a month later another episode scared us into moving out. The house behind us was a crack den and usually there was no trouble from it. But one autumn night, a gunfight broke out and bullet spray came through the back of our house. A student named Linda was studying in her room, and a bullet went by her head and stuck in the wall behind her. Bullets broke several windows. By this time, there had also been an attempt at breaking into the back door of my car when I stopped at a traffic light, and my car was heavily vandalized on the rare nights I left it parked on the street. Usually I parked in the university garage and had a police escort drive me home, but occasionally I was too tired and lazy to wait for them.

Larry and I had had enough. My student loans had finally come in, and I told him I was leaving the ghetto fortress before our luck ran out. He decided to come with me. Butch, Larry, Jazz, and I moved into a great little row home in the Mt. Airy section of Philadelphia where we happily lived out the rest of our student years.

There were a few things in the first two years of medical school that didn't sit well with me. Some instances during class still come to mind: the first being a lecture on colon polyps. The professor went through all the different types and then told us that colonoscopies were necessary to detect and remove them. Someone close to me had recently had a colon polyp diagnosed and removed, so I had already been thinking on polyps. I asked, "How did we know that polyps never go away on their own? What do we know about polyp regression?" After all, moles fall off the skin, and blood supply can be cut off from any growth. I wasn't suggesting he leave polyps alone and watch them; I was just asking if they ever regress. He drew up very tall, and curtly informed the class that, "No! They definitely don't regress and go away . . . in case anyone else wondered." I walked away feeling unsatisfied that he couldn't even consider the possibility that they didn't know everything. He was not aware of any animal studies where animals get polyps and after different treatments or changes in diet, are then followed to see if regression ever happens. Perhaps polyps do regress, but nobody bothered to look, so no one knows the answer. We know that cancer generation in the body happens all the time and is often dealt with by the immune system and we never even know it regresses. So why so much certainty? Perhaps his retort simply came from a career of hacking away at colons.

Two other incidents occurred during a surgical class in the auditorium, in second-year medical school. The subject was gender reassignment and assignment surgery. I don't much care what adults do with their genitalia but when it comes to babies and children, certain things really upset me.

The first incident was assigning gender to babies born with ambiguous genitalia. We were shown many photographs of before and after genitalia. Sometimes genetic testing and some pelvic scanning can lead the surgeon and parents to choose which gender to leave the child. But what struck me was that if there was ambiguous genitalia and ambiguous genetics, the surgeon and parents would chose to assign the infant to be a female because the surgery to make a female is easier. One slide was presented of such a child and the surgeon put it up and proudly said, "Now she looks like a proper little girl." And I thought, but what if she doesn't feel like a proper little girl, but feels like a boy? You've just hacked away at what was there and it will be of no use.

The questions that remain are: Who would have seen the genitalia before the child had the time to form an opinion of whether they felt like a girl or boy? Why do doctors need to make up so many excuses to play God? Where is the common sense? And why do parents agree with this senseless mutilation? The answer, of course, is that doctors are thought to know more than parents. The problem is that doctors mostly lean on traditional methods to do things, and rarely think outside the box.

The second incidence that upset me greatly was the first circumcision. This turned into one of the most traumatic psychological experiences for the infant, and me. It made me furious and full of questions. It was performed by one of the male obstetricians, who did it as if he was just shaving his beard in the morning. Perfectly routine: strap the baby down so he cannot move at all, cover the body except for the penis and cut off the foreskin while the baby cries into a huge blue spasm. It still infuriates me, and I take every chance I can to educate parents beforehand to what the function of the foreskin is, suggest they watch a movie called *Cut*, and watch a medical circumcision video before going ahead with it. Most of the time they decide not to circumcise, but some still do because they think they are bound by religious commitment.

Two years into medical school, students begin full clinical rotations. Halfway through the second year, as an introduction to clinical medicine, we learned to touch and interview real patients; to document things in proper order, maybe even think about what could be going on, and formulate a differential diagnosis. Life gets easier in one way, because there are no more regular tests, but harder in another way because the hours awake are long, and determined by someone else. On top of that is the stress of having to get used to a new set of 'chiefs' every six weeks. And the truth is that some of them are just blatant assholes. But mostly I just floated through, did my work, made my passing grades, and moved on.

Third year began with all the clinical rotations, with a new medical specialty begun every six weeks. Again, we learned a whole new set of hierarchical rules and expectations from different people. In some ways, the hierarchy of medical education works well, so long as the people involved have integrity. Every so often, perhaps too often, that integrity is nowhere to be found, and then life can get quite difficult. Several such instances occurred. I had moments of clarity where I realized that there was something missing; something wrong. As time passed, I had a nagging suspicion that the end result of all these years in study and training might not be what I hoped it would be, but I couldn't define why, or what I was hoping for.

The first moments of clinical doubt happened in my fourth year of medical school, in the form of two women: One was a very beautiful wealthy woman, with a rich powerful husband, except when it came to her illness he might just have well been a pauper. She had gone from regular specialists (our medical team) to genius specialists at the world's finest institutions and back to us again . . . for help with her ulcerative colitis. The genius specialists waved their hands in blessing towards what we were doing, and sent her back. All any of us knew to do, was to prescribe from the pharmaceutical mainstay of 'gold standard' treatment protocols for so many conditions: antibiotics, steroids, and anti-inflammatories. The only result was that this wealthy woman became dependent on those drugs while the ulcerative colitis steadily worsened anyway, in between transient remissions. The specialists then wanted to surgically remove part of her bowel.

Today, doctors have a new alternative that is supposed to be a revolution. We used monoclonal antibodies in nephrology for years, but now they are being diversified and used for many other diseases. They call these drugs "biologics" which to me, is a total misnomer. They are animal-derived antibodies that dampen the immune system so that cell-mediated autoimmunity drops to very low levels. The problem is that just like every drug, there are non-specific effects. In this case, overwhelming infection and death is not uncommon. Basically, the drugs induce a clinical case of AIDS and I've personally seen the disasters that can happen using monoclonals for autoimmunity. Just recently, the founding member and guitarist of the Eagles band died after treatment with such agents, at the premature age of 67. While his case was widely published, death from monoclonal antibodies is a daily occurrence in hospitals.

The other woman I remember, was really young and had had encephalitis at one point, kidney lupus, and severe lupus-associated bowel problems.

Both of these women were put on the steroid after steroid after steroid treadmill—IV, oral, or whatever suited the need. Worse, they were recommended a totally bland fiber-free diet called a "low-residue diet" consisting of over-cooked meat, bread, margarine, Jell-O, and foods with nothing alive at all.

My immediate thought was, "How could that diet be good for anyone's colon? How can that possibly work?" It felt backwards but when I questioned it, I was told that fiber would make everything worse. I didn't yet know enough to understand why that tray of food sitting in front of that sick patient would not help very much—but I saw that even if it stopped things getting worse, it still wouldn't help to cure her underlying problem. In 2015, a medical article was published which showed my insight was probably correct. The results were that the Crohn's disease patients who ate more fiber had fewer flares and the study calls for a re-evaluation of current practice in feeding IBD patients.[12]

The gastroenterology doctors taking care of her didn't talk about a dysfunctional gut caused by prescriptions of serial antibiotics, how what we eat can control the immune system, or how the gut flora influence the immune system, even though there was medical literature on that at the time. The only discussion was, "Use X, Y, Z, drugs, at A, B, C dose." Both these women would be discharged, and return within days or weeks for a repeat, be discharged, and come back for the next escalation of more aggressive or invasive therapy. Patients like that were called "bounce backs".

I just remember thinking that this was really depressing and up-setting for these patients. Instead of getting better, the colon people eventually ended up with colostomies and heavy-hitting drugs.

---

[12] Brotherton, C.S., et al., 2016 "Avoidance of Fiber Is Associated With Greater Risk of Crohn's Disease Flare in a 6 month Period." *Clinical Gastroentoerology and Hepatology*, Aug; 14(8): 1130-6. PMID: 26748217

The thinking behind all this felt limited and costive. As I looked at my training, and the principles upon which diagnoses and solutions rested, I knew that something important was missing.

The problem is that as fourth-year medical students, we didn't know what we didn't know. In some ways taking apart a cadaver in year one, seemed to instill a mindset that NOW we know everything about the body, so it's just a matter of fixing what is wrong. What I didn't fully appreciate, was that these four years were a bit like taking apart the hardware of a computer, and learning which bits were connected, but never really knowing how to run the programs of the software, the coding that made everything come together, or even the interchange between electrons and why electrons behave differently in different conditions.

All we were doing was identifying a problem we had dissected, with a diagnostic tag, and then applying either a chemical cosh to it, or cutting it out, without really understanding how the problem came to be, or what else could be done.

I also started to see that so much of medicine was about doing one thing with one hand that resulted in having to do another with the other hand, often with nasty spin-offs as a result.

For example, with heart-failure patients, it was a game where the left hand would give diuretics. Then when the kidneys shut down because of dehydration, or the potassium and magnesium fell too low and arrhythmias occurred, the right hand of the medical system would give fluids and minerals to try to fix the dehydration and demineralization caused by the diuretics given by the left hand. This was the heart/kidney failure seesaw, but back then I didn't understand heart failure, kidneys, mitochondria . . . or anything more than medical school biochemistry. We all simply played the dynamic game of "Is he 'dry' or is he 'wet'?" and acted accordingly.

I felt helpless, and grieved that this was the best we could do for people. Yet the very reason I wanted to be a doctor, was to help people.

Rotation Realities

Nuts and dolts of psychiatry

During my years as a lab technician, I had a spell of therapy with a PhD, Gestalt-trained psychologist, after a relationship breakup. One thing that the psychologist helped me to realize was that though I loved my parents, there was a toxic element to our family dynamics, which is discussed in more detail later in this book. Up until I began therapy, I had not made the links as to where various stresses stemmed from, because as children, our families of origin can be the only reality we know.

Realizing some of those links, helped free my thinking from the constraints my parents put on me. I became more analytical, independent, and confident. When medical school came onto the radar as a possibility, my first thought was that it would be very satisfying to help people understand the reasons why they are mentally stuck in seemingly tough circumstances. So while I knew I wanted to be a doctor, initially there was a strong pull towards becoming a psychiatrist . . . until I saw what psychiatry was really all about.

One psychiatry rotation at Temple University was the locked inpatient ward where the most flagrantly psychotic and difficult patients were treated. Those six weeks amounted to a valuable learning experience in a school of very nasty knocks.

As a medical student I was permitted access to all patients at any time, and was specifically assigned to four patients with whom I had to visit twice daily, write a chart note on, and attend all meetings that discussed their progress.

All of the psychiatrists were very nice to me. The worst person I had to deal with was the North Philadelphia black version of the white Nurse Ratchet from the movie *One Flew Over the Cuckoo's Nest*. If I had understood history or racism like I do now, the Black Panthers poster with Angela Davis hanging on the wall in her office would have signaled a warning. Naïvely, I thought if I just did a conscientious job, that we would get along fine. However, Nurse Hatchet stalked me and hooked into any little thing she could use to belittle me.

One day after talking to one of the patients for longer than she thought was necessary, she ripped strips off me. I cried tears of anger and frustration, but was defended by one of the psychiatrists who was also black and knew that Nurse Hatchet had extended her tentacles farther than her job description allowed. Once I settled back down, I continued my work, knowing that Hatchet was watching my every move, looking for something to crush me over, but that someone else had my back.

Aside from Hatchet, those six weeks were, for the most part, interesting, sometimes highly amusing, and other times quite tragic.

One patient was an African-American Muslim woman who would not answer to any other name than Madonna of Fatima. She would walk the corridors praying and seemingly talking to herself. She was a peaceful woman who did not seem to belong there. Since she was not directly under my care, I do not remember her diagnosis or the finer details of her weeks at the facility. What stands out in my mind was how she dealt with the psychiatry staff.

All of the male psychiatrists wore bow ties. First rule is not to wear a noose around your neck when dealing with potentially homicidal people. The head psychiatrist was the only person that Madonna of Fatima would speak to. But she would only speak to him if he knelt down in front of her and said "Madonna of Fatima will you please speak to a lesser being?" and remain kneeling during the conversation. I have to hand it to this man because he did what needed to be done in order to move the process of her 'recovery' along. Every morning when I arrived to the ward, he was there in the hallway, kneeling, and discussing different things with Madonna. She spent the entire six weeks there and I don't know when she was released or what 'progress' she made.

Next was Maybelle. One day while walking down a sunny corridor I heard in a musical tone of voice, " 'Scuze me doctor but can I aks you a question?" I stopped to see a small rotund lady in her 40s sitting on the bench. "Of course," I replied. "Well . . ." Maybelle began, "what do it mean, 'A rolling stone gather no moss'?" Figuring that I could have got in trouble if I answered, and that she was just messing with me, I responded, "I think it is a saying that is asked a lot around here." In rapid fire, my answer was followed by, "And doctor what do it mean, 'No use cryin' over split milk'? And doctor what do it mean, 'People in glass houses shouldn't throw stones'? What do it mean, 'Rome was not built in a day'?" She was playing with me, asking me the questions that all patients are asked in a mental-status examination. Knowing that I should not fraternize, I simply kept my answers to shallow one-liners. So as not to be totally rude, I asked her her name, and after she answered I stood there and talked about a few other light things like weather and the food in the place.

Little did I know that Hatchet had heard every word. She stormed up to us with belittling questions and comments about who did I think I was, talking to HER, and did I know how much trouble I could stir? Maybelle was perfectly calm and friendly through our whole talk, but when Hatchet approached, Maybelle went into riot mode, yelling, punching Hatchet right in the face, wanting a good fight. Three of the largest male aides were summoned to restrain Maybelle at Hatchet's command. I was astonished, not just at the horror of what Hatchet had done, but by the strength of little

Maybelle when she went ballistic. Those men had a right hard time holding her down. A body net was thrown over Maybelle and she was given two injections, after which she melted into a lifeless blob. She spent the next three days lying flat in her bed, restrained and sedated, all because Hatchet took a hateful power-trip just to throw her weight around.

Another of my patients was a very obese white lady, around 30 years old, from Fishtown in Philadelphia. Her name was Margaret and she smoked like a chimney. She was very difficult to communicate with because she was so psychotic and angry, but she was not violent. The thing I remember vividly was that her father used to visit every day, bringing cakes and cigarettes, and he would sit there while she yelled at him, "You are an evil criminal!" He remained quite mellow, accepted it, and let it roll right on by. To begin with I started to feel sorry for him. One day when I was talking to her, I asked her why she thought her father was an evil, criminal and, after about 10 "Because he just is" answers, she told me about the sexual abuse he had done to her growing up.

I queried this with the psychiatrist, suggesting that perhaps her father was a criminal and someone should look into his history with Margaret. I wondered why, if he had NOT done it, he would just sit there, every day. Was he just keeping up appearances, or was he so loyal to his daughter and convinced of his innocence to the point it just washed off him? The answer I got was that they had investigated and determined she was just psychotic, and that she lives with him and would have to be permanently institutionalized if she did not return home to him. Somehow, this just felt to me like a cursory flick-off. By this time, I had seen that the system was such that assumptions often determined action. Those assumptions might depend on who had investigated and who was most believable. My enthusiasm for psychiatry was rapidly dwindling, so I let the issue go.

Once Hatchet loosened her grip, I was assigned to work with a nurse named Beth, who was a breath of fresh air to me because she was kind and really cared for the patients. One day she and I went to the weekly assessment meeting. This was a ritual whereby each patient who was up for review was invited into the conference room and sat at one end of a long table, with the head psychiatrist at the other, and the rest of the nurses, aides, and students down each side.

Jessie was a young African-American man about 28 years of age with movie star good looks. He was committed by his mother whom he was living with. Apparently he took to dismantling the plumbing pipes and toilets in his psychosis. Aside from that, he was perfectly lovely and easy to deal with in the ward. The head psychiatrist that day was a humorless bowtie-wearing white man. He asked Jessie if he was ready to go home. Jessie said, "Yes sir," with a huge happy smile. Dr. Pokerface asked, "Okay, do you know why you are here?" to which Jessie replied, "Yes, because I was taking apart my mother's plumbing." Dr. Pokerface: "Are you going to do that after you go back home?" Jessie: "Yes sir!" Dr. Pokerface: "Why will you do that after you go home Jessie?" Jessie replied with a big innocent smile, "Because I am the Ty-D-bol man."[13] This response hit my funny bone totally by surprise and I stifled a giggle. Beth sitting next to me also began to giggle a bit.

Everyone else remained poker-faced. I thought I had myself under control but then Dr. Pokerface asked something else which I can't remember and Jessie replied, "Yep, good for a thousand flushes." At this point the flimsy wall that held back my giggle broke down completely. Even though I knew Dr. Pokerface and Hatchet were glaring at me, I could no longer hold it in and had tears streaming down my face. Beth was also laughing so hard she was crying, but Dr. Pokerface and Hatchet never saw anything to smile over. Fortunately, nobody ever said anything to me about that outburst of laughter and we just carried on our work for the day.

---

[13] A popular TV commercial advertised a product that clips on to the toilet and cleans and deodorises it. The TV commercial usually ended with "Good for a thousand flushes!"

There are many more stories that could be told from those six weeks. What struck me was that most sad cases had perfectly reasonable explanations as to why the psychosis started. The foundation was almost always a history of extreme abuse at an early age, lots of drugs, both prescription and street, and years of bouncing from jail to psych ward to group home. There were psychotic people with really high IQs who were so insightful they almost seemed like mind readers.

The biggest problem I had there was that I didn't think everyone was irreversibly damaged. Sometimes what we saw in these patients was akin to post traumatic stress disorder (PTSD) in soldiers, but for those people talking things through often started the healing process for them. As I progressed through the rest of my rotations, I started to see people outside of the psychiatric wards being treated with psychiatric drugs at the slightest hint of a problem. I was saddened to realize that for psychiatrists the solution was never to talk about anything meaningful, but to try one drug after another or some sort of manipulative behavior therapy that mostly didn't work.

Any dream I had of going into psychiatry was stifled during that rotation. Instead, I chose internal medicine because psychology is part of every branch of medicine, and rather than being obligated to deal with every patient's mental mess, I could choose which patients to get involved with more deeply, and just deal with the physical problems for everyone else. Analyzing people and looking for the 'best' drug to alter their minds may have value in some instances, but drugs for everyone was not an acceptable career path for me.

Years later, when I lived in Maine, I became friends with a Scottish child neuropsychiatrist, who had just moved to Maine from Nova Scotia. Even though she was given a real sweet deal, in an area of high need in Bangor, she only lasted about two years before going back to Canada. She said that the drug prescribing to children in the USA is, in her estimation, child abuse and she could no longer participate. Every time she tried to stop drugs that she considered unnecessary, her colleagues just got on her case.

Today, one in four to five adults in the USA are estimated to have taken at least one psychiatric medication during the year. More than 1 million children in the USA now take antipsychotics each year, and tens of thousands of them are under the age of 5. Across the USA, 7.5% of children aged 6-17 take a prescribed medication to treat emotional or behavioral difficulties. My Scottish friend said that, in her opinion, most of the drugs were not necessary. She was treating conditions that could have been easily dealt with through better family nutrition, resolving parental conflict properly instead of screaming and violence, and more time for children to play. She hated the fact that parents wanted their children on drugs because they got more social welfare benefits if the children had diagnoses requiring drugs. To make matters worse, further drugs were often prescribed to treat the effects of the first drugs, which were simply Band-Aids, because the real problems were never constructively addressed. She was an esteemed neuropsychiatrist but nobody would listen to her, so she packed her bags and left, because at the time Canada was more open to keeping children off drugs.

My psychiatric-ward experience was just one more to add to all the others that would show me that former Merck CEO Henry Gadsden meant business when he said in a Fortune Magazine interview that he wanted Merck "to be more like chewing gum maker Wrigley's". Gadsden said it had long been his dream to make drugs for healthy people, because then Merck would be able to "sell to everyone." His dream has become a depressing reality.

The surgeon in training

When a surgeon is needed and has excellent skills, and knows when and when NOT to operate, they have something very valuable to contribute. Time and again, at the cliff face of accidents, including my own, surgeons save people's lives. Like every specialty, there are the good surgeons, the passable, and the bad. Every medical student has to spend several weeks among a surgical team of some sort. Some choose to do it more than once, with different types of surgeons. I spent six weeks in obstetric and gynecologic surgery, six more in general surgery, and six more in trauma surgery. Seven years later, I was to be on the receiving end of surgeons, which has left a few memories and questions that remain to this day.

One incident, which echoes loudly, occurred during my general surgery rotation. I was the lowly student holding a retractor to keep the huge laparotomy incision open for the surgeon to work, while suctioning up blood on command when necessary. All of a sudden, the senior resident at the helm of the operation, and the highest of rank in the room, shouted "Shit!" He had torn open his outer glove with a suture needle but did not puncture himself. Soon thereafter, there was a loud snap as the surgeon impatiently ripped his outer glove off, without moving away from the surgical field. The snap was followed by a puff of white powder swirling above the open abdomen, illuminated by the high intensity light. The nurses knew exactly what to do, and immediately had a new set of gloves ready for him to slide into. Nobody said anything after the surgeon's expletive. In disbelief I uttered, "The powder is going into the abdomen!" which was totally ignored. For years after that, I mentally buried the scene, thinking they must know something I didn't. Perhaps sterile talc settling inside an open body cavity was just fine.

Later when working through my pulmonary rotation in New York, I learned about a procedure called pleurodesis. This is where talc is used in some cases of collapsed lung disease to intentionally cause an adhesion of the lung to the body cavity. I realized that that patient probably had problems with adhesions post-operatively because of one surgeon's thoughtlessness. But it was probably just attributed to the surgery itself or to bad luck.

In another instance, a woman's abdomen was open for a bowel operation. The surgeon in charge had every student and low-ranking resident put their hand into the abdomen to feel the liver. She wanted us to feel the texture and pulsation of the live liver. Next, she instructed the senior resident, who was performing the elective gall bladder operation, to remove the appendix. They inspected it, determined it was perfectly normal, and then removed it. The attending physician told me they do this often in order to give the younger residents practice at appendectomies. When I asked how they justified it, they said the consent form covered it and that they would state in the operative report that the appendix was 'dusky' in appearance. Their reasoning was that if they said it had any evidence of being abnormal, they could justify its removal on the grounds of not having to return to the operating suite at any time in the future to remove an appendix that could be taken out then and there. After that, I started to notice how many organs are considered disposable by the surgical and medical professions.

Ob/Gyn

Even today, obstetrics remains a branch of medicine dominated by callous men. Sorry, but it's true. Kudos to any woman who gets through it with an ounce of understanding of how a normal birth should happen, and how to deal with the most common female medical issues without immediately intervening with pharmaceutical drugs and/or surgery. Most of the women ob/gyns were not much better, and never delivered a baby in a way that resembled the natural births I later came to appreciate. I spent six weeks between the delivery ward, the operating room for general gynecology, and the clinic for both general gynecology and obstetrics. Then another six weeks in family practice with yet more gynecology and obstetrics. The ob/gyn rotation left me frustrated, angry, and embittered at the callous disregard for both mothers and infants. It's not a field I could have entered, because I could not have kept any composure in the face of what looked like psychopathic arrogance, and barely legalized abuse.

The most memorable flaming asshole in medical school obstetrics was the self-named "racist bastard from Georgia". He hated women, especially women of color, and made no excuses for himself. One day when he was particularly ramped up, my best friend on rotation with me (and who was of African-American/Native American mix) asked him why he was such an asshole. Perking up proudly, he twanged, "Because I am a racist bastard from Georgia."

The racist bastard from Georgia (RBFG) entered every exam room and surgical suite as if everyone in there had been waiting their whole lives to see him. Telling a young Asian woman "Darlin', just lie back and relax," as she winced through an unnecessarily rough bimanual exam, was his baseline demeanor. She left the office very angry but did not lodge any formal complaint. Undoubtedly she felt violated. If he was woken up in the night for a delivery, he became even more animated. A young black couple were in the delivery suite, the head of the baby just starting to crown, as the RBFG gavotted in, turned on the exam spotlight, told her to open her legs, and shined the light on the crowning child while loudly humming the theme to Johnny Carson's *The Tonight Show*. It was appalling. The father did not retaliate because he didn't want to put the wellbeing of his child in any more danger than it was already in.

After witnessing many such instances from this RBFG, my friend and I, who were just completing our six-week sentence in the House of Stupidity, reported him with detailed accounts of what he did, including names of the abused patients. We didn't have much hope that our report would have any effect. However, it seemed that ours wasn't the first complaint lodged, and he was dismissed from his residency. It's quite possible the RBFG found another residency and went on to abuse more women: the medical system is quite forgiving and accommodating that way. The brotherhood buddy network encourages widespread tolerance of both incompetence and bad behavior in the lower-level institutions that have no choice but to hire the worst of the physicians. Then they can move up from there.

Other practices that were routine in my ob/gyn rotation, did not seem wrong to me until years later, when I learned better. Like routinely pulling on the umbilical cord, slowly twisting it around a cylinder with traction, in order to deliver the placenta. Or putting a hand past the dilated cervix to scrape the placenta away manually from the uterus. I recall clearly one New Year's Eve, when a white mid-level obstetrics resident delivered a 10-pound African-American baby boy at midnight. She thought it was funny to call him "Bullfrog". The mother was not amused by that at all. Then the resident decided to speed things along and put her hand and forearm halfway into the woman. When the woman startled, the resident said with a laugh, "Yes, that's my arm," as she scraped away at the placenta that was not being expelled fast enough for her liking.

None of the manipulation of the cord and placenta would even be necessary most of the time if the cord was not clamped and if the blood was allowed to move where it belongs: into the baby, allowing the placenta to shrink and peel away from the uterine wall. I was later to work with Nicaraguan midwives who understood that, but why didn't the experts? I remember asking a first-year ob/gyn resident why everyone jumps so fast to clamp the cord as if it is an emergency. He replied that if we didn't, the blood would drain back to the mother. I wonder if he is still walking around with such a physiologically wrong, moronic idea?

Episiotomies were commonplace. I was taught that if you hold the scalpel just right as the perineum is stretching, you get the best cut. And that episiotomies are better for the mother, because they are so much easier to sew back up than natural tears. Never mind that the reality for women is the exact opposite. There was no discussion about relaxing, or oiling the perineum and using warm rags to relax it. There was no thought that, just maybe, that unnecessary pudendal block preventing the perineum from stretching, was the reason for the tear in the first place. No consideration was given to either the stress the medical system puts mothers under, or allowing labor to progress at its own pace. It was considered good to strap monitors over the gravid abdomen of the woman stranded on her back with feet in stirrups, and gather around to watch the monitor tracing that came out. The crowd mentality was narrowly focused on the machine, waiting for that first, preset sign of distress. Then, mentally attuned only for catastrophe, they would leap into action, do a scalp cut into the baby for some blood, or take the mother for a c-section. Nobody, not even me, considered this circus in the room to be a tragedy. But it was. C-section rates have risen greatly since 1990, and it is no wonder why. I never saw any delivery in US hospitals where the mother was encouraged to have self-direction, to walk, squat, get on all fours, or have her lower back strategically massaged. Laboring mothers were treated as patients always in need of white-coated heroic doctors rushing to the rescue.

Today, I am well aware that the tension of that fear-laden mindset can trigger distress in both mother and baby. In retrospect it is kind of miraculous that as many women as did, managed to give birth vaginally in those days. Most of those who did, came into the hospital already well progressed and probably didn't need us for much other than to clean up afterwards.

Abortions were done frequently and especially by one particular ob/gyn. Dr. Nosebest was a tall, slow-moving, bearded, fat old granddad type who had earned the affection of most of the staff, and was a bit easier to like than most of the other doctors. He thought the students needed to observe some of his abortions, since he was using a technique we may not see anywhere else. Back then, I never thought there was any problem with abortion. I was enough of an advocate to take a course from Planned Parenthood during my residency, with the prospect of doing early embryo evacuations; which was the polite, PC term for abortion. However, there was a little voice of hesitation that never shut up and thus I never completed the training and didn't get certified. Perhaps an indelible memory supplied by Dr. Nosebest two years before in the operating room, had something to do with that.

Dr. Nosebest considered it a service to the world to do abortions on any embryo or fetus that was unwanted. He thought it better to kill the embryo or fetus rather than allow it to be born unwanted, into a gang or to a drugged-out mother who would not take proper care. So he did abortions to all-term fetuses. Though most of the abortions were done on fetuses 24 weeks of age and under, there is one I will never forget, which was a third trimester baby, probably within a few weeks of its due date. The procedure was called saline-instillation abortion. The woman was totally unconscious, but not under general anesthesia, and the cervix was chemically dilated. A large syringe with hypertonic saline was injected into the amniotic sac. I thought that would instantly kill the fetus but it didn't. A lot of writhing began immediately and could be seen on the outside of the abdomen. Then Dr. Nosebest began dismembering the fetus limb by limb, pulling out arms and legs using a Sopher clamp. When it finally stopped moving, he pulled out the body without the limbs or head, and then the crushed skull. Then all the pieces had to be closely examined to make sure nothing was left behind. I was shocked, silently traumatized, disgusted, and speechless. The worst part is that Dr. Nosebest justified the procedure under the category 'danger to the mother's life', and said he did it all the time. He was considered a hero in North Philadelphia, where he continues to practice, for providing this service to poor women.

When I think back on this now, I realize that by the third year of medical school, my heart was already in critical condition, on its way to a numbed out coma that would masquerade as depression but, at the same time, save me from implosion in years to come. A normal response to that abortion would have been outrage and total non-acceptance. Dr. Nosebest deserved an equally, if not more scathing report than we gave the "racist bastard form Georgia". Instead, my friend and I just left the operating suite in silence like a couple of zombies, and didn't say a word to each other or anyone else.

One of the biggest obstetrics puzzle, was standing in a room full of men intoning, "All clotting during menstruation is abnormal." Period. "Any woman who complains of clotting during menstruation needs further evaluation and probably a D and C." Most of us women scratched our heads.

In the midst of uteri of octogenarians falling out, still attached but lying like dry jerky meat on the table, and beyond uterine hemorrhages, hysterectomies were among the gynecologist's most common surgeries. When in doubt, they just took it out. Sometimes a trial of hormones was first prescribed. Most of the time a D and C was done first, but always the women did whatever was recommended with no questions asked. Every older woman in my family had a hysterectomy. It was almost like a rite of passage in the 1970s and 1980s, and as I learned in the Bronx during a later ob/gyn rotation, not much had changed. I never saw a woman argue back against the recommendation.

Another ethical issue that arose for me, was that surgery consent forms omitted most of what a patient needs to know. Nobody was told that, while anesthetized on the table pre-operatively, they would be examined by up to eight different doctors and students. I'm quite certain they would not have agreed to that, and that that is why nobody ever asks for permission. I was told it was the best way to feel the ovaries and uterus because the woman was totally relaxed, so tense muscles would not be in the way of palpating deep pelvic structures. While this may be true, the practice was revolting to me and I stood aside after the first two times. Later in my internal medicine practice, I felt hundreds of ovarian sets and rarely had trouble feeling them or making whatever diagnosis needed to be made, and I don't thank those operating room exams. They were totally unnecessary and a violation to the unconscious woman.

The missing link

During a neurology rotation, we treated a patient after he nearly killed himself by leaping from a rooftop after taking a hallucinogen. Fortunately, the landing was soft enough that only one bone in a leg was broken. Treating patients on hallucinogens can also be a regular part of trauma medicine.

While reading that effects of PCP (phencyclidine – a hallucinogen) are felt within 30-60 minutes, and last 6-24 hours on the brain, something clicked. The symptoms of paranoid delusions, temporary schizophrenia, audiovisual hallucinations, and delusions of superhuman strength fitted my behavior on the night of my arrest to a T. So did the worst hangover ever.

PCP comes as a powder and is one of many powders such as THC, LSD, mescaline, and methamphetamine that people have used to spike alcohol drinks. It was the only thing that made any sense. My escapade at the bar and racetrack in 1986 was probably due to PCP intoxication, from someone spiking my drink.

12

Guatemala
And Nicaragua

Guatemala

My post-graduate assignment was to be in the Spanish-speaking Bronx, so it was logical to get myself schooled up in the language. In medical school I met many cultures, but had grown up with just about no cultural diversity or travel. While there were local classes, I thought that going away to a Spanish-speaking country would make me learn faster.

There was an organization in Philadelphia, mostly Mennonite, which was into Liberation Theology. They arranged a Central American rotation with Temple University for interested medical students. She made an announcement one day to our class, and I pounced on the chance to be the first student to do it.

After months of anticipation, I began my journey to the unknown, starting in Philadelphia and stopping over in Mexico City, then landing in sooty, smelly, loud, and polluted Guatemala City. I was met by the nephew of the owner of a remote Spanish-language school in Quetzaltenango. I chose that city because total immersion was guaranteed, with few tourists or English-speaking people. Learning Spanish as quickly as possible was a matter of necessity. I was as green as could be when I got there, with my only experience of Spanish being a course I began on tape, just to get some basics.

José, the nephew of the school's owner, spoke fluent English. He was a very polite brown-skinned young man. Driving from the airport to my hotel La Posada Belén was uneventful. The following morning in his truck, on the way from the hotel to the bus station, he was quite talkative. In his chatter, he said to me, "Do you know what the problem with Guatemala is?" I answered, "No". He replied: "Indians". That answer mentally knocked me over. In all my naïvety, I said with total honesty, "But you have Indian blood coursing through your veins." He sat up straighter, tightened the look on his face, and said angrily, "Yes, but that was a very long time ago." As I got out of his truck at the bus station, José's 15 USD rate escalated to 60 USD, which was a fortune for Guatemala, even in that era. I was miffed but kept silent, even though the course work of his aunt's school that I was attending, supposedly centered around indigenous culture. But it was possible that his activist aunt had also forgotten her indigenous roots, and mentioning anything more might have given someone even more opportunity to treat me badly.

Two very colorful chicken buses later, I was in Quetzaltenango: a remote highland, mountainous, and antique region with vast surrounding beauty and live volcanoes that spat steam through various parts of the day. After registering in the small building located in one of the brightly painted curved alleyways, I was introduced to the family whom I would stay with, eat with, and try to talk to for the next two weeks. The daytimes were filled with one-to-one tutoring at the school. My tutor was a 20-year-old named Freddie, who I had to endure for two weeks. Though he was a decent Spanish language tutor, he did not speak a word of English and had a very different idea to mine of what physical boundaries were. I gave him the hairy eyeball after one too many gropes and he fortunately got the message.

Walking around the city, I always had a list of new words that I would turn over and over in my head until I learned them. I tried to make every minute of my waking day count towards learning as much Spanish as I could.

The parents of my host family were about 50 years old or so, and had two sons. The older son was 30 and scared me a bit. The younger son was six years old, and took a fancy to my Timex Triathlon watch and swiped it one day while I was at school. Again, silence seemed the best response. Every day when I was leaving, the older son would say "Con cuidado," which took me about three days to catch onto. "Go with care." Yes, of course I went with care. For the most part.

The family was highly amused when a mild earthquake occurred one night. I'd never experienced the helpless feeling of ground shaking beneath me. I ran outside trembling saying "whoa, whoa, whoa, whoa", as the house contents rattled around, thinking that if I went out in the open, at least nothing would fall on me. Once they were finished laughing at the silly American gringa, they went back to sleep. Apparently that was just a minor tremor by their standards.

My weekend off was a time to do some more traveling on the buses through areas where you could supposedly get murdered or wake up without any kidneys. I somehow escaped both of those endpoints, met some fellow gringos on the way, and sat with the peasants who think nothing of tossing a cage of chickens on the roof, sitting down next to you, handing you a baby, and falling asleep on your shoulder. Personal boundaries and social norms were altogether different in the highlands of Guatemala. In back-country travel, buses were often stopped and everyone had to get out; the men were searched, sometimes they were taken away, and the rest of the bus went on without them. There were many mysteries about the militant government, police, and Guatemala's war-torn past, which I never figured out.

Roadsides were occupied by women weaving on looms that could extend 20-30 feet. Markets for local crafts offered the most beautiful and intricate weavings at pathetically low prices. I have moved and traveled a lot over the years and gotten rid of almost all of my belongings, but I still have two Guatemalan blankets. They make any room beautiful, no matter where they are.

The first adventure I embarked upon was to a very high very remote place called Todos Santos Cuchumatán. I probably chose that place for its altitude and the fact that very few gringos ventured up there. Because the trip was long and far away, an overnight stay in Huehuetenango was necessary. On the second part of the cloud climb, the bus took us skyward, with frequent stops on cliff edges while the driver's assistant would leave his usual hanging place outside the entrance door, in order to move a big rock out of the way. Amid the beauty of green mountains, some of which were wild and some speckled with native Guatemalans in traditional garb, often with babies on back, working the mountainous farmland, was also the reality of a society with some first-world conveniences but inadequate waste facilities. The rest stop was a roadside, where the men went to one side and the women to the other, and anyone who needed bowel or bladder relief did it in the open, in an area about 30 feet by 30 feet that was dug out by hand. It kind of looked like a mass gravesite that was never used. Instead it was filled with all sorts of human waste and flies. Some of the steep drop-offs were colored with every type of plastic bag imaginable. Any plastic that was not burned was dumped over the cliffs.

A little bit short of breath, I arrived at the peak and walked into a small village of girls, women, young boys, and old men. Men between the ages of 16 to 55 were conspicuously absent. I thought either they had been killed for not agreeing to fight or they were recruited for whichever side invaded the little highland hamlet first. Peasants were pawns in the battles that took place in Guatemala and like most civil wars, if anyone was suspected of helping the other side, they were punished. I knew that there was mass genocide against the Mayan people in 1986 but nobody was talking about it by 1993.

Travelers stayed with locals on whatever floor space was available or, if you paid a little more, an old bed or couch. Showers didn't exist. Instead, there were primitive wood saunas, for the locals only. One night was enough for me to explore the area, see all the most-amazingly dyed fabrics, buy a few things, and head out on the morning's descent. Taking the long way home, I stopped off at Chichicastenango and then began school on Monday, with both kidneys. Strangely enough, the only trouble I ever encountered in my years of Central American travel, were from USA males.

Public safety regulations in Guatemala were nothing like the USA. On another sightseeing trip to Lake Atitlán, which was very undeveloped back then, there were two near misses. The road around it was not yet built and only one little town called Panajachel was accessible by bus. If you wanted to see any of the other little villages, the only way was by boat. On one passage, a terrified man came running towards me yelling "Su brazo!" just before my arm was about to be crushed between a wooden pillar at the dock and a railing on the boat. I noticed and pulled it away.

But that was not the only close call. Unbeknownst to me, an area I was walking along, at night, with two other tourists in Panajachel, was under construction. There was no yellow tape, no lighting, no sawhorses . . . nothing. As the three of us were walking, they said I just disappeared. The hole in the walkway over the beach was open enough for one person to fall in. The fall felt like an eternity and as my arms and legs flailed in attempt to find stability, all I could think of was, "What is going to be at the bottom of this pit?" Eventually I landed upon sand and rock. With the wind knocked out of me, and in a lot of pain, I answered their calls. The two others walked around and down to meet me and assisted me to a place at the lakeshore where I could safely sit and gather my wits. They just kept saying things like "holy shit", "wow", "Oh my god", and "Are you sure you are okay?" I was alive and nothing was broken but the next morning, and for three days after, I had near-incapacitating aches and pains. That jarring landing to the bottom of the 20-foot pit marked the last week of my trip to Guatemala.

Guatemala was more of a working holiday than anything else. I loved it, and would return many more times in the future, observing how fast a little country can go from quiet beauty and affordable tourism, to an ecological nightmare. When I first went there, it was raw and beautiful. There was no pollution and very few roads . . . But later, the roads that were put in, ended up eroding away the mountainsides and ruining the coastline at the lake. Foreigners came in and built, and the natives who lived there started adopting the worst of tourism. Instead of just living their lives, they tried to work the tourism market in ways that were leech-like. The whole social and ecological tone changed.

The real purpose of being in Central America was to do my medical rotation in Managua, a totally mysterious place where no medical student from my school had ever gone before. Today, according to Temple University's website, the foreign rotations have expanded.

Nicaragua

My lodging in Nicaragua was all prearranged by the church in Philadelphia that sponsored my attendance in Managua's medical facilities. Upon arrival to the Nicaraguan capital's shack of an airport, I was taken by taxi to meet my host. Doña Coco was a tough, bone-thin lady and the widowed mother of two grown children, and she ran her house like an army barracks. Once she got to know me a little better she asked in a soft voice, as if the secret service could be listening, "Estás Sandinista?" To which I replied "No sé." I had no idea if I was a Sandinista sympathizer, or even what a Sandinista really was. That was the wrong answer. Despite our rough start, we got on well for the next four weeks. She always frowned and disapproved when I headed out of her house on my own towards the bus stop, or wherever my naïve sense of curiosity took me during my weekends off.

One part of my rotation in Managua was working in a bombed out, poorly staffed hospital called Hospital Bertha Calderón Rogue. All my work was alongside midwives, who delivered the majority of babies drug free, in every positional variation known, and with no stirrup table in sight. Those midwives taught me the mastery of calm normal birthing. They had a deep understanding of the variations of the natural physiological process, and easily adapted to a mother's unique needs. American obstetricians should have a compulsory sabbatical there, with handcuffs on and their mouths duct-taped while the experts birth babies naturally, so that they can understand how many 'high-risk' situations and perceived distress signals they diagnose in the USA are babies that can actually come into the world normally.

It was routine to watch babies emerge foot first, or with a cord wrapped once or twice around the neck. I was initially panic-stricken, but the lay midwives just found the cord early by feeling for it, then slipped it around the neck, or did a somersault maneuver, delivering a perfectly normal baby. The cord was left unclamped (something I thought at the time was just lack of equipment and personnel) and the baby put on the mother to begin feeding. There was none of the alarm, immediate cord clamping, or a NICU team stealing away the baby as seen in developed countries. Most American obs have pathologized birth, creating many irrational fears between doctors' ears, so that they see danger and intervene prematurely when it could often be avoided. Part of the problem is that like so many other situations, American doctors are primarily educated for the worst possible scenario; and without the diverse knowledge base understood by the watch-and-wait, experienced Nicaraguan midwives. I was miseducated for a very long time, too, and it was an eye-opener and a privilege to see natural physiological births, with none of the first-world hype and drama considered normal and essential in the USA.

While the main drive towards the natural births in Managua was probably the sheer lack of personnel and facilities, the benefits to the women were enormous. Beds were nothing but a mattress with a plastic cover. If someone had enough resources, they brought their own sheets with them to the hospital. The hospital was forced to rely on apprenticed midwives and lay people—who, to their credit, did a great job. The only people I saw in the hospital were those who came in to give birth, and those who came in to die. We were reusing Vacutainer tubes and needles under the most primitive conditions. The one c-section I attended was atrocious. I was handed a pair of dirty covers for my shoes and a set of used scrubs while a terrified pregnant woman lay helplessly on her back awaiting the general anesthesia to take effect. That was the only form of knockout they had on hand. I watched the procedure with great trepidation, thinking it would be a miracle if that woman did not end up with sepsis.

Knowing what I know now, it is obvious that the USA could do much better. We have the resources to do a safe c-section WHEN necessary. The problem is the warped perception of what 'necessary' really is. Hands-down, Nicaragua had the natural birth process much better established. There is every reason that the best of both worlds should be combined.

My time outside of Bertha Calderón hospital in Nicaragua was spent in a church-based clinic. In retrospect, I was probably on a medical mission trip. I got the requisite shot of immune globulin in each side of the gluteus maximus that Dr. Tedaldi said I needed. I was up to date on all my other vaccines, having taken on a high-dose protocol of Hepatitis B vaccine as a guinea pig before medical school, and I took the prescription for chloroquine to Nicaragua. After a week, I decided that since the Nicaraguans could live there without poisoning themselves with antibiotics, so could I. I didn't get malaria anyhow. Instead I opted for the 'simple' form of dengue fever probably from a house mosquito. After a week of severe headache, fevers, body pains, followed by a spell of sleeping around 16 hours per day, I recovered.

The rest of my working time was spent in the church-based clinic stocked with expired or nearly expired USA pharmaceutical drugs, treating desperate people who called me "Doctora". "But wait! I am not a doctor. I am a fourth-year medical student and I have no idea what I am dealing with down here," was the thought in my head. There was no equipment to check blood tests, look at urine or stool, or x-rays. All I had to go on was my instinct, a physical examination, and a closet full of expiring drugs carried down in suitcases. On some days there was a Nicaraguan doctor of whom I could ask questions, and get validation for my choices, but most days I was winging it with newly learned, medical Spanish and one church member translating when I needed it.

Was I doing more harm than good down here with my limited supply of drugs, interfering in something I didn't fully understand? I sent children home with antihistamines and antibiotics, and the elderly home with analgesics for their arthritis, antifungals for foot fungus, and lots of practical advice that most people probably could not afford; like wearing clean socks and eating more protein. I was flying blind for the first time in my career, but it would not be the last. The whole experience was beyond stressful. I was totally beside myself wondering how things went for these people in the weeks and months to come. I later wrote a letter asking how certain people did after I gave them medications and the secretary told me that as far as she knew everyone did fine. Gulp.

I visited the headquarters of a social project in Managua called the soy project. They were making soy paste sandwiches on commercial, soft white bread and distributing it to children in need. I had a taste and realized how hungry even I had become. It felt good as it hit the bottom of my stomach, but was something I would never have touched in my luxurious American life at home. Kids need healthy food and love everywhere on earth, but in postwar Managua, both were scarce.

Returning to the USA, I had a renewed appreciation for all we take for granted: walking the streets in safety, hiking the mountains, roads with painted lines, men who are held to a higher standard of politeness, electricity, hot showers, sanitation, well-fed healthy dogs, computers, and no serious mosquito-borne illnesses. I remember thinking that the perfect cure for first-world doldrums would be to spend a few weeks in Managua, seeing dirty unkempt toddlers walking on crumbling highways and begging at stopped cars. The average home was a hut with corrugated metal roofing— yet strangely, most always with one appliance—a TV, usually playing old American action movies and bad news.

The air was blackened in patches wherever people lived. All day and night, smoke would drift from small bonfires, as people cooked the house chicken or stray dog, or burned trash including plastic. Hot showers were a nonentity. The water was only turned on three days per week by the city, so anyone who could, saved water in a drum for sparing use as needed. My host's home was luxurious by Nicaraguan standards, and my bath consisted of using one bucket of water out on the patio in sunshine. My student digs in the USA, would have been considered a castle in post-war Nicaragua. By the end of two visits, I had met several American activists and songwriters, who were Sandinista sympathizers and had gone there to live, help and join the revolutionaries, at least in spirit.

Nicaragua back then, was a harsh place that God seemed to have deserted and left as fodder for the Devil. It was my first taste of a place where any sensitive person could bleed their heart dry. Developing at least a light callous was a matter of need. Survival meant acting familiar on the streets, dressing down, and smoking cigarettes, which helped with the stress, but also—I hoped—helped me appear less delicate. It was a mixed experience. Human hearts are essentially the same everywhere. Babies are born into the worst environments and they draw out whatever love is leftover. The sad, desperate look in a sick old woman's eyes defies any cultural boundaries. The green snot on the face of a sick two-year-old in a tired mother's arms was the same in Managua as it was in the USA in 1900, or in ghettos anywhere. A fellow American traveler, who was doing some farming, told me that Nicaragua was so poor they could not even afford seeds.

I went home and, for the first time, felt deep in my gut, what an easy life I had had. My worst traumas and upsets were nothing compared to what I had witnessed in post-war poverty-stricken Managua. I knew my government was responsible for most of the trouble in Nicaragua, yet when I got off the plane, I was still relieved to be back on USA soil, ready to start my final six-week rotation before being crowned with a medical degree.

Nearing The Finish Line

Last rotation: trauma surgery

Many of my patients never got to go home. Watching people die was something that grieved me in the early years, especially the ones who were not expected to die. But the worst deaths to watch were the hemorrhages.

During my emergency trauma surgery rotation at North Philadelphia's Temple University Hospital, I saw plenty of horrible deaths, like the eight-year-old with smoke inhalation, who arrived at the ER dead. He looked perfectly fine except that he had some charcoal marks on his skin from the blaze he was trapped in. We tried everything to save him, including an open-chest cardiac massage. He never came back. I thought, "Wait! Eight-year-olds are not supposed to die." I heard my first wail of grief, but not my last. There is nothing like the sound of a mother being told her perfectly healthy eight-year-old son was suddenly gone forever. It still brings chills to remember.

The same month, we worked on a 22-year-old man. He was strong, fit, and brawny with long thick red hair and beard. He and his friend were messing around with a pick-up truck. One drove while the other stood in the back at high speed. The friend slammed on the brakes and tossed the redhead out of the truck, sending him 12 feet into the air and crashing into a tree with the back of his head. He looked normal too, until I picked up his head. The back of his skull was missing, and clotted blood and brain spilled out all over the stretcher. His brainstem and heart were still on line so we did what we could to keep his organs perfused while getting consent for organ donation, from another wailing mother.

These events were part of any day in a trauma service in a busy city hospital. Because tragedy is what you deal with all the time on a trauma service, the passage of time prepares you for most things, no matter how shocking.

Leaving the hospital on the last day of medical school was surreal. I was done and I had made it to the end. Many students didn't. One friend developed a flare-up of bleeding ulcerative colitis and had to drop out because he thought the stress was the cause of his flares. Another had to drop out after a brutal assault on the subway one block from the house I lived in. His facial bones were badly crushed and the physical trauma in the brain was enough to take him out of school permanently. But even more students could not pass the course work in the first two years, despite the school's best attempts to help them. I remember feeling really bad for one of the women, Hazel. I knew her because her last name was close to mine and we were in the same anatomy lab group. She just could not grasp the course material. Maybe she had a really bad case of self-doubt that simply did her in, because I knew she really was smart enough.

One of my favorite people was one of my housemates, Willy, a solidly built, tall African-American man. He made us feel safe in the house and sometimes walked me home or to school. After being left back three times, he landed in my class, but still couldn't get passing grades. It must have been horrible to have accumulated all that debt and then not be able to get the degree.

Despite my non-academic beginnings, and initial lack of self-assurance, I made it. Standing at the top of that little hill on the way to the final precipice, I took in the view, and smiled, savoring the moment.

In just a couple of weeks, I would start climbing another three-year mountain, and then, another . . . I had no idea back then, that at the end of the long mountain range, after drinking from the nectar of the gods, I would end up spitting it out.

14

Coronation Day

The bliss of that sunny day in May, when I was awarded my MD, was one of the happiest times of my life. The knowledge that, "I'm now a doctor," temporarily over-rode tiny feelings of disquiet, and the bitter distaste that had begun to grow while watching people be diagnosed and 'treated'—then get sicker and sicker, and while watching 'nice' doctors do unethical things, and creepy doctors getting away with blatant abuse.

Even so, I had hope, because there were some really amazing, brilliant, heart-centered doctors too. With letters after my name, I would soon be able to adjudge 'best practice' for myself and become a doctor who achieved more than feeling helpless. I was determined that I would help sick people find their way back to health. Decades later, making people better is still the most important goal, as it will always be.

Because I saw something wrong with the general way medicine was practiced, I wanted to try an alternative medicine type of residency. During medical school, I went to New York City's Bronx borough and did a rotation elective there to be sure that was what I wanted. I really liked the people because they were open-minded and trying to do something different. Of course everyone was on his or her best behavior, but even so, I thought I got to see how the residency worked. It wasn't until I actually joined them, that I got to see how it didn't work so well.

Temple University Medical School graduation, 1993

15

Internship
And Residency

I went to a social medicine/internal medicine program in New York, hoping to learn something unique that didn't just throw drugs at people. But there were not many significant differences between this residency program and an ordinary internal medicine program. The social medicine program offered a clinic with continuity, where patients always saw the same doctor instead of dealing with a random resident who was scheduled at the time, which is what happens in most residency programs. There was also an emphasis on what was happening in the home and socially in people's lives and how that impacted illness, but that should not be unique to a social medicine program. Considering how lifestyle and cultural norms or differences impact health, is just common sense in my opinion. There were opportunities for research, and there seemed to be more acceptance of non-pharmaceutical medical interventions in the outpatient setting.

The biggest difference was that we had a separate outpatient clinic in the South Bronx and had extra meetings at the social medicine building, where there were guest speakers, peer review sessions, and video self-review conferences, among other things. All the rest of the training was identical to the other medical residents. Like any internal medicine residency, there were choices on how much intensive care acute medicine vs. more outpatient-based 'health maintenance' or chronic medicine we could choose. Beyond 12 weeks of obligatory acute-care medicine, most of my electives were in the sub-specialty internal medicine areas.

We were able to choose which electives we wanted, but not when they happened. Timing was determined from on high and I suspect that social medicine residents got last pick as to the order of our rotations. My first rotation as an intern was the most dreaded one, the Cardiac Intensive Care Unit (CCU). To make it even more interesting, it just happened to be the month that the terror of cardiology, was the attending physician on service.

The Thunderbird, a legendary senior cardiologist at Montefiore Medical Center, was of German descent. She ruled with an iron fist exacting the most rigorous academic standards. When she was upset, her fist would hit the counter, the neck veins would bulge, and everyone around her would tremble. Or worse, her fist would point towards you, or the finger, or occasionally, a medical chart could fly in your direction. Everyone did his or her best to make sure that didn't happen. Sometimes a tyrant only needs to show their might once, in order to get the masses to comply forever, because the legend lives on.

With the legs of a 20-year-old, she wore short leather mini skirts almost every day along with three-inch stilettos that she seemed to have a second nature to surf upon and, the ever-present, just-a-little-bit-too-open, undone top three buttons of her blouse. Often there was the top of a breast, or even the edge of a lacey bra peeking out. She was built like a supermodel, until you got to the face, which looked every bit of her 70 years, and erased the image one got from the back. Scars behind her ears, gave away the secret to her taut eye skin. Image and authority were everything to The Thunderbird. Nobody ever messed up around her, or dared to joke about anything. The only jokes were hers, and she laughed the loudest. Apparently, if you publish enough high-impact medical papers, and get to be renowned for your academic prowess, you can be as much of a sadist as you wish. This was to become a recurrent truth in my various specialty rotations.

There were rules that some of us never figured out. "At least one liter of fluid to every patient every day," no matter how bad the congestive heart failure or kidney failure was. She never explained why. But when you are a legend like that, nobody presses you. The intuition of a guru is enough to have everyone doing as they are told. So while interns and residents spent the nights fighting off congestive heart failure, myocardial infarctions, arrhythmias, and more, The Thunderbird got her beauty sleep, which she proudly admitted was often induced with temazepam, especially when she went on holiday to the alps. Every morning the nurses, interns, residents, and fellows went through the same ritual of gathering the charts, putting them in the wheeled rack, having all lab values on hand with a fully detailed report of the night, and a morning progress note written with the physical exam detailed. If she agreed, she would bless the note with her signature. If she didn't agree, we would get a lot of pointed questions.

There was a second-year resident named Mukesh Patel who saved my hide, day in and day out. He had a seemingly supernatural ability to know exactly what to do in every circumstance and how to answer. Mukesh nearly always had everything working like a well-oiled machine, and shielded me from the wrath of the claw-drawn Thunderbird.

Most of the patients who were conscious, were glad to have a strong older doctor overseeing their medical care. But once in a while a patient only has the ability to give an innocent, natural response. During morning rounds, we stood at the bed of a very elderly Jewish woman who had just a pinch of dementia. When The Thunderbird gave the usual "Good Mawning Meeses Rrrrosenbeag" to a half-sleeping Mrs. Rosenberg, Mrs. Rosenberg startled with a jump out of bed and a loud scream. After a short uncomfortable snicker, The Thunderbird carried on her routine, while the rest of us stifled uproarious laughter.

The nights in CCU were speckled with short naps, curtailed by our ever-present pocket pagers that would give a shrill beep, followed by a muffled operator telling us which four-digit number to call. Most of the time, a page required a walk back to the CCU to monitor whatever arrhythmia had occurred. After treating as indicated, we could return to the on-call room for another nap, if we were lucky.

One evening, an 88-year-old woman, who had had a massive heart attack that interrupted her conduction system, was trying to die. Since her living will stated that she wanted everything done, we were tortured all night with one arrhythmia and unstable hemodynamic situation after another. I remember waiting for the elevator to arrive, wishing she would just die, so that I could get some sleep. This is not something I feel proud to admit and it was not the last time that keeping someone alive artificially, who was bound to die anyway, sent my mind into that place. It's just reality for all but the most superhuman of medical trainees. She died a few hours after I signed off my shift.

The CCU was the beginning of three busy years where anything and everything could happen. In 1993, the Bronx's teaching hospitals had only a skeletal phlebotomy service, and limited special services. We, the medical house staff, did everything: arranged social services, transfers, ordered all medical testing, personally drew all of our own blood samples, set up IVs, did our own EKGs, hung blood transfusions, performed lumbar punctures, and arranged hospital discharges. You name it; the house staff did it. I don't regret that at all, because I think it made me a more skilled and competent doctor.

In 1989, New York state adopted the Bell Commission's recommendations that residents should not work more than 80 hours a week or more than 24 consecutive hours. In addition, attending physicians were supposed to be physically present in the hospital at all times. But my experience did not line up with those regulations—at all. We went home when we were done, and sometimes that was 36-48 consecutive hours of work later. But later, as a full-attending teaching physician, when I saw the quality of the new residents that emerged from the kinder, gentler regulations, it was evident that 'kinder and gentler' did not produce as knowledgeable, competent, or experienced medical doctors. There is nothing like a ground zero to learn in, and the Bronx NY was the perfect war zone. It was a very busy city hospital system, which provided patients of all ages, diseases, and walks of life, from all around the world. Despite sleepless nights and the sleep anxiety that emerged as a result, and year-long clinical depression, I'm grateful to have had the education I got there, because nothing can replace hands-on reality.

As for the depression, it was easy to forget that someday we would all emerge from the position of overworked, sleepless minion, to have some quality of life again, and be able to be the boss. The light at the end of the tunnel seemed an eternity away during the first, and part of the second, years of internship, and the things I saw and the work required seriously messed with my head at times. But I can look back and say it was all part of a valuable learning experience, from the school of hard knocks. From those above me, I was often reminded, "That which doesn't kill us, makes us stronger." And that at least, "I was not a patient and I got to go home alive and healthy," no matter how bad the work was. They were right. I also learned that half a cup of strong coffee mixed with a quarter can of chocolate Ensure made an okay café mocha. That recipe saved me from wasting 30 minutes in the cafeteria getting breakfast, and kept me going for six hours on busy mornings.

There were some encounters during residency that lingered with me long after I went home at night. Exsanguination is the technical term for bleeding to death. Blood has a subtle smell you never forget, and the room fills with that smell during exsanguination. And for some reason, those deaths were particularly hard for me to stomach. Probably the helplessness in the middle of a fully equipped hospital is one reason it was difficult.

A 50-year-old obese Hispanic woman was taken to cardiac surgery at North Central Bronx hospital. After her operation, she was put in the ICU where the resident physicians took over her care. After a few hours, she began to ooze blood from the chest wound. We applied pressure, checked her coagulation status, and monitored her vital signs. The oozing worsened and the surgical team was called. This was when I first learned that consultants and surgeons don't always jump on a problem with the same degree of urgency that I would like. We never did see a surgeon that day, and spent the next hour pouring blood into Mrs. Santos, just trying to balance what was pouring out of her. I felt that the senior resident didn't know anything else to do except keep pouring blood into her. I think there were around 12 units of blood used to keep her systolic blood pressure above 80. By the end of the hour, she was gone and once again, our feet were stained in blood. Mrs. Santos was not a guinea pig, but rather the victim of incompetent surgeons and residents. We were doing the best we knew how to do, but I have always felt that she could have been saved. Outwardly, hammer and nail medicine seems to make sense to a novice. If someone is bleeding, you infuse blood. If they are infected, you give them antibiotics. If they can't breathe, you give them oxygenated air. If they can't eat, you give them liquid calories through a nasogastric feeding tube or parenteral nutrition. If they can't move their bowels, you go in with an enema and/or pull the fecal matter out manually. Today, outside the walls of the ivory tower, hammer and nail medicine often looks savage, because I now understand more and know better. However nobody around me knew any better back then.

After Mrs. Santos' death, I'd been part of enough 'codes' and exsanguinations, to have worn down my calloused heart. I remember breaking down in my kitchen, on one of my days off and having a good cry, and then lighting a candle and thinking of God and all the souls that left on my shifts, and asking God and the souls of the dead to forgive me for anything I did wrong or for my shortcomings that meant I could not save them. This became a regular practice, crying after so much sadness and death had built up, lighting candles and praying . . . even though, at the time, God was mostly an afterthought in my spiritually agnostic life. Like everything else, I was covering all the bases I thought I knew—or didn't know.

A young man with AIDS came into the hospital, emaciated and infected with pneumocystis pneumonia. In the midst of his treatment, he began to bleed from his nose. The third-year medical resident on call, whom I can only remember as The Savage, packed the nose was as per routine. She was really good at technical skills but she could have been working on her enemies for all the hostility she emanated. The man kept bleeding down the back of his throat, and spitting it out, which frustrated The Savage. We transfused him and gave lots of IV fluids but because he was a former drug injector, his veins could not tolerate all the fluid and they burst. We were left with no IV access. The Savage attempted to place a femoral vein central catheter, but every poke and stick meant more bleeding. It turned out that his platelet count was in the sub-basement. Eventually, after a lot of stabbing and cutting by The Savage, central vein access was established but the bleeding just never stopped. The code was started, CPR, and all the chemicals were used per protocol by the robotic Savage, but to no avail.

In the end, a handful of young residents, sweaty and red-smeared interns, were left standing in a pool of blood, looking at an emaciated dead man. The Savage left, knocking the paper cloths and plastic trays off the table as she swooped up her white coat, and gave orders to the minions to fill out the death certificate, clean up the mess, write a note, and enter all orders for the drugs we had used. I sometimes wonder where she is today: Perhaps a busy city clinic, shuffling patients in and out, hating them every second, while dispensing elixirs as a matter of routine. Or maybe she grew a heart, once her own post-traumatic stress had eased up.

This was life in North Central Bronx Hospital. The patients were all poor and mostly of color and they used to get angry because they felt like guinea pigs. In a sense they were guinea pigs because we just did all we knew how to do. It is possible that a more senior attending physician would have done things differently than a cadre of minions under The Savage's tutelage.

Patients were guinea pigs for lots of reasons, even after they died. Mrs. Geneva Brown was one such patient. A 50-something, robust looking African-American woman, she walked into the emergency room complaining of some trouble breathing and a cough. Days before, she was enjoying good health, a birthday cruise around the New York Harbor, and her normal life, with two dedicated adult children. Her daughter, a taller and thinner version of her gorgeous mother, was at her bedside until her untimely death. Mrs. Brown had a 'fever of unknown origin'. On day two of her hospitalization, she required mechanical ventilation and after one week, we were feeding her through a nasogastric tube. The fever raged on, despite three different powerful antimicrobials, a cooling blanket, and our best efforts to diagnose and treat her. The infectious disease team came every day, scratched their heads, ordered more tests, changed antibiotics here and there, and never made her any better. Every genius within consulting range was called upon for an opinion. This is one of the cases that still haunt me. I can still see her struggling, sweating and looking really uncomfortable as she fought the battle against some mysterious illness. All of our scans turned up nothing. She died after three weeks in the intensive care unit. I was gutted because I thought we missed something and she should not have died. And while I was alive, part of me also felt dead. There was a yawning cavern of emptiness inside that seemed to get deeper the more we failed.

My attending physician was Dr. Gerber; a physical giant of a man who was also a really warm, humorous, and caring cardiologist. When life became noticeably stressful, he used to break the tension by talking in a high-pitched voice with a German accent, ala The

Thunderbird. He cared for us as residents but not so much for patients. All he focused on was whether or not we got the post-mortem autopsy. I hated to ask Mrs. Brown's family for that after all they had been through. Knowing they would cut her from neck to pubic bone and take all of the organs out for inspection, cut her head open and subject her to more desecration, I could not bring myself to ask the family. I thought if they wanted her to have an autopsy, they would have asked us. I never did arrange the post-mortem examination. I cared about her too much. Perhaps I shortchanged my education and that of the other residents, in case the pathologist had turned up something on examination. But we sometimes have to make the choices we can live with. I made my choice.

Taking a nap with Jazzie, 1995

16 The Arrogance Of Ignorance

Patients were also guinea pigs because there was still a lot we didn't know about AIDS. I remember browsing through a bookstore with my best friend and constant companion, Dick. He was perusing new novels and I went to the medical section. A book jumped out at me called *Inventing the AIDS virus* by Dr. Peter Duesberg.

At that time, Duesberg was not viewed as a fringe quack without a medical degree. He received a Nobel Prize. He was, is, and, despite the unbridled anger thrown in his direction, continues to be a professor of molecular and cell biology at the University of California at Berkeley. Peter Duesberg is a pioneer in retrovirus research and was the first scientist to isolate a cancer gene. He is a member of the National Academy of Science and received the Outstanding Investigator Award from the National Institutes of Health.

I bought the book and read it from cover to cover and then some. Based on what I was seeing around me, I could go along with the fact that the people I saw were immunosuppressed prior to being infected with HIV. Many of the NY patients were constantly on antibiotics. Promiscuity, in both males and females, is immunosuppressive. Their lifestyles were suppressing their immune systems so much that any virus, including HIV, might have the potential to cause havoc. Duesberg had a point: that to begin with, retroviral drugs were making things worse because experts had no idea what doses to give and inadvertently gave toxic doses, at more than twice the amounts given to patients today.

Comorbidities and toxic retroviral drugs at the inappropriate old dosages, made perfect sense to me and I felt that it unlocked a mystery that had been bothering me for some time. But there is also no doubt that when given the correct doses, patients got better and their T-cell counts rose. Later on in my career, I would see an HIV patient respond so well to treatment, that he was successfully given a kidney transplant. My understanding today of HIV and AIDS is far more sophisticated, but that is not relevant to what I thought 22 years ago.

As a clinician, I knew what I saw when treating HIV patients. What caught my attention was that by reading a book by a world-renowned, Nobel Prize-winning, tenured professor from one of the world's biggest academic power houses, and giving thought to some of what he said, I was met with a mountain of hostility by people who outright refused to even read his book. I had no reason to doubt everything he was saying or automatically toss it all out as rubbish.

Today, I know that there is a huge population of HIV-positive people who are actually falsely positive on testing, for various common reasons. There are also many who were once sick, had HIV positivity, low CD4 cell counts, but have had vastly improved health and are disease-free by virtue of changing their habits and implementing good nutrition and appropriate vitamin supplementation. Duesberg's theory may not be true for every AIDS patient, but what if it was true for even some? Wouldn't doctors want to know that?

At that time, it was also becoming clear to me that many of my teachers in residency, and even my best friend Dick, were making careers on the AIDS virus by solely focusing on all sorts of new drugs in new combinations with the goal of prolonging the CD4 T-cell population. I didn't see much attention given to lifestyle, comorbidities, or the effects of constant prescription-drug treatment on every other opportunistic pathogen these people were fighting off. Part of me believed then, and believes now, that the HIV virus wouldn't have been nearly so famous had doctors promoted better lifestyle choices, that have the potential to make life very difficult for the HIV virus. At the very least, the outcome for these people would have been far more optimistic at that time.

On considering this bigger picture, and the fact that my colleagues were only functioning with narrow reductionist thinking, I thought, *"What would happen to all these doctors who are building careers around HIV drugs, if addressing lifestyle and nutritional issues changed the need for this expensive mountain of drugs we are now prescribing? They would have to find new specialties or adapt their focus towards looking at total health, rather than correcting a bad test result. Do they really want a treatment for AIDS that could mean they have to find new work or change their narrow focus?"* The answer, of course, for most of them is NO! If there was any other treatment, would they even believe it? The only focus they could allow to influence their biased thinking, was that HIV is a dangerous virus that needs to be eternally drug-treated like a chronic disease. And that they would have a life-long secure job through a patient base constantly dependent upon drugs they prescribed, monitored, and adjusted to suit. Making themselves even partially redundant isn't the goal of a "successful business model". The same thinking is operative today in the pharmaceutical treatment of infectious diseases, chronic disease, and cancer.

In my naïvety, I made mention of this book to Dick, who refused to read it, and was disgusted with me for suggesting such quackery could be real. Nobody would read the book. Many other people rolled their eyes without any curiosity. One of my former professors felt the same, and said, "Yeah, most of what I hear is that everyone just wants him to shut up." To them it was their way, or the highway. **If only Duesberg would just shut up** . . . Without reading or rationally considering his facts, they 'knew' that no variation or broader thinking should be considered or tolerated.

Little did I know that decades later, I would be called a dangerous quack for writing a book, by people who have probably never read it. However, I have received emails from some doctors who have read my book with an open mind, and checked out what I say.

It would take my own personal experience as an outlier doctor, butting heads with mainstream ignorance and medical religion, for me to realize that cancer, high blood pressure, infections, kidney disease, heart disease, autoimmune diseases, arthritis, and joint disease are all pathways to career success. It should have occurred to me much sooner that doctors, industry, and academia work together to build careers[14] around the blood of sick people, and that a true cure for many conditions is not only unprofitable, but also undesirable. For hundreds of thousands of medical professionals, the drug focus ensures lifelong academic claim and tenure, and is worth billions of dollars to them, and their industry. There is no real incentive to pursue either knowledgeable lifestyle preventions, or a true cure by those who hold the purse strings.

Duesberg was in the ivory tower club, receiving awards and accolades, until he challenged the widely accepted belief that HIV is the fundamental cause of AIDS and argued that HIV is a passenger virus. From there on, he became a nuisance at best and a dangerous quack at worst in the eyes of the mainstream medical model, most of whom probably refused to read his thesis enough to even have a rational educated conversation. Duesberg was not alone in his skepticism around the HIV-AIDS connection. Kary Mullis, who was awarded a Nobel Prize for his role in the development of the improved polymerase chain reaction, has expressed sympathy for Duesberg's theory, as have several other outspoken scientists. Most people who question the HIV/AIDS relationship are categorically

---

[14] National Vaccine Advisory Committee, 1997 "United States Vaccine Research: A Delicate Fabric of Public and Private Collaboration," *Pediatrics*, Dec;100(6):1015-20. PMID: 9411380

tossed into the conspiracy bin, regardless of their scientific reputation or accomplishments.

Unlike virus denialists, Duesberg never denied the existence of the virus. Duesberg, and most of the many scientists who have sympathy with some or all of Duesberg's views, still hold tenured positions in academia.

About 20 years after reading Duesberg's theory, I was immersed in poliovirus research. My study revealed to me a similar situation with poliomyelitis, in that there are numerous published scientific studies that disprove the central dogma that ONLY poliovirus caused paralysis. There are either cofactors along with the poliovirus or no polio virus at all, found in the majority of people who have been diagnosed with poliomyelitis. Other enteroviruses, such as Coxsackie B, are often found in paralyzed people with no trace of polioviruses. There are published cases of lead poisoning, which were initially diagnosed as paralytic polio. I found recent papers linking agricultural chemicals to a polio-like paralysis. In China, what was originally thought of as polio was later diagnosed as Keshan Disease, the underlying cofactor was selenium deficiency. In the 1990s, the CDC was rampaging through Cuba, determined that the paralysis they saw was polio, but again, it turned out to be selenium deficiency augmenting a coxsackie virus—yet in other areas of Cuba, where there was no selenium deficiency, antibodies to the virus were widespread, but clinical disease was absent. I found all this information startling and published some of it in a 70-page chapter on polio in *Dissolving Illusions: Disease, Vaccines, and the Forgotten History*[15].

Ironically, I was later verbally dogpiled by an anti-vaccine coalition that denies outright the existence of any infectious viruses, stating

---

[15] Humphries, S., and Bystrianyk, R. 2013. *Dissolving Illusions: Disease, Vaccines and the Forgotten History*. Available on Amazon.com

that they are detoxification elements. This is obviously ridiculous, given the ability to type all sorts of viruses genetically, and the experimentally demonstrated contagion of so many viruses like measles and varicella.

17

The Bane Of Bad Apples

Another intensive care specialty I rotated through for six weeks, was the pulmonary or lung unit. A senior physician named Dr. Pinsky gave me one of my most valuable lessons when it came to dealing with obstructive nurses. While most nurses are your allies, every doctor becomes subject to a bad apple in the barrel. My nemesis was a veteran nurse there who came to work every day in her military-perfect whites with the old-fashioned white nurse hat. She could be considered the black nurse version of The Thunderbird.

I must interject here with some history. I was raised believing that all people are equal regardless of the color of their skin, the texture of their hair, or their education, because the most important part of a person has nothing to do with any of those things. I still believe that. I was never a race discriminator. Race never even entered my mind as a modern issue. I knew there were poor disenfranchised people all over the Americas and that slavery had taken every form and been perpetrated upon every race, including white people, some of whom were from my own Irish lineage.

One of my very first friends, at the age of five, was African-American. We were both fascinated with each other's hair. Almost simultaneously, we touched each other's heads with curiosity: her hand to my dark brown locks and mine to her bushy afro. Then we just carried on as good friends. My high school was at least 50% black and some of my best friends were black. Growing up, there were always black, brown, and non-Caucasian people in my circle of friends, and there always will be. My best friend in medical school was half African-American and half American-Indian. I lived my life treating people as people. All lives are precious and important. End of story.

When I was 19 and working in the nursing home, Roz the nurse, took me to an all-black bar in North Philadelphia. She wanted to show me what it felt like to be the minority — the only white face in a sketchy part of town. But being the only white person in the bar didn't faze me any more than being the lone gringa in Guatemala or Nicaragua. I knew the horrible history of slavery in the Americas and how nasty the Africans were treated after their emancipation and that there were still racist bastards among us — one of which lost his job because of me. I was not an ignorant white person of privilege. I had grown up with less money than most of the blacks I worked with. None of us can live our lives constantly focused on what we think we don't have.

Fast-forward to the Bronx in 1993-1996, and Dr. Pinsky who presided over the pulmonary unit, where apparently there was still a nasty race war going on. That same race war also went on in my social medicine residency building, where a cadre of people of color pushed to have the white chair of internal medicine fired. I agreed she needed to be fired, because she was a total ditz, and had no right to be the head of anything—not because she was racist or white. She was incompetent and daft, and she infuriated me just as much as she infuriated everyone else.

The response to the race war resulted in a culture of white people trying to appease the angry black and Puerto Rican nurses, patients, and anyone else who had a complaint about Christopher Columbus or any other white character, past or present. The problem was that any appeasement was never enough, and only seemed to cause more anger. Part of the social medicine program was appreciation of cultural diversity, and discussion and training ignorance out of everyone, in order to provide the best medical care to the local population.

O.J. Simpson was on trial during this time, and the division among some of the secretarial staff, nurses, and doctors shocked me. The black people in my midst simply refused to believe that O.J. could have killed Nicole. The day the judgment was handed down and O.J. was vindicated, secretaries and doctors of color partied, dancing in the social medicine building like it was New Year's Eve. Watching the whole thing unfold in slow motion with streamers, glitter and music floating in the air, I was startled that I had missed these undertones living in the hearts of some of my favorite people. I saw one of my favorite secretaries dancing and thought, "Clearly there is something I don't understand." So I listened and watched and spent time trying to work out what I had missed. But really, I didn't miss anything. O.J. is a monster. He is finally in jail where he belongs, because he continued a life of violence and crime.

I remember being the only person willing to say something that was not politically correct, because actually I was not a racist. Only a racist would have said nothing. There were all sorts of discussions regarding the fact that Mark Fuhrman had not done a clean investigation. During one of our sociology meetings, I was encouraged to talk about it by one of the psychologists who was part Native American, named Dr. Chinita Fulchon. She thought honesty in conversation was important. So, in a meeting among many people of color, including Chinita, I asked, "So because it is okay to kill your wife if you are white, it should be okay to kill your wife because you are black?" Everybody found someplace else to look and I never got an answer. Maybe it's just not okay to kill anyone in a fit of jealousy or rage—ever, no matter who you are. So why was anyone celebrating when we knew two people were brutally murdered?

O.J. got off on a technicality. It would have been one thing to just shrug and say alright, that's working the system to your advantage, but to celebrate his acquittal as if a landmark civil rights victory had been won, was revolting to me.

If you have a hospital where a certain sector of the black population are busy hating on the white population and making lives miserable—because they actually had the power to do so—lives can be lost as a result. As interns and residents, we were very much dependent on the ward clerks, the radiology technicians, and the nurses, any of which could whip out an, "I'm not going to help you spoiled white brats" attitude, even if it meant simply not doing their job. Fortunately, the majority of hospital workers were not that way. However, just as it takes a little bit of yeast to impregnate the whole of a loaf of bread, it's true that the bad apples on the ward can not only stall progress and ruin the day for good nurses and doctors trying to do their jobs, but also threaten the lives of patients in many different ways. Several such instances happened.

The most memorable was in North Central Bronx Hospital radiology department, where I was the intern on call. My pager went off and I was summoned to the sixth floor where a patient I had never met showed new signs of paralysis on half of the body. He seemed stable to me so I called the radiology department, were I was met with the usual obstinacy and doubt as to whether or not I had filled out all the work orders perfectly. One of the radiology technicians was particularly hateful at baseline, and he was on that night. I arranged help to have the patient transported, and went down to the basement with the transport personnel and the patient on a stretcher. Once we arrived, we were sent back to the floor by the tech stating that we were early and he was not ready. He was eating. Rather than have a huge fight while a patient was having an active stroke, we brought the patient back to the floor. Once we were there, we were told by the ward nurse to go back downstairs because they were ready for us. We went back down and were told the same thing, that they were not ready. He was still eating and there was a lady with him this time. By the time the transport assistant and I arrived back on the floor, the transport assistant was practically in tears because of the ludicrous injustice and insanity of such despotism. I told him it wasn't the first time, and wouldn't be the last. Complaints were lodged by many people but the workers were all unionized so nothing was ever done.

Those months were not pleasant, particularly concerning a certain female ward clerk who made it her personal mission to make every intern cry at least once. I don't recall her name, but I recall one of her habits, which was to suck her cheek with a clicking noise when she was sneering at an underling doctor. When I was an intern, she made me shed tears of outrage and frustration. But by the time I became a third-year resident, I wasn't going to let her do the same to my intern. She tried though and, when I saw the intern near tears, I decided to intervene.

The ward clerk was hassling the intern over the labels she was trying to stamp, and was delaying the delivery of the samples to the lab, which needed to be processed 'stat'. I picked up the tubes of blood and the urine sample, went behind the counter and set the samples on a piece of paper on the file cabinet and opened the drawers, and took out the forms and bags that the clerk was provoking my intern over. She sucked her cheek really hard, began twitching and said, "You can't lay those samples on the counter like that." And I said, "Apparently I can. Look they are just sitting there and I put them there." I bagged the samples, stamped the paperwork with the patient's card, and handed them to the intern.

Later in the week, I was led into a private meeting room by the head nurse in her starched whites. She told me what a bad girl I was, after which I explained the position of my intern and the malignant ward clerk, turned on my heel and left. Behind my back, the clerk and some nurses named me "Dr. Bitch." Dr. Pinsky pulled me aside one morning with a grin on his face, like a parent who has to correct you even though they are actually proud of you. He said "Suzanne. Nursing is a paramilitary organization. When a nurse tells you something that you don't like, you say 'Yes ma'am' out loud. And then in your head you say 'Eff you'." I agreed and we moved on.

Most of the nurses in my career earned enormous respect from me and many became my friends. One nurse even followed me to Maine to work together in dialysis for nearly 10 years. Once again, I never paint any group with the stroke of one brush, nasty or nice; whether they be black, brown, tan, white, yellow, or red people . . . or nurses. I have always seen the human beneath the façade and acted accordingly. It is one of the things my mother taught me, which has held me in good stead. I admire all people who do an honorable job, no matter what the job is; we are all needed. But of those who didn't honor their patients or the people around them, I tolerated very little. The same went for doctors, though it wasn't until later in my career that I began to notice which doctors needed to be challenged and reoriented.

Nurses teach doctors at least half of all the practical things they learn on the job. And there is nothing more valuable to either patient, or doctor, than an experienced, compassionate, and seasoned RN. Years later, one of my long-term patients, Mr. R. Bean, was gasping for his last breaths—in my opinion, at too young an age for death. He asked the nurse on the cardiac intensive care unit to call me up from working in my office. I went and held his hand and talked to him and his wife, and he asked me to just keep him comfortable because he had had enough. As I went to the nurses' station, sobbing and nearly incapacitated with grief, it was an RN who dictated the exact orders for me to write for the morphine drip that was to be administered 'to patient comfort'. He never once sucked his cheek or belittled me for needing his help. Thank God for those nurses.

Retrospection

Residency was about gaining experience, learning, and keeping one's mouth shut unless pushed too hard. They were the years of "see one—do one—teach one": the apprentice method that all young doctors learn by. Whenever someone challenges me today for doing something new without having years of practice, like treating babies for whooping cough with vitamin C, I remind them how much of my career was expended in the absence of a gold standard method, experimenting with different protocols. I also reiterate the reality that my second lumbar puncture was done after I just watched the first one, and my third one was done by a resident or student below me, as I supervised. It's how we all learn. And much of what we learn is some person's inspiration and experience guiding us in what to do, or not to do because we don't have a controlled study to back it up.

I learned that medicine was not all it was cracked up to be and that some doctors were more than human, and some were seemingly subhuman. And that people die of natural causes but more of them die after protracted illnesses, and being kept alive artificially until death simply becomes stronger than all the tools of the doctor.

There were instances where I thought something didn't seem right, but because there was so much insecurity as the underling, I usually said nothing. For example: endoscopies with instruments that are reused and reintroduced into hundreds or perhaps thousands of successive patients. Every specialist has their bread and butter procedure; the one they think is of high yield for information . . . and which also happens to lend itself to higher billing status.

Cardiologists have their cardiac catheterizations and stents and, as a result, they often can't see the forest for the trees. Their ingrained passion is to get patients to the cath lab and later entertain the differential diagnosis and more intellectual processing. Surgeons have surgery. While a good surgeon performs well under the hot lights, an excellent surgeon knows when to say no to surgery.

Dermatologists have their favorite tool: the liquid nitrogen burner. When in doubt they sample the lesions for cancer and when not in doubt they sear it off with a freeze. I happen to love my dermatologist so don't get me wrong. She has taken sunspots off my face and made it so I don't have to use cover-up anymore before going on camera. But still, that's just how it is. My profession has kidney biopsies, which are done far too often in my opinion, and I was sometimes questioned for not being aggressive enough on that front. Nephrologists also run dialysis units, and that extra income helped keep our year-end bonuses rolling in.

Gastroenterologists have colonoscopies.

A colonoscopy is done with a long fiber optic snake, which is passaged up the anus, rectum, and sigmoid, to the transverse colon and finally past the hepatic flexure towards the ileocecal valve. Air is blown into the intestine to blow the walls outwards for easier visualization. Before the endoscopy, the colon is washed clean with multiple enemas and a drink named GoLytely, which I always found to be rather ironic. I used to call it go-all-nightly, because there was nothing light about it. The other option was vile-tasting Fleet's Phospho-Soda for a good clean out. My point regarding the clean out is that, in addition to flushing out stagnant stool from the colon, whichever method is used also flushes out considerable volumes of beneficial bacteria that protect the body and the colon walls. That washout depletes protection and increases infection susceptibility. After a sick person has an endoscopy, rarely is any infection that follows thought to be associated with a reusable endoscope. Yet when a healthy person goes for their religious five-year sightseeing tour by the gastroenterologist, problems can appear out of the blue.

About a week into my gastroenterology rotation, I had a good look at the endoscope. While the surfaces of the snakelike instrument were mostly smooth, there were areas that looked like a potential niche for microbes to hide and evade sterilization. In addition, while the operator tries to only use one hand on the anus and scope and the other hand on the camera, there is often two-hand use of both ends, contaminating the complex jointed camera. I thought to myself, "How can they possibly effectively sterilize that device from top to bottom for the next person?"

In the following years, my own patients often told me of the infections they acquired just days after getting a colonoscopy. Ironically, one of them was a patient of the chief of medicine in Maine who thought I was mad for questioning the safety of vaccines given to acutely and seriously ill patients. Not only did I hear from patients of his who had vaccine reactions but one who was given antibiotics for a Campylobacter jejuni intestinal infection one week after his colonoscopy! While this is usually a self-limiting infection, it can also be quite severe.

In the years since then, there has been an outpouring of medical validation to my early concerns over unsterile colonoscopies and resultant infection risk. The risk is real and now you can read about it on the internet from peer-reviewed medical literature[16] and popular media. The CDC website[17] states *"more healthcare–*

---

[16] Kenters, N., et al., 2015 "Infectious diseases linked to cross-contamination of flexible endoscopes," *Endosc Int Open*, Aug; 3(4): E259–E265. PMID: 26355428

[17] Centers for disease control and prevention. Healthcare Infection Control Practices Advisory Committee (HICPAC), Guideline for Disinfection and Sterilization in Healthcare Facilities, 2008. http://www.cdc.gov/hicpac/Disinfection_Sterilization/3_0disinfectEquipment.html

associated outbreaks have been linked to contaminated endoscopes than to any other medical device". But, back in my medical residency days, such an idea was considered to be half-baked nonsense from a naïve novice's over-active imagination.

You can also be sure the reported cases are tiny compared to the actual cases, just like vaccine reactions. Someone has to notice them, make the connection, and then report them. In 2015, the news[18] reported that superbugs are spreading in hospitals as a result of duodenal endoscopes.

When infections are noticed, there always seems to be a logical explanation or some unavoidable circumstance. *"Studies have found that, despite adherence to cleaning and disinfection guidelines, endoscopes can remain contaminated, leading to infections. Defects, either during production or during use, such as a loose biopsy-port cap, can cause outbreaks or infections. Lack of maintenance also can lead to contamination of flexible endoscopes."*[19]

I suspect that most infections are with normal colon flora and never become symptomatic. In recent times, however, upper endoscopy has led to numerous deaths and infections from hospital superbugs called Carbapenem-resistant Enterobacteriaceae (CRE). Dozens have died, and thus there is more focused attention on the cross-contamination issue. I am not suggesting that colonoscopies should be stopped. However, given that endoscopes are mainly used on people who have usually been on serial antibiotics that can result in serious gut dysbiosis issues leading to gut colonization with superbugs, one should never assume total safety, total sterility, or that you will suffer no consequences from 'routine screening'. All medical procedures carry an inherent risk, sometimes from the skill

---

[18] Huff, E., 2015 "Endoscopes are spreading superbugs in US hospitals," *AlignLife*. https://alignlife.com/articles/infections/endoscopes-are-spreading-superbugs-in-us-hospitals

[19] Ibid. Kenters, 2015.

and carefulness of the operator and sometimes from the maintenance of the equipment. Risk factors should be weighed against possible procedure risks.

Dr. Nice Guy not so nice

Swollen testicles, penile discharge, erectile dysfunction, lumps, blood in the urine, or can't pee? When it comes to male medical issues, men prefer a male urologist, and that's what they usually get.

Women had no choice for a long time, but today they do—at least electively. I think the fields should be restructured and women should be primarily doing women's obstetric, gynecologic, and urological medicine, and men should continue doing the urologic and reproductive medicine for men. It should not be the case, that a woman in acute distress is only given the option of a man to examine her in emergency situations. I've borne witness to too much subtle abuse from even the 'nicest' guys that never gets reported.

Dr. S. was my senior resident at Montefiore Medical Center. I was a second-year resident and he was in his last year. We had worked together one year previously, when I was a new intern, and he was by far one of the smartest and kindest people I worked with during my residency. So the following event took me totally by surprise and I still have regret for not doing more for the elderly Croatian woman who unnecessarily ended up feeling violated in the emergency room. Mrs. C. was brought to the ER by her daughter for having pelvic pain. Women who present acutely with pelvic pain get the following tests: urine analysis, rectal exam, fecal occult blood test, general abdominal exam, vaginal/pelvic exam, and pregnancy test if applicable. Mrs. C. was totally okay until she asked, through a translator, to have the pelvic exam to be done by the "lady doctor". The male doctor took this personally and said, "No, I am the doctor and I will do the exam." I weakly protested in the moment and said, "Why don't you just let me do it. She is clearly very distressed at being examined by a man." To which Dr. S. grew more determined and said, "NO." He told the translator to have Mrs. C. put her legs into the stirrups and open them. He went on to do the speculum exam, swab, and bimanual hand examination. Mrs. C. cried through the whole thing. I was so angry with him after that, I could barely look at him, and have never forgotten it. I doubt Mrs. C. ever forgot it either. That is what the nice guys are capable of . . .

I had a first-year intern on my service when I was a third-year resident. He was an attractive, moderately arrogant young man, who was quite good at fudging an answer when he didn't know it. It was obvious to me that he was dishonest and a bit slimy and would need extra monitoring. We were called to the emergency room to evaluate a beautiful 22-year-old woman for abdominal pain. The medical intern took me aside and said, "Can I do the pelvic exam? Please, please, please?" I asked him how he would like to be in an emergency room with abdominal pain, if behind the scenes, a young gay male intern was begging me to allow him to do the genital, rectal, and prostate exams—saying 'Please, please, please?' He went silent and I assigned my second-year resident to do the exam.

Some doctors become callous jerks over time, but some of them start out that way. I am sad to say that the field of medicine does not require any psychological testing to ensure that doctors released onto the unsuspecting public, are the sort that patients deserve. This is unforgiveable, particularly given the huge amount of research done on medical students by the Johns Hopkins Precursors Study[20]. This was started by Dr. Caroline Bedell Thomas, who wanted to look at 1,046 medical students and follow them, from the start of medical school, through their careers. One of the first tendencies they noticed was the very high rate of suicide[21]

---

[20] Weiss, E. F., June 2001 "The Study of a Lifetime," *Johns Hopkins Magazine*. http://pages.jh.edu/jhumag/0601web/study.html

[21] Thomas, C. B. 1976 "What becomes of medical students: the dark side," *Johns Hopkins Medical Journal*, May;138(5):185-95. PMID: 940252

amongst medical students and doctors, something that continues to this day. Many papers have been published since 1951, looking at pathological tendencies in medical students, both physical and psychological, and how that can impact on how a patient is treated. So you would think that screening to weed out those susceptible to suicide, and identifying those with psychopathic, sociopathic, or uncontrollable tendencies would have been in place decades ago.

During medical school, there was a small quiet woman a year ahead of me, who landed in my class. When I asked her what happened, she told me how a classmate raped her during a study group. She was not dating him, interested in him, or flirting with him. She pressed charges but, because she did not go directly to the emergency room for a sexual assault exam after the rape, the classmate was exonerated. He went on to become an ob/gyn and she lived in upset over the injustice and was set back an entire academic year by the psychological trauma.

In those years, I tended to all walks of life from all over the world, with just about every type of illness seen in the developed world. Most of the time, the house staff worked on their own. Attending physicians showed up in the morning to debrief the admissions from over night and the day before, but the rest of us were just house staff winging it the best we could. We saved most people who came in to be saved, but not all of them. Teaching hospitals are a double-edged sword, in that you get lots of attention as a patient, but it's not always the attention you would choose. During the overnight hours, there was no internal medicine attending physician in the house. If we had a question, we could wake one up. Most of the time they were gracious, some of the time they were tired and short, and hardly ever did they give us any new ideas. Their words were more of a ceremonial blessing. Holidays, overnights, and weekends are the most likely time a patient will get the worst treatment. Years later, I fractured my jaw in an accident and experienced first-hand what being a patient in a New York teaching hospital was like on a holiday, and how even a doctor-patient who needed immediate surgery can just be left to sit around for three days. Even though I was on intravenous antibiotics the entire time, the delay resulted in an abscess forming inside an open wound that went from the inside of my mouth to the outside of my chin. The result was an extra operation and four extra weeks of jaw wiring.

Patients thriving and healing is not on the medical priority list. Getting patients out to home or rehabilitation, any way possible, with a freshly tweaked list of drugs is most important to the majority of overworked, dead-hearted house staff.

After the three-year postgraduate residency was over, I could have moved on and gotten a job. But by then, I felt trapped in a maze. I couldn't go backwards and stop being a doctor even if I wanted to, because my loan was now even higher than when I left medical school. No medical student commits to a student loan that will amount to half a million dollars, unless they believe that their study brings value to the people they are trying to help.

So, I kept making course corrections. I could go left, forward or right. What to do? This time, I decided maybe 'up' was a better option, so I opted for yet more study towards a sub-specialty, which resulted in even bigger student loans. The increasing total of an already huge student loan burden didn't bother me nearly as much as the sense of creeping deadness.

Nephrology
Fellowship

There's scarcely a doctor alive who doesn't know about the huge number of interns and residents who, deep inside, react to their medical training by feeling bleakness and desperation. Too many doctors land up on drugs or taking their own lives.[22] And they often countenance the mantra that it is just a cranial chemical imbalance, which needs a prescription. Most doctors simply take anti-depressants to cover the pain, in the hope that at some point they can make sense of the quagmire of never-ending illnesses; palliating, treating, tracking declines in health, creating new diseases, and hoping for temporary remission or an upturn in bad situations. After hopping onto that magic carpet ride myself, I quickly jumped off.

Why would doctors get depressed? Despite expensive, extensive training, we rarely if ever cure anything except the occasional infection. But even that is a bit of a reach to call the result 'cured' when the answer is usually to toss antibiotics into the body, never considering the downstream ramifications. There are times when antibiotics are the right treatment, but often, they are unnecessary and simply given to 'do something', while the effects of the treatment are universally ignored.

---

[22] Boyle, Kristin, 2015 "Making a bad thing good," *Life in the fast lane* blog. Personal testimonial of doctor depression and the situation in the medical profession. This is described globally as well.

So, with the knowledge of what was in (and absent from) my medicine bag, I chose to move upward, specializing in nephrology (kidneys). My logic was that I could help people who really needed lots of drugs—because these are seriously sick people whose situation can be desperate. I thought that prescriptions and medical procedures might actually help them and give them a better quality of life.

Highly toxic drugs are regularly given to kidney patients because, to this day, there aren't too many options that a nephrologist has for someone with a late-stage, very nasty autoimmune disease, who has got sick blood because the kidney filters are under attack. Those drugs and procedures usually get people out of crisis. That was a little better, because I thought, "This poison at least has a purpose and I can use it for the best interests of people, and try to limit the toxicity."

Nephrology was also attractive because it offered the opportunity to deepen my critical-care skills, which I thought were slightly lacking after a residency program that was more heavily weighted towards outpatient medicine. Best of all, I loved renal physiology and still think that kidneys are fascinating and important organs.

The nephrology training years were happy ones, medically, because I loved what I was learning and worked mostly with really smart, kind people. Having passed my internal medicine boards, I was no longer just a minion in the eyes of the hierarchy. I now had some status in the food chain, being an attending physician, so perhaps would be more able to make some more meaningful contributions.

The training program was two years long and it was served between two of Philadelphia's hospitals: Hahnemann University and the Medical College of Pennsylvania. The program chair was a brilliant and benevolent woman named Dr. Sandra Levison. She was an ideal leader: personable, fair, and strong. I doubt any of her secretarial, nursing, or fellowship students would have a negative thing to say of her. She is rightfully known in Philadelphia as a local legend in medicine. It was an honor to graduate from a program she chaired. Dr. Zia Ahmed was another amazing teacher in the program. They stand out in my mind as very influential and kind-hearted people that I was blessed to learn from.

Then there was Dr. Charlie Swartz, another legend, of a totally different breed. The first meeting, in a conference room with a long table at Hahnemann University hospital, was to meet the staff. Charlie walked in 10 minutes late. He was a white-bearded, round-bellied man with a very slow pace in his walk, and hardly ever seen without his long white coat hanging lopsided on him and a Diet Pepsi in hand. He entered the conference room without saying anything, loudly clicked his Diet Pepsi can onto the table and put his feet up. He always wore Wallabee shoes, a shirt unbuttoned at the top with no tie, and usually the collar scrunched up beneath his white coat. If he did wear a tie, it was as loose as a necklace, and a sop to a dress code that he would rather do without.

At the meeting, his pager immediately rang and he got up at the speed of an earthworm, picked up the phone, dialed four numbers and yelled "Swartz". Then "Yes, yes, yes, okay." Click. At first I thought, "Who is this arrogant slob?" but I would come to appreciate Dr. Swartz for the unique warm-hearted genius that he was. Indeed, he had earned the right to dress any way he wanted and put his feet on the table. He was the last of the old school nephrology physiologists, and well into his 70s when I first met him.

Dr. Swartz started the dialysis program at Hahnemann University back in the days when dialysis was done using parallel plates and a bathtub. He watched as the field of 'Endocrinology and Metabolism' (which was an intellectual pursuit in which doctors studied physiology and then had careers in clinical medicine), morphed into 'Nephrology and Hypertension'. According to him, the new way was fast becoming a drug/dialysis-based set of protocols implemented by automatons writing prescriptions and dialysis orders. He was very disturbed that the knowledge he and his colleagues worked so hard to bring about and publish was getting lost.

One day he announced out of the blue, "Nephrologists today don't understand physiology or how we came to know the things we know about kidney glomeruli and tubules and electrolytes. I intend to change that." So every Wednesday morning from then onward, Dr. Swartz held a teaching session in a classroom. He filled our heads with real physiology and a deeper understanding of why, when, where, and how much of today's physiology knowledge was born, as well as intricate and complex details of things that even most nephrologists squint at, like the countercurrent multiplier system in the kidney; a complex physiologic mechanism involving specialized blood vessels and kidney tubules. There is an expenditure of energy that creates a concentration gradient. This is of importance in the process of urine concentration, without which we would all be running to the toilet every 15 minutes and drinking gallons of water per day. It is just one of the many fantastic aspects of the kidney. Nobody left that fellowship program without being able to eloquently describe and appreciate this beautiful system, thanks to Dr. Swartz.

In addition to being the kind of teacher you could listen to all day, as he tossed out fascinating pearls of scientific and clinical wisdom when you were with him, Dr Swartz's patients loved him. When a fellow in training walked into the room, patients would tolerate us, but always they would ask, "When is Dr. Swartz coming in?" They knew he really cared and would do his best to fix them.

Sadly, the life of too many food calories washed down with a continuous flow of Diet Pepsi caught up with Charlie, and he got pancreatic cancer. After I graduated from the fellowship, I was invited back to a big retirement party to honor him when he was dying. About half the size he once was, I'm not sure I would have recognized him on the street.

I gave him a big hug, an impromptu speech and told him that I would never forget him. The speech was about my experiences, and I named Charlie the Scarlet Pimpernel of Nephrology because he was always sauntering around looking scruffy and acting like a daffy old man but, in reality, he was a genius with an enormous heart of gold; totally dedicated to his career, his patients, and his students.

I recalled being a brand new fellow on call and phoning him, nervously presenting a difficult case. Then I sheepishly ended by saying, "I think she should be dialyzed." He abruptly yelled, "So dialyze her!" and then he hung up. I wasn't sure whether to laugh or cry, but that was just Charlie. He was colorful, funny, honest, brilliant, and blunt.

So those were the best of the best. There were others but they will have to be left unsung.

Now for the worst of the worst: It's nearly impossible to go to a two-year postgraduate training program as large as mine was, without encountering at least one person you'd rather not have met. Dr. P. was a relatively young nephrology professor, hired around my second year of training. He thought he could get away with abusing us all and mistreating the foreign fellows. He was soft-spoken, so few would have picked him for the prick he turned out to be. He was serious, stern, and very committed to immunology and transplantation. Making rounds with him was akin to trekking a desert in sunshine. Laborious lectures, diagrams, and endless questions, and then he would write out a long note in what could only be Catholic school handwriting. I know because I once had the same writing. Hours later, rounds would end so we could finally get on with the patient care of the day.

Rounds on the sicker patients would then happen again at the end of the day. He was mostly polite to me, though I saw fangs poke through his gums once in a while. One might have thought that all this time he spent with us was of great value, but I rarely learned anything of use. His teaching was more of a way to browbeat us over molecular minutiae that he knew, and thought that we didn't. It was rarely of any clinical use or interest academically. His distasteful and hostile delivery was something we all could have lived without. It was nothing like being with Dr. Swartz.

It was explained, by some other attending physicians, that he had personal issues with his young bride. After meeting her, I could tell that she was way out of his league and that most of his general hostility was probably a result of him being rejected. But I didn't care any the more for knowing. It is all too common for people in power in medicine to think they can take their frustrations out on, or shaft anyone, beneath them when they have personal problems. It's just another version of kicking the dog.

One day I entered the fellows' conference room only to see the guys looking upset and talking passionately, but quietly. I was the only woman in the program. All but one of the fellows was of Eastern descent and most were Muslim from different parts of the world. One was an Indian Sikh but Dr. P. probably didn't bother to figure the difference. They were all targets for his pent-up aggression. These guys had been verbally abused, harassed, humiliated, and mistreated for months on end. It was all going on while they were alone, on call, and this particular day they were comparing notes. I asked what was going on and they reluctantly briefed me. They would not have said anything because of fear of losing their J-1 visas.

On other occasions, at conferences, Dr P. had 'pimped'[23] them really hard, to the point that Charlie Swartz would shake his head and suggest he stop it. Pimping is done for variable reasons; to show the

---

[23] The well-known term for asking serial questions until you can't answer anymore. A method of learning in medicine, akin to the Socratic method, but with an air of nastiness.

student who is smarter, make the pimper feel big, or to teach. With Dr. P., looking big and smarter was always clearly his focus. Humiliation seemed like his end-point goal.

After hearing them recall several outrageous instances of abuse, I suggested they talk to Dr. Levison because she would never allow that kind of abuse if she knew the extent of it. Finally they realized that was true. Dr. P. must have gotten a stern warning from Dr. Levison because he never abused them again. He was still a prick within the bounds of what was acceptable, but he implemented some restraint.

There were many aspects of fellowship that we all loved. Case conferences were frequent and quite helpful to broaden our knowledge: learning to interpret various different biopsies by electron photographs and direct microscopic visualization. In various conferences, we got to compare notes on how different diseases were being treated by other doctors and to present our own interesting or perplexing cases.

My fellowship research paper[24] was published in the *American Journal of Hypertension* in 1998. The subject was the relationship between dietary magnesium and insulin resistance in black Americans. The paper has been cited in books and other medical journals. Yet, at the time, I had little idea how significant magnesium really was in so many diseases, not just insulin resistance. Later, when I started practicing 'quackery', seeing the results of replenishing this important element, and reading more on the total body effects, I understood more. Magnesium therapy is still not an accepted practice in mainstream medicine. They don't know how to measure for true deficiency and when they do find a deficit they use a form of magnesium that has low bioavailability.

---

[24] http://ajh.oxfordjournals.org/content/12/8/747.short

Sometime near the end of my fellowship and the beginning of my first job, I got it stuck into my head that I wanted a fig tree. Why? I love fresh figs, but the real reason was festering fury at things that seemed just plain wrong. I had gone from being really respected and cared about during my fellowship, to a job where I could be verbally and emotionally sniped any time, by someone on a power trip. There was pent-up fury in me, which had no outlet.

Caring for the fig tree soon after purchase. Note the figs and leaves that were initially present.

Completely out of left field, and without a rational context, I recalled a story from school days of Jesus cursing the fig tree and making it die. I knew it was about judgment but saw it in the context of a corrupt, judgmental, and hypocritical church, and similarities within the medical system. I decided that Jesus was a jerk on a power trip. If he was such a hot shot, why didn't he just fix the tree? Why couldn't we just fix patients? I had a green thumb with other plants, so thought having a nice fig tree would be a cinch. At the very least, I could do that!

Promptly, I went to an Italian farmer in New Jersey and purchased a moderate size tree, put it into my Jeep Grand Cherokee, drove home, carried it up to my fourth-floor roof garden, transplanted it into an appropriately sized pot, read about care of the fig tree, and meticulously looked after it.

20

First Job: Professor

During the second year of my fellowship, I had to start thinking of what I wanted to do next. I was going to be released; freed, able to finally start to pay off those loans, make a living, maybe later have a house, some investments, and build some savings.

There are two major categories of medical doctors: Those who are filled with confidence and ready to practice as soon as possible, knowing that they will figure out anything they don't know along the way; and those who feel that core knowledge isn't enough and want to continue growing alongside more experienced people with the aim of eventually knowing the subject as widely and deeply as possible. I was definitely in the latter group, partly because I like the apprentice system, but partly due to insecurity. I had seen far too many SNAFUs happen to new graduates and even older doctors, to feel seasoned enough to completely trust my own ability as a new nephrologist. I had also seen enough treatment failures to value the experience of older clinicians. The field can be very complicated and curve balls come along all the time. Working alongside older, practicing, scholarly doctors, and being a teaching professor seemed the most logical way to give myself the most knowledge and confidence, and therefore, my patients the best care. So I set my sights on doing that.

Philadelphia is a nice, manageable city compared to New York City and by 1998 I had spent a good chunk of my adult life there. It felt like home and I enjoyed the diverse culture, excellent dining, the city parks system, and the relative ease in getting around and having a car. There were many different neighborhoods that I had lived in and enjoyed; all offering something different. There was no reason to relocate, because the area is loaded with teaching hospitals, so I looked for a local academic position.

The South Street section of Philadelphia, where my lovely fourth-floor roof garden apartment was, is right near the Delaware River. An opportunity arose on the other side of the Delaware, in Camden, New Jersey, which was a convenient reverse commute across the Ben Franklin Bridge. Cooper Hospital is a university medical center and part of the Robert Wood Johnson Medical School campus. Funnily enough, I was born there. My family lived close by in New Jersey and they were happy to know that I was staying local. I knew that academic jobs did not pay as much as clinical practice but thought I could live on that while I built my knowledge and taught at the same time.

There was just one problem. When I began to fill out the New Jersey medical license application, there was the question, "Have you ever been convicted of a crime?" The exact reading is:

> Have you ever been arrested for, formally accused of, charged with, indicted for or convicted of the commission of any crime or offense, whether state, federal, or in other countries, including offenses categorized as misdemeanors, high misdemeanors or felonies? (NOTE: If you have been arrested or had a conviction for which you have been informed the record has been expunged, please verify that the expungement has in fact been implemented prior to answering "No" to this question.)

My heart sunk into my feet. I was going to have to discuss spiked strawberry daiquiris with an attorney. Could that cost me this job? I thought I should mention it, because I was going to have to deal with this stain on my record anywhere I applied for full licensure. It turned out that I had plenty of time to get the issue expunged and could have stayed silent, but I didn't know that then.

I interviewed with the head of the nephrology department, whom for legal reasons will be referred to as The Magpie. She and her physician husband were part of the old establishment at Cooper's University Hospital. At University Renal Associates, which The Magpie cleverly named UREA, my job would include seeing hospital patients and inpatient dialysis patients, and teaching medical students, residents, and fellows. The university clinic was located across the street. In addition, there was another busy dialysis unit with an attached private nephrology clinic in Cherry Hill, about 20 minutes' drive from the hospital. We also covered four community hospitals on the outer regions, but sometimes there were none of our patients there. Overnight call would be one in five nights and every fifth weekend. The annual pay was 90,000 USD, which at the time seemed like enough, but I hadn't factored in that, as an unwed person with no dependents, nearly 45% of that income would go to income tax.

The Magpie was socially adept and easy to talk with in our one-hour interview. Only later would I realize that the reason she was probably so good at interviewing, was because her staff turnover was astronomically high. She rapidly drilled into my psyche and my personal life, trying to see what I was about. Unbeknownst to me, she had a report on me, which the chair of internal medicine had sought out, regarding my nephrology fellowship. The most important figures at the fellowship program, like Dr. Levison, had sent shining reviews of my work and abilities.

However, there was a private physician from Hahnemann named Joe B. that I was obliged to work with from time to time. Mostly the relationship was such that the fellows did his work, before he strolled in like the king and arrogantly imparted a few 'pearls' upon us, most of which we already knew. He and I mixed like oil and water. When questioned by The Magpie as to why he hadn't written a totally glowing report about me, I said that I found his rudeness, and the fact that he used us, distasteful. Joe B. had not written any negative comments on my fellowship evaluations. He couldn't—I did my work well, which earned him money. The benefits were all his. Most of the private staff knew that and therefore were very respectful to the fellows.

At the interview, The Magpie smiled and confided that it was a mark of good repute, in her eyes, that he gave my attitude a bad review. She happened to know him and his group and felt the same. Joe B.'s cowardly attempt at underhanded sabotage had failed.

I was introduced to the rest of the nephrology physicians and nursing staff, toured the hospital, and was invited back for a second interview.

At this point I told The Magpie the whole story of my arrest in gory detail. She listened and came back with a surprising answer. "Well we've all done really stupid things. I have too. You just got caught. Get it taken care of." I had already started the process, which took until about two weeks after the interview. She followed up with, "And one more thing. This better be the whole story and you had better not have anything else that you are not telling me about. If I am going to go to bat for you to take this job, don't make a fool of me." I assured her with a totally clean conscience that I had no other skeletons in my closet.

After hiring an attorney, all charges were brought before a judge again, to have my record, behavior, and life examined. The judge completely wiped all the charges off my record: **<u>expunged</u>**. Now I was free to apply in good conscience and check the 'No' box.

The Magpie called me at home to offer me the job. I thought it was all totally amazing; I got the exact type of job I wanted, didn't have to move and uproot again, and was going to work with this smart, cool professor who had the same distaste I had for one of my cowardly critics.

Thrilled at the job offer, I accepted without even considering negotiating the salary, because I could hardly believe how easy everything had fallen into place. I forgot that, as my father used to say . . . if something seemed too good to be true, it might be.

The Magpie was a graduate of top medical programs, and constantly reminded everyone where she had studied and that she was "very well trained". She was technically bright and ran the department with a sledgehammer. The other doctors there seemed reluctantly accepting of her often haughty and entitled penchant for detail.

We used pre-printed forms to keep track of inpatient data and history. The forms were passed to the doctor on call or when changing over patient service duties. Such forms made sense and were helpful. The only problem was that if they were not precisely and perfectly updated with every detail The Magpie thought should be there, she would become antagonistic and confrontational. The forms were a means to exact control over us, to micromanage and nag about any trivial element that could be missing. Upon turnover, she would scour every detail, ask questions and, if we knew the answer but had not put it in, she would rant. In the real world, and everywhere else I have ever worked, such nitpicking is never done. The Magpie seemed to get much pleasure from haggling us over anything that didn't conform to her standard of perfection. Those forms used to be a thorn in our sides. Her second in command, Dr. W., was the best at kowtowing to her demands in his pretty fountain-pen cursive.

However, one of the doctors, Dr. R., flat-out refused. He would only put the name of the patient and the hospital stamp with logistical information, leaving the rest of the forms blank. The full sign-out was handed over verbally, with great detail, while the recipient took notes, which is the way it is done in most medical groups. The

Magpie insisted on nice, legible handwriting, which was a shortcoming of Dr. R.'s. But that was not the real reason he wouldn't fill out the forms at The Magpie's decree.

Dr. R. was a really, really bright and talented nephrologist. He had a conscience the size of Brazil and very strong work ethic. As a seasoned physician, and because of his stature, he had a lot of negotiating leverage when he was hired, and he refused to be browbeaten the way the rest of us were.

As a conservative and very observant Jew, part of the deal when he was hired was that he would get sundown Friday night until sundown Saturday night off when he was on weekend call. It was a bit of a pain for us, but it meant he took more weekends on call but just shorter chunks. In addition, he took charge of an outlying hospital and was based in a clinic near there. So, by not doing rounds at the university hospital or attending all the meetings we did, he was spared the continual direct haggling by The Magpie.

Eighteen months into the job, at a Monday morning conference that all the nephrologists were expected to attend, Dr. R. changed how I dealt with The Magpie. The Magpie had picked on something totally petty, to really throw her toys around the room, and Dr. R. wasn't in the mood to take it. He stood up to her and was getting really upset as they argued. The Magpie would not cave or allow Dr. R. to have his say or the last word. They went at it for what seemed an eternity while we three bystanders sat and said nothing.

Dr. R. was visibly shaken but he didn't cave as The Magpie stormed out of the room. I said something to him and he whipped his head towards me and said, "Yes and you said nothing Suzanne. Nobody said anything. And when you all let her act like this and don't say anything, you are colluding and allowing it to go on. Neutrality is complacency with her irresponsible, provocative, unprofessional behavior."

I felt totally internally convicted. He was absolutely correct. I had been a total coward.

From then on, I made it my business to talk back to her when she was being pushy and never allowed her to needlessly or aggressively roll over me again without putting up a sound defense.

The Magpie treated the secretarial and nursing staff as her own private minions, who were born to serve and make her life run smoothly. The only problem with The Magpie's servitude mentality was that she lacked the etiquette or finesse to keep her staff happy. Frequent outbursts were the norm when things didn't go the way she thought they should. She could cut anyone down with her words, temper tantrums, and self-righteousness, and she regularly pitted one doctor against another, until we figured out what she was doing and stopped agreeing to be manipulated.

On the plus side, we had the most amazingly competent transcriptionists and secretaries. These were grown women; mothers with children at home. They were very good, experienced workers, yet everyone would hear her regularly tearing them down in the administrative area, as if they were bad little children. It was vicious and torturous. She verbally brutalized them, even more than she walked all over the nurses or doctors. Sometimes they would last for six months or more, but at least a dozen office staff left in the three and a bit years I worked there. But that is how it often is in the hierarchical world. None of her support staff had a kind word or feeling about her when she was not in the room.

As all this unfolded in front of me, I wondered how she managed to set the whole thing up and keep it going for so long. As time went on, it became obvious that she carefully sought out really bright doctors who were humble, hadn't really found their niche yet, had low self-esteem, or who didn't quite have the experience or courage to defend themselves. Or so she thought. Because staff turnover was constant, very few people opened their mouths and warned anyone else, which, as Dr. R. said, leaves the abuser protected by silence. But if you kick all your dogs for too long, one might eventually bite you where it hurts.

After one particular occasion when The Magpie had publicly taken a chunk out of me, I was licking my wounds in my office. The Magpie's second-in-command entered the room, sat down, and said he was sorry I got hurt, and acknowledged what a difficult person she was. Then, he quietly said, "Just remember, you can't reach her through me." In other words, I was on my own. While Dr. W. was a wimp when it came to The Magpie, deep down he was a compassionate doctor who really cared about all people. The way he dealt with her terrorism was to keep her very close.

Another significant event that illustrates the perniciousness of the old boys' club mentality that The Magpie had little problem being part of, occurred early in my employment. I saw an elderly woman in the cardiac care unit one morning. She was a chronic dialysis patient but had an acute heart issue and was admitted with atrial fibrillation and a heart attack. The cardiologist on duty was another of the boys' club who had been in the system for a couple of decades. I never saw him that day. He drifted in some time during the day, wrote a short illegible note, then left. This particular morning, the surgeon Dr. Mosley was also in the room when I arrived, because the woman's normal dialysis access had clotted off and we could not give her a treatment. I wrote an order for dialysis and left. The surgeon decided to take her to the operating room and put a neck catheter in for dialysis.

That evening, I was attending to my 13-year-old dog Jazz who was ailing and doing so poorly that I had decided she needed to be put out of her misery. At her latest vet visit, her degenerative arthritis was so crippling that I had asked the vet to give me something to drug her up for the next visit, when she would be euthanized, because she was very nervous at the smell and sound of the office. I didn't want her last memory and experience to be so negative. Now was that time. I was not on call, but had forgotten to turn off my pager when I arrived home. I gave Jazz her last meal; a meatball sandwich with about six Thorazine pills which were supposed to sedate her and make her unaware of her surroundings.

All was going well. She started to doze off and relax into my arms. I was crying softly as she became more unconscious. Then the pager went off. I should not have answered it. I got up to take the call, leaving Jazz lying next to a friend. On the line was the old cardiologist who proceeded to say, "You have murdered the lady from the CCU! There was an unauthorized dialysis catheter placed today and it was the cause of her cardiac arrest and you are responsible!" He was really angry and I was shaking and trying to answer him the best I could, and was really sobbing by the end of the call.

Jazzie, in her final year.

My dog, who had become nearly unconscious, suddenly became more aware and ineffectively attempted to crawl closer to me. She became upset at hearing me in distress and was trying to comfort me. So her last memory was not a peaceful one, but one of significant upset, thanks to a cardiologist looking for a scapegoat and my inability to tell him off because my thinking was not clear enough to do so.

The following day I arrived at work, only to be interrogated by The Magpie who had heard the whole story from her husband who got an earful from the angry cardiologist. It turned out that either the rich lady or her husband was a hospital board member (I can't recall the exact details), so heads were expected to roll—and mine was chosen to be placed on the chopping block.

It wasn't until The Magpie was interrogating me, that I remembered that I actually had nothing to do with the catheter being placed at all. The only surgical interaction was between Dr. Mosley and the operating room. All I had done was write for the dialysis session, which she was due for, and really needed. She never made it to the dialysis because she arrested in the surgical suite, which for some reason was assumed to be my fault. The family never made a complaint, but the cardiologist decided that because I was the lowest member on the totem pole at the time, I should be chosen to take the blame. Even though my non-involvement was clearly provable, there was never any sort of recognition that I had been wrongly accused of murder, nor any apology for such unwarranted harsh treatment by the good old boy of cardiology.

It is much easier to rebel and become intolerant of an outright abuser. But when the abuse is subtly cloaked between seemingly generous and kind acts, you can be deceived into inaction, thinking the person might be turning over a new leaf, and perhaps coming to their senses. The Magpie was not a blatant, consistent abuser. Her abuse was tactical, and careful. In between being needlessly handed my head, favors were given—always the kind that everyone else knew about and that made her seem like a generous person. We underlings were indeed conditioned to be grateful for mediocre treatment.

During this time, my depression deepened. Psychotherapy had done nothing and I was getting desperate inside. I'd gotten involved in the music industry, sat in a professional recording studio with friends, went to more live music at clubs, and met lots of singers and musicians. Now that I was no longer in training, there was lots more time, and I loved having the space to socialize and discover new types of rock, pop, jazz, and soul music. It was also a time of mixing with more politically minded people. On the surface it was all very exciting, but inside was a different story. The emptiness was so bad that there was almost no limit to what I would have tested, spiritually. So around December 1999, I wandered into an occult bookstore on South Street in Philadelphia and bought some books on paganism and earth magic. Totally naïve, I began doing some of the rituals and incantations, one of which involved the Egyptian god of wisdom, Thoth. After all, what else could happen other than someone tell me that it was superstitious idiocy?

Weekend call was a social and family life nuisance, and one that The Magpie didn't have to deal with if she didn't want to. Being wealthy, she could afford to pay another young nephrologist and myself to take her weekend call. Given that we had huge student loans, and could use every last cent, we took the opportunity gladly. The Magpie somehow had us both feeling grateful and privileged, when in fact it was a drop in the bucket for her to buy herself a free weekend for 1,000 USD every five weeks. And, she set our bargain basement salaries that kept us so desperate in the first place.

The Magpie also had her other benevolent moments, as Saturday, May 13, 2000, would later show.

My father died in December of 2000 and it was one of the most emotionally traumatic times of my life. I knew I needed at least three days off, but when the long weekend was over, I still could not function. I called The Magpie and told her I just couldn't do it. She understood completely and issued a week off for me to recover. When the week was up and I was still not myself, I asked her to ask everyone not to mention anything about my father so that I could hold myself together. She did. In addition, she sent a large tray of sandwiches and flowers to the funeral. Such kind deeds were always appreciated.

The fig tree that I purchased about a year earlier didn't thrive. No matter what I did, how I watered it, or where I kept it, the leaves fell off, one by one. There would come a point where one leaf would hang on, and then that one would fall. I kept expecting it to die, but it would slowly recover and gain a few more leaves, but refused to bear fruit.

21

Wired And Bugged

May 13, 2000 was a holiday weekend and the first hot day of the year. Early in the day, I'd taken advantage of the weather and ran five miles in Central Park in New York, but the day turned into a scorcher. After becoming quite dehydrated, I drank water, but not enough. All day I felt a bit out of sorts, but fought through it and drank water when I thought of it. I went out to dinner with some family and friends, and felt worse afterwards, but kept drinking water and ignored the light-headedness.

While strolling down the sidewalk in the evening, on the Upper East Side, my vision began to change. Everything turned orange and then yellow. I kept fighting. There was no place to sit down so I kept pushing mentally to stay conscious and keep walking. I had never lost consciousness before and thus had no idea what it felt like to faint. In one moment, the rest of my life changed as a wave of the most strangely blissful feeling swallowed me up. In one second, I slapped forward like a rigid plank with no outstretched hand or bent knee to break my fall. The white cement sidewalk buried itself into my chin.

The next thing I remember, were bystanders screaming, "Holy shit!" "Is she alive?" "Someone call a fucking ambulance!"

The paramedics wanted me to lie flat on a board and be strapped down. I said, "No way, I am going home." I was feeling what I thought was a tooth in my mouth, only to be told that it was my jawbone. After a bit of bargaining, I agreed to be taken to an emergency room as long as I did not have to be strapped down and could sit up. My blood pressure was 60 over palp—very, very low.

Lenox Hill Hospital was the closest trauma center. Being a doctor got me absolutely nowhere other than with the paramedics, who respected my wishes enough not to be strapped down. Once in emergency, I was treated like an idiot, immediately vaccinated by a nurse who said, "Here is your tetanus shot," as she was injecting it, and then jammed an IV into the top of my wrist. I still have a scar from where it later became infected. I was repeatedly chided for not allowing myself to be strapped down in the ambulance. The angry attending doctor kept upbraiding me, "Why did you refuse to be strapped down?!" I replied, "Is my neck broken?" He said, "No." I said, "So what's your problem? Leave me alone now."

A brain scan showed a subarachnoid hemorrhage, which explained my new headache. There was also a large fracture of the right sinus even though the fall was on the left side of my chin. From the outer part of my left chin to the inside of my mouth was basically a hole, later described as "dust" by the surgeons. That pretty well describes the shear forces my entire head endured.

Even though the books say this type of fracture—a comminuted mandibular fracture—should go to the operating room within 24 hours, I didn't go until four days later. So much for best-practice medicine during emergencies on holiday weekends . . .

As I became more aware of what was going on, I could feel the jawbone protruding deep into the inside of my mouth and several loose teeth. I knew I was lucky not to have broken my neck, but the enormity of how screwed I was hit like a tidal wave. "What a mess," was all I could think and I began to sob out of control. No human words or touch could lessen that feeling, which just had to gush out all over my face and shirt until it was done. Then I rallied and dealt with it. There was no more crying for another 12 weeks.

Looking back, I think I was suffering from adrenal fatigue after years of constant stress, walking a knife-edge, and always wondering who at work would be keelhauled next. I had no understanding of nutrition or the value of vitamin C. I had become an insomniac; ruled by a pager, and with no ability to sleep deeply. So it was little surprise that I had hit a breaking point. The subsequent full cardiac workup was negative.

Once my cortisol level from the acute trauma dropped down, the pain became enormous. I was started on IV penicillin and IV morphine by self-dosing pump, with acetaminophen for breakthrough pain. From there I was taken to the trauma ICU to be closely monitored for mental status changes with frequent neuro and airway checks. I sat and slept upright, with my hand constantly operating the suction tube to remove the bloody saliva that I could no longer control. The oromaxillofacial (OMF) surgery team evaluated me the next day, which was a Sunday. No attending physician was on duty so all of my OMF team members were resident trainees.

Ice packs initially kept the swelling down a little but by Monday I had become an unrecognizable blimp, featuring bruising, scrapes and swelling on my entire face, neck and chin. All I could handle was a liquid diet. The trauma surgery attending kept close watch and allowed me to be transferred to a private room on Monday morning. Several CT scans and panoramic x-rays later, I was finally seen by the OMF attending, who outlined two surgical options: a permanent metal plate implanted into my chin, which would leave me with no sensation on the chin, or my teeth and jaw wired shut for six weeks. I chose the latter because it was less of an invasive procedure.

On admission, I had told the hospital staff that both parents had severe anaphylactic penicillin allergies, and that because I had never taken penicillin on the recommendation of my pediatrician growing up I didn't know if I had an allergy to it. They started me on penicillin anyway, assuring me that because I had never had penicillin myself, I should be fine. I was too messed up to argue. Monday, late in the evening, my skin turned red in patches, my neck was swelling more, and I began having fevers. After asking the nurse five times to call the OMF doctor on call, he finally showed up in his scrubs, appearing annoyed and short tempered. It was obvious that I was either becoming septic or was having a penicillin reaction. At first he tried to brush it all off as related to the fracture. I told him that sepsis could be related to the fracture, but we should know why I was febrile. If the penicillin wasn't covering the infection, we also needed to know that. Begrudgingly, he listened to my request to order blood cultures, stop the penicillin, and start me on clindamycin instead.

On Tuesday morning, surgery finally took place. I woke up in the post-anesthesia care room to two Filipino nurses yelling at me. "Dr. Humphries, wake up." "Dr. Humphries you have to stay awake." But my drug levels were too high in my brain and my desire to sleep was overwhelming. Each time I fell asleep, the low oxygen saturation alarms went off, but I never heard them. After the shift change, a male nurse took over, and he kept looking into my hospital gown, which pissed me off enough to keep me awake better. Once fully conscious, I was taken back to my room for observation, unable to open my mouth at all. For the next 12 weeks all of my nutrition came through clenched teeth.

If anyone wonders, I do think there is a place for antibiotics, and this was one of them. Having a New York City sidewalk invade your jawbone and gumline introduces anything from the bottom of millions of shoes to dog excrement, which is a regular on those walkways. On Wednesday, as I was leaving Lenox Hill Hospital, I asked the doctors why I was not being discharged on antibiotics because there was heat in the jaw, I could feel jawbone in my mouth, and the lower jaw still felt unstable. They told me that was normal. I asked to see the attending physician but was told he was in surgery all day. Just wanting to get away at that point, I was discharged home on oxycodone and a liquid diet, driven back to my own apartment and to my own La-Z-Boy chair, which was a partial relief. It was great to be home in my own cozy apartment. The first place I went was my roof garden, to get some sun. The tomato plants were thriving, as were the herbs and flowers. But the fig tree was stark in its nakedness, with three leaves, which fell off one by one in the next week.

The first order of business was to consult the OMF surgeon for the Philadelphia Flyers ice hockey team, Dr. Guy Lanzi, who agreed to see me on Friday.

The fevers continued and the pain worsened. That Friday, Dr. Lanzi took one look at my chin, felt around the jaw, and casually asked, "Have you eaten?" I replied, "No, why?" He said, "Because you need to go back for more surgery . . . now. You have an abscess from your outer chin that tracks into your mouth and I need to go in and drain it. They do things a little different at Lenox Hill than we do [protecting the brotherhood]. I would not have wired it the way they did."

The second operation went okay. A couple of days later when I was being placed into the tube for an MRI, I asked the technician if having wires on the jaw was going to be a problem. He looked confounded and said he had to make a phone call. Fifteen minutes later, he returned and told me that it would probably be okay and that if I felt any heat or if I saw any sparks to put my hand up and they would turn off the magnet. The anxiety that comment left me with was huge, but it turns out you can magnetically scan someone with wires in the jaw without incidence.

Because the second surgery took place at the hospital I worked in, I was given a private room at the far end of the surgical floor and was pretty much left alone with my morphine pump for five days. The antibiotics were continued and I slept, sipped, and pressed the morphine button as often as I could. At one point, I was requiring 100 mg of morphine per day between the IV and oral dosing. On day three postoperatively, I was sent home to begin recovering again.

Living on a fourth-floor walkup was a nightmare because I had to stop to rest at each level, sitting on the landing before I could move up. I knew nothing then about vitamin C or replenishing the microbiome properly after antibiotic use. I was depleted of ascorbate and my mitochondria were seriously weary. The rest of the week was spent in a recliner, day and night, reading when I could, and sleeping a lot. It was two weeks before I could lie flat in bed because the tension on the jaw was too painful and the feeling of potentially choking was too frightening.

The projected time of six weeks with teeth wiring stretched out to 12 with concern was that my scrawny frame might lose around 15 pounds during that time. Because my mother and friends brought all sorts of creative blended meals I ended up gaining weight, which at that time of my life was a good idea. It was amazing how good a piece of pizza blended with some tomato juice tasted, or rice, beans, and sour cream. I drank four to six bottles of Fresh Samantha almond soy beverage every day on top of all else that I blended. Fresh Samantha was not the wisest choice because of the soy, but it felt good in my stomach and was easy to bring to work. But nothing felt as good as the first drop of real food after the wires came off.

The Magpie was totally cool about my mishap and never once put pressure on me to return to work. I put the pressure on myself though and, during the third week, decided to cold turkey the opiates and return to my teaching duties and clinic.

Halfway through the first day back, I felt like a freight train had collided with me and I went into my office, shut the door, put my head on the desk and started crying. At first I was confounded as to why I felt so horrible all of a sudden, with pain occurring in places that didn't previously hurt. Was it just the stress of being back at work? Sitting up, I calculated the opiates I had been on, and realized that my receptors had become so accustomed to 20 mg of oxycodone daily, that zero was making them scream.

So I took five mg, which was just enough to take the edge off the withdrawal, and immediately called Dr. Lanzi to say I thought I had a problem. A few phone calls later to a friend of his, who specialized in opiate addiction, and they both determined I could continue to work and wean myself off opiates. Chiropractic care was long a part of my personal health maintenance, and I had a great DC in Philadelphia. I called her and told her I need more adjustments and asked to begin an acupuncture regimen to help get off the opiates. She strategically placed some adhesive ear dots, after a comprehensive needle treatment, and told me to press the ear dots when the symptoms occurred. That three-day weekend felt like an eternity, with shakes, feeling like bugs were crawling over me, and sweating buckets of water. Then it was all over. I had new empathy and understanding for opiate addiction.

By the fourth week after the fall, I was back at work with no drugs, giving lectures to students and going about life as if talking and eating through clenched teeth was perfectly normal. Once in a while a new group would need an explanation that my jaw was actually wired closed and I was not just angrily grunting words through my teeth.

As the weeks wore on, the jaw wiring became claustrophobic. The opiates had helped with that, but by 10 weeks the trapped feeling was becoming unbearable. I called Dr. Lanzi and told him I was going to cut the wires off myself, so I could open my mouth, but would leave the wiring between the teeth of the top and bottom jaw in place. He said, "Sure, you can do that, but if it's not healed, you will have to start all over again." That threat was all I needed to press onward. On week 12, I was put under sedation in his office, and had all the wires removed and was woken up by the nurse afterwards. It was a colossal relief when the mouth moved a little bit and knowing that I had gotten through the 12 weeks. The resultant sound that came out was a deep anguished sob that had been withheld for 12 weeks, overlain with tears of relief and gratitude that that part was over. Now to deal with the mess inside the mouth . . .

The space between my upper and lower jaws was only about a half-centimeter, but it was something. It took months to regain the ability to fully open the jaw hinge, but I returned to work that afternoon, with a food I had craved the whole 12 weeks. Watermelon. Inserting tiny full-fibered slivers of watermelon, through a five mm space between the upper and lower jaws, was pure bliss. The feeling of food dropping into the stomach was nearly orgasmic after living on liquid for so long. I would have never guessed what a loss it is to not have solid food for a regular diet, but it is.

There followed numerous dental appointments; to clean and restore the fractured teeth, preserve a dead tooth with root canal, extract teeth that died months after the ordeal and could not be preserved, remove old amalgams, and file down the rough edges after my jaw had regrown into its new shape. About a year later, I had a pain in one of the remaining lower teeth and went to an oral surgeon who x-rayed the tooth and took it out. The root had a large hole clear through it. Because he thought it a bit of a dental phenomenon, he refused to give me back my tooth and lied, saying that it was against the law for him to return it to me.

For a while I had a partial denture but it was uncomfortable and pulled on the one tooth I have left in the bottom left quadrant. I canceled my appointment for dental implants twice, because I couldn't bear the idea of screws placed into the fractured area. The oral surgeons and dentists said I needed to have bone transplanted from my hip to the jaw and that if I didn't have the surgery, "Your face is going to collapse if you don't get something put in the empty space." Sixteen years later, their prophecy has still not been fulfilled.

My face is now asymmetrical with my smile and teeth not as good as they were before that awful day at age 35. My gums have receded to that of an 80-year-old leading to significant neuropathic pain, and there is bluish-gray scar under my chin that has never faded. Missing a quarter of my teeth makes eating more difficult. My face makes me appear about a decade older than I am—worse on the left. I attribute part of that degeneration to stress, impact tissue damage, toxic metals, drugs required for the treatments, and my ignorance about nutrition and vitamin C.

Now, every bite of food I take in, every time I brush my teeth, serves as a reminder of what happened, and the good and the bad of what medicine has to offer. I was on the other end of student doctors over a holiday weekend, whose last concern was treatment protocols, and who really just wanted me out of their hospital. And I learned the value of an experienced and compassionate surgeon who would go the extra mile, even on a Friday afternoon. However, my wires should have been totally redone the day Dr. Lanzi noticed the problem. So, I also realized that even a good doctor would still protect the brotherhood and not go the full mile from the beginning, like he should have.

Amongst all this, was my father, someone who had stood by me through thick and thin and who now needed me, as he was dying.

Finality

Dad was diagnosed with cancer after a long and terrible ordeal. There were signs of trouble in October 1999, while at Disney World with my sister and her family. According to my sister, he appeared fine, but my mother kept saying he was winded and didn't seem right. He went home from that trip and changed his death benefit on his insurance policy, so he probably knew then that there was something wrong.

On Thanksgiving 1999, he had the worst pain of his life, radiating from his back to chest. Being a life-long heavy smoker, there was reasonable cause for concern over a potential heart attack. Most chest pain in a 64-year-old smoking male is cardiac ischemia until proven otherwise. Even though he had none of the classic signs of heart attack, like EKG changes, or elevated heart enzymes, the doctors did a heart catheterization on him, diagnosing severe multi-vessel disease. They told him that the pain was "an angel tapping on his shoulder" and that he should have immediate heart bypass.

Two days after his acute pain, I arrived from out of town, went over the charts, talked to the cardiologists, and asked them what the big rush was because there was no evidence that the pain came from his heart. The catheterization found diffuse disease but was it really the cause? Did he really have unstable angina? He was placed on a mix of drugs that made no sense to me. Since becoming a nephrologist, I was well acquainted with acute cardiac patients and all their drugs. Cardiologists send nephrologists a lot of business because their drugs and procedures often shut down the kidneys. Upon questioning, the attending cardiologist backed down, stating that my father may not have had a heart attack, and that he had time to further consider his options. Dad was on once-daily hydralazine; a drug that made no sense in any way, because when taken daily it can set up rebound hypertension. The cardiologist recanted and stopped it. I told my father that he could go home, think about things, relax, and regain his strength first, but the doctors had so deeply planted unnecessary, scary words and unfounded fear into his head, that he ignored his daughter, and went immediately to surgery.

His surgery turned very complicated when they found his emphysema was worse than they expected. My father returned to the recovery room six hours later. I immediately wanted to see him, but the nurse warned me that he wasn't looking good. I thought, "Don't be ridiculous. I am a nephrologist; used to seeing death, and the worse types of dying people." She was right. He was as gray as a corpse, everything swollen from fluid shifts, and didn't even resemble my father. I felt sick, weak-kneed, and panicked, and astonished at my situational frailty. But then, nobody I loved that much was ever at the other end of my stethoscope, either. This was only the beginning of my realization that we can't handle family the same way we can handle patients.

A week later, my father left the hospital in very weak condition. Dad had become diabetic and was placed on oral antiglycemic drugs. I kept saying, "Why is Dad suddenly diabetic? He is thin and this just doesn't make sense?" The cause would later become clear.

One week after noticing lumps cropping up on the back of his neck, the doctor diagnosed a disease called Gardner syndrome. I thought, "You have got to be kidding me! What a totally bizarre approach and differential diagnosis." The neck lesions were worrisome to me as they were fixed, hard masses that had cropped up very fast. The rule when it comes to skin and body lumps is that if they move, they are not likely to be a problem but if they are matted or fixed, they are.

It turned out the doctor was also certified in colonoscopy so, as a matter of convenience, my father had been given a drive-by colonoscopy, as well as a biopsy of the lesions on his neck at the same time.

The colon was 'clear' on the exam but the pathology on the neck was a poorly differentiated neuroendocrine carcinoma. That bought him an oncology consultation with lots more biopsies and tests. The primary lesion was never found but assumed to be from the lung. It also explained his new diabetes.

I shifted his care over to the hospital where I was employed, and referred him to my favorite oncologist, who did a conventionally conscientious job from start to end. To make a long story short, my father underwent two rounds of very toxic chemotherapy, the first of which probably bought him about eight months of good quality life, but the second had no effect on tumor shrinkage. By March of 2000, I knew my father was heading to the grave and I wouldn't need to stay around Philadelphia anymore, so I began looking for jobs.

The first interview was with a group in Waterville, Maine, which is about an hour's drive from the capital, Augusta. The group was very welcoming and kind and I could have worked with them except the geographical area was just too isolated. The only real cultural stimulation there would have come from an exclusive, small private college called Colby. The professors from the college and doctors from the hospital did a lot of socializing. Outside of that, the population was spread thin around the outskirts of the little city. I thought it would be too much isolation and culture shock, so declined the job offer.

In July 2000, Dad had a burst of quality life, when he finished radiation. He went to visit my sister in Texas and played hard the whole time. Everyone but Dad and my two-year-old niece got a vicious stomach bug and so he took care of my young niece for two days, playing basketball and having tea parties with her until everyone recovered. But by October of that year, my father had developed bilateral pleural effusions, lost significant weight and had dementia from tumors in his head. A CT scan in late-October revealed massive space-occupying tumors everywhere in his chest, abdomen, and pelvis, so much so that the radiologist said he had never seen a scan like it.

It was obvious the battle was over, and he was going to leave this earth. Hospice was brought in. My brother and I were handed a bottle of liquid morphine and told we could give him all we wanted once he started to have trouble breathing. Once he died[25], I found myself sobbing, lying over him, and hugging him. I wanted to be left alone but the undertakers, like buzzards, were waiting outside the room in their black suits with a stretcher. They came in and said, "Okay, we have to take dad now." I didn't want to interfere if there was something important that had to be done, but in retrospect I know they just wanted to get it over with and get home. He was not embalmed and after the closed-casket funeral, I just needed to leave Philadelphia and The Magpie, and thus I started my job search again.

It really hit me that I had indeed been hired for a pittance. I had also come to realize that not only did The Magpie collect bright doctors who couldn't stand up for themselves, but that the pay was far lower than it should have been. You would think that after this level of education, I should have been able to manage to pay my bills, but with 45% income tax, and my high interest student loans snowballed even higher, I was barely treading water and felt stifled. Even with implementing meager raises, my loans would not have been paid off for another 30 years and I would not be able to purchase a home in Philadelphia. Enough was enough.

---

[25] November 13, 2000

Over the months while keeping an eye on Dad and feeling that it was time to quietly move on, I had asked for, and was provided with, excellent recommendations.

I called the New England Health Search 'head-hunter' I'd dealt with the first time and asked if the Waterville job was still available, thinking at least it was a place to start. But she said there was an even better job advertised in Bangor and I should immediately go up to interview, which I did.

Dad, Mom, and Aunt Sara

23 Life After Death

While the working years in Camden, New Jersey weren't all bad, they were bad enough. Before my father died, I had begun to try to find a way out, because that was easier than constantly dueling with The Magpie's ego, risking getting fired, and being handed a bad reputation by default. The whistle on the roof of my tolerance had reached screaming pitch with her management style, and my jaw was a constant reminder of how stress can contribute to a seemingly small thing like fainting, which can have a huge outcome.

After Dad died and I was in the process of leaving, The Magpie had some sort of a spat with upper management and covertly tried to move her practice to a new location, taking other physicians with her. Her maneuvering was mostly done behind closed doors. There were other doctors who told me they were offered the chance to go with her.

However, unknown to any of us medical people, in the process of her jumping ship she was allegedly copying patient charts from the hospital nephrology department, with the plan to also take patients with her. If true, this would have been in violation to her contract. The crazy part was that the very same secretarial staff that she systematically bullied and demeaned, were the ones that she allegedly insisted illegally copy the records for her. Like I said before, if you abuse people enough, just maybe one of them will bite you . . . and so it turned out. Somehow, the chair of medicine got wind of illegal file duplication and the office spaces were examined immediately. We were informed that all the evidence was found and the secretaries confirmed what they were being coerced into doing. During the investigation, The Magpie's office was sealed off with yellow forensic tape and nobody was allowed in for any reason until everything was legally settled. After these events, her office staff were terrified because of the threat she could come back and make things even worse for her whistleblowers. She never did.

The air in the department was tense because nobody really knew what had happened or what would happen next. But on the other hand, everyone suddenly worked and breathed much more easily. The relative peace stood in stark contrast to her previous constant reign of verbal terror. One of the janitors passed by around 5:30 PM and, looking at the yellow tape, said, "Should have happened a long time ago." Her bullying attitude had seemingly been directed at the janitorial staff just as much as, if not more than, the rest of us.

While the investigation was going on, The Magpie came into the satellite dialysis unit and found me. Shedding rivers of crocodile tears, she detailed how she had been wronged, how much she had done for the hospital and all those who worked for her, and how people had lied about her. I said that I only knew what I had been told about what was going on and that presumably justice would be served. She continued to cry and rant, but I just listened and then excused myself to go see my waiting patients. I figured that if she had done nothing wrong, she would make sure we would all soon know with unmistakable emphatic pithiness. I heard that she had attorneys at her house, around the clock, after her dismissal. My gut feeling was that she came in order to sound me out and see what I knew as to who had blown the whistle on her.

Eventually the department's second-in-command took over her job. I had already given my notice and was due in Bangor in a couple of months. I had nice recommendations from everyone at Cooper months before The Magpie's mess evolved, and was ready to move on.

Because of the sudden shortage of nephrologists at Cooper Hospital, one spring day a FedEx envelope arrived at my apartment from the university, offering me a promotion and a pay raise. They really wanted me to stay and offered me a yearly salary of 115,000 USD. I said I could not stay because I was already committed to Maine and was actually looking forward to my new life up there. I counter-offered to stay until mid-August, to give them more time to find staff, if the hospital paid me an extra 4,000 USD. They agreed. They were a pleasant few weeks with spring in blossom, and a new, quiet work atmosphere.

Always the opportunist, The Magpie went on to reinvent herself outside Cooper's system.

A few years later, at Dr. Charles Swartz's dinner banquet, The Magpie popped up unexpectedly. Nephrology is a small world even in a big city like Philadelphia. The Magpie swooped into a conversation I was having with Dr. Levison, taking me totally by surprise. I had no idea she knew or cared about Charlie. Judging by how she had treated her peers and colleagues, I figured The Magpie had shown up to schmooze and play the political game for the sake of career rebuilding.

By then I had grown a backbone and told her that I had nothing to say to her. She replied, "Suzanne I can't believe you are acting like this! We had a good relationship." To which I responded, "Like I said, I have nothing to say to you, nor any desire to speak to you at all. And I don't have to." She walked away in a huff, mumbling to herself in disbelief, which indicates that even years later, she had little insight as to her effect on others.

That was still not my last encounter with The Magpie. My dear Aunt Sara, who was more of a mother than an aunt, was a bilateral amputee, afflicted with diabetes and peripheral vascular disease. Her kidney function went up and down over the years during any illness. They always sprang back, however, and my aunt had more than nine lives. Around life number four, she was in one of the private community hospitals with sepsis. I was my aunt's medical power of attorney and, when I was phoned, made it clear that when nephrology was called, The Magpie was not to be the consulting physician. I specified which practice I wanted consulted and my aunt also knew my wishes for her, because Dr. W. had seen her in the past.

The Magpie was always a career-building businesswoman above all else. I'm pretty sure she had a mechanism in the hospital to monitor who had elevated creatinine (signifying decreased kidney function) because she strutted into my aunt's room before any order for a nephrology consultation had even been logged. My aunt was startled and put into an uncomfortable situation because she knew of my turmoil with The Magpie. It had been a big deal in my life, and my whole family had seen how tortured I had felt during the years of being her minion. So when The Magpie entered, my aunt said to her that her niece only wanted Dr. W.'s group from UREA to consult and that her niece was clear that The Magpie was not to do the evaluation. The Magpie then launched into a tirade about how nice she was to me, how we had such a good relationship, how well she thought of me, and how she couldn't understand why I would not talk to her or want her to take care of my aunt.

I was incensed at the audacity and called the attending physician who was in charge of my aunt's care and reiterated whom I wanted consulted. He told me that The Magpie had approached him and asked if he wanted her to consult, so out of convenience he said yes. I should not have been surprised because, in the years I worked for her, The Magpie was always trying to drum up business in ways that I was not comfortable with. She had wanted me to schmooze with other doctors in the lounge and on the wards of the private hospitals, so we could get the business. One of the reasons I left Philadelphia/New Jersey, in addition to the abuse from The Magpie, was that there was so much competition for patients. People were constantly accusing each other of purloining their kidney patients. I had got to the point where I wanted no part of any business that ran like that.

So that is the story of The Magpie and me.

In 2001, I was looking forward to finally making a dent in the ever-growing pile of student loans, which were crippling my freedom. I was, and am, a doctor, not a marketing businesswoman. I wanted to be where doctors were truly valued, respected and needed, and not living in a cutthroat medical market like Philadelphia.

In late-August of 2001, I made my way up to Maine to begin a new life.

Not wanting to take my dying fig tree to Maine, I asked Mary, a dialysis nurse whom I had become friends with, to take it to her house. Her husband was very clever with plant grafting and they thought they could keep it alive. So they came and took it, planted it in their yard, and kept it warm over the winters.

Maine: Eye
Of The Storm

The Bangor metropolitan area is home to about 150,000 people. A large tertiary-care medical center with a Level II trauma team, large dialysis unit, and several satellite dialysis units, serve the area. Tufts medical school is affiliated and there is a family practice residency program, which offered some teaching duties to me.

A long-term relationship was heading to an obvious end, and it looked like I was going to be alone in Maine. One of the things about city living was that I always felt safe because so many people were around, day and night. Even in the Bronx, people used to worry for me but I never worried. My A-frame house next to the Kenduskeag Stream was set on bedrock that had been dynamited out in the 1980s and the rocks were arranged around the house into perennial rock gardens. Move in day was September 1, 2001.

I really loved the quiet in Maine, but being so much more isolated in my big house was a totally new experience. I did not feel safe at night and because I had always had dogs, I had started a pet search before I left Philadelphia. I only wanted to go to shelters, not breeders, and definitely wanted a really big dog. A Rottweiler in a New Jersey pound seemed scary enough. The only problem was that I was actually a little scared of him. I was going to take him anyway, figuring I'd find a way to communicate with him and be the boss, when the shelter called to tell me they were not going to adopt him out because he had too much food aggression. I figured it must be pretty bad if they said that. The search continued in Bangor shelters but I was kind of picky as to what I wanted. One day, while switching my driver's license over, I wandered into a pet shop next to the Department of Motor Vehicles and there was a little golden retriever puppy. She was really cute but so incredibly bitey that I put her right back down.

As I was turning around, a large fox-red colored puppy in another cage in the back of the store caught my eye. He'd been there for nearly eight weeks and was now 12 weeks old. He lay there, really sad, leaning up against the cage side, head buried between his paws and not paying attention to anything around him. The shop owner was delighted that I was interested, because he was getting too old for the shop and so he was putting him on a big discount. I googled fox-red Lab and sure enough, it is a breed of Lab, so I knew he would be large enough. I took him home with me. At first I thought this was the easiest puppy on earth but, after his depression lifted, he became much like all the others, though not as destructive. The biggest problem was that no matter what training techniques I tried, he whimpered, barked, and got diarrhea anytime he was left in a cage. I tried leaving the cage door open with treats inside, but he never went in. Eight weeks of confinement was enough.

His name, Henry, came to me immediately. As he grew, the universal comment when anyone saw him was, "He's so handsome." With his square jaw, square head, and the most beautiful red-colored dog hair I've ever seen, he just kept getting more healthy and handsome as time went on.

Not happy with leaving him alone during my long days of work, I enrolled him in a therapy dog training program with Don Hanson, a really talented trainer up the road at Green Acres Kennel, who taught the click-and-treat method. After the first 12-week puppy training basics, which taught Henry how to walk on a leash without pulling, heel, wait, sit, and lie down etc., we went into the next level for therapy dog training. Henry loved the game of figuring out how to get the click sound, with the attendant treat. Because Henry was a lot more like a hound than a retriever, food rewards were quite effective. He had to learn things like: not reacting to loud noises, like the 100-year-old squeaky wheelchair Don used for training, or a pile of books falling to the ground; not licking; not going for anything if I said "leave it", "sit and stay", or "go to the mat"; and to walk a path lined with the most amazing smelling meats, without making any moves towards them. Optional extras were funny things like taking a bow at my feet. Clicker training was an attractive method because there was no negativity, no "No," chain yanking, or anything unpleasant for the dog.

We worked hard, but only around 20-25 minutes per day, and got great results. After that, he was registered as a therapy dog, which allows a dog into medical institutions for visits with patients.

Henry was loved by everyone. The nurses and office staff spoiled him and gave him lots of attention. Everyone more than made up for his first 12 weeks of life and he enjoyed working with me anywhere I went. I took him to Presque Isle dialysis clinic, three hours north, and because the owners of the bed and breakfast I frequented had three golden retrievers, Henry was a welcomed guest too. After work, he got to romp and get good and tired.

I'm quite sure that Henry increased my clinical show rate. On the rare days that I left him home because I was in a hurry, I was berated, "Where's Henry? Why didn't you bring him in? I've looked forward to seeing him for three months . . ." So I stopped leaving him home, and he went wherever I went.

As a regular fixture in the dialysis units on weekends, the nurses were more than happy to keep watch on Henry while I made hospital rounds. Patients on dialysis asked for Henry to go to them, and I was actually surprised that the blood and the dialysis lines were never the slightest temptation to him. He knew to be gentle, and would approach the patients in recliners, turn so his back was towards them, and sit. Occasionally he would crane his neck around and look as if to say, "Go ahead and pet me." The dialysis patient waiting room was another place he was especially warmly welcomed.

In all the 10 years that I took him between offices, dialysis units, and the hospital, only one patient asked me to keep him away from her, because she was terrified of any dog. She had been viciously attacked as a child and had the scars on her face to prove it. Eventually she asked me bring him over for a pat and within a year, she was hugging him.

Henry at home, 2003

Not only was Henry the best office companion ever, but I credit him for getting me out of a speeding ticket. Around eight months into living in Maine, I was driving on a road that had frequent changes in speeds. In an area that limited speed to 35 MPH, I was going 45 and a police officer pulled me over. It was an early spring day and the windows were open in the back. As the officer was asking the usual "Do you know why I pulled you over?" Henry popped his head out the back. The officer started petting him and before I knew it, he was kissing Henry and hugging him. He turned to me and said, "Please slow it down ma'am. Have a nice day."

On the morning of September 11, 2001, I was making rounds in the intensive care unit, when the televisions began repeatedly showing the traumatic images of the planes flying into the World Trade Center buildings. My first thought was "What a brilliant form of warfare. We are in real trouble." Then the reports of the Pentagon and crashed Pennsylvania plane followed.

One of our practice doctors, Dr. K. S., was up in Presque Isle that day, but strangely, the weekend before, he had asked me to cover for his weekend call. Dr. K. S. was a strange man, and we didn't really mix well. He was also pushy to the office staff, and I decided early on that I was not going to be manipulated by him. I had had enough from 'Magpie'-types in my past, so I refused his demand that I had to cover for him on my weekend off because he "had to pick up some guests".

The nurses in Presque Isle said that he had nervously paced back and forth from the exam rooms to the TV all day on September 11. Shortly after that, he announced that he was needed "back home" and took long leave, not giving any return date. I was suspicious of him, because the job recruiter who brought us both to Maine had once innocently told me that Dr. K. S. had no debt, no credit cards, and he paid cash for everything, including his rent. I noted that he was irrationally nervous after the bombings. He fitted the profile of a terrorist sleeper unit to a T. I called the government hotline to tell them what was happening, but they just asked stupid questions like: "Did he ever exhibit any aggressive or anti-American behavior?" I just sighed and hung up after giving them the information, knowing that they really didn't care. Dr. K. S. dumped everything he had ever had in Maine, and never returned.

Years later, I considered all the known facts, as the truth of the New York City events unfolded. It is possible that K. S. just knew the kind of ignorant bias he might be subjected to following the blame on Islamic terrorists. However the timing of his weekend demand upon me still has me wondering what really happened.

The sudden departure of Dr. K. S. left only three of us covering the whole nephrology practice, which was difficult at first. I asked Dr. Mediumspeed for more money, for doing more work, and he agreed to raise my salary to 160,000 USD.

In time, we hired another doctor but he only lasted about a year.

We later hired two more to help with the growing number of patients and the expanding area we were covering.

By 2005, I was earning 190,000 USD and was made a full partner. Shortly thereafter, our group agreed to raise our salaries to 210,000 USD and disperse any extra at the end of the year as bonuses.

Our peritoneal dialysis nurse put in her resignation. This is a very specialized nursing position and our practice was seemingly up a creek. So I decided on a long shot and called my friend Mary from dialysis in New Jersey, who was an ace peritoneal dialysis nurse, and told her the job was available. Much to my surprise, she showed an interest and her husband happened to have family in Maine! She applied, came for the interviews, and was accepted. By the end of the year, she was working for us, but her husband took longer to come up as the house had to be sold and the move was rather extensive.

I asked about the fig tree, which we had named Figgie years before. She reported that it was doing great and bore lots of fruit in summer. In order not to lose it all together, they brought up several cuttings and gave one to me. My wall of windows let in sun just about all day, even in winter, so it was an ideal situation for plant life. All my other plants thrived there so there was no reason Figgie would not.

Arsenic
Au Lait

Spring of 2003 put me on the cleanup crew of a bizarre tragedy in Maine's history. On Sunday, April 27, members of Gustaf Adolph Evangelical Lutheran Church in the hamlet of New Sweden, in Aroostook County, were sipping coffee, as they always did. They loved coffee and drank lots of it, but apparently, like most Mainers I knew, they were not coffee connoisseurs and would drink any brew so long as it smelled like coffee.

This coffeepot was unlike any other they had ever experienced, as it had been heavily laced with arsenic, which as most people know, is a nasty poison.

One 78-year-old church member, who had had quintuple bypass surgery a few months before, deteriorated so quickly he couldn't be moved and died at the local hospital, Cary Medical Center. Cary Medical Center, which didn't have the necessary critical care facilities, was over a three-hour drive from Bangor. Another patient at Cary died but was resuscitated by the medical center's doctor, stabilized, and then helicoptered to our hospital in Bangor, along with another five critically ill church members.

I was the only nephrologist in town that weekend, and received an urgent page to go to the hospital. Several people were put on ventilators in intensive care; one of whom had drunk two cups of the vile brew. This fellow, who had never been sick in his life, had made the coffee himself. Though he noticed it was unusually strong, as a former member of the Navy he was used to vile coffee, so he just shrugged and drank it. Shortly after his admission, his kidneys shut down completely.

One of the ventilator patients had to be placed into an induced coma with a tracheotomy for just over two weeks.

I spent the night and morning figuring out who needed immediate chelation and repeated dialysis vs. who could be treated with just chelation. It wasn't a simple dialysis technique required, either. Normal dialysis wasn't going to work.

Arsenic poisoning is something most doctors should dread treating, because it disrupts the ability of mitochondria to produce energy, resulting in dysfunction in the heart, liver, and kidneys. It's a huge metabolic cluster bomb and potent oxidative bonfire anywhere it goes. With the degree of ingestion the critical care patients had, it would have been fatal without proper life support. Barrier filtration, and membrane functions fail, all over the body. Even in the face of profound dehydration, the kidneys continue to leak massive amounts of dilute urine because the cells that normally reabsorb most of the urine after it is filtered, become paralyzed. Massive amounts of potassium and magnesium are required. We were giving doses of electrolytes that most normal people would have trouble handling yet, in these patients, we were barely keeping up. Phosphate, which is vital to a molecule called ATP—an energy source for the majority of cellular functions—is bumped off that molecule by arsenic, and then lost in the buckets of urine that leak past damaged tubules. Cellular function seizes up, so massive amounts of phosphorous are required for infusion.

It's interesting to look back upon this with my renewed eyes, because it is now so obvious how much the anti-oxidant properties of vitamin C would have helped. Most of the time with fulminant kidney failure, we have to be really careful over the dose of electrolytes we give as too much phosphate and too much fluid in the body is a problem. This situation was a whole new ballgame and unlike anything I, or anyone else in attendance, had ever encountered. We were going where no one had been before, learning fast, and writing orders for massive amounts of lifesaving fluids and electrolytes.

Even the church members who reported immediately spitting out the coffee after noticing how foul and bitter it tasted, had significant symptoms requiring hospitalization, though not kidney failure.

The evening I was called, I was briefed by Dr. Toby Atkins, a veteran family practitioner, who told me he had talked to poison control and we were going to be starting with an old drug called British anti-Lewisite, a chelating remedy for poisoning. It's a horrible, painful injection, which both stinks and burns. One patient in Cary had an anaphylactic reaction to it, so we all knew that wasn't going to do the job. Nonetheless, it was where we started.

Strangely, as I now know, many medical doctors on the outskirts of convention have been doing chelation safely for years. They had much better solutions, but conventional medicine, at that time, was for the most part just discovering chelation's value, and only willing to do it under the threat of death. Aside from that, chelation was considered quackery.

We trialed an 'investigational' chelation drug called Dimercaptopropane-sulfonic acid (DMPS), which is supposed to bind to arsenic and send it out through the urine. Because it was efficient and well tolerated, DMPS became the mainstay of our chelation therapy and we eventually received a delivery of as much as we needed, from pharmacies all around the USA. The patients not on dialysis, were given huge amounts of chelation pills, washed down with milk.

This was one of those unusual circumstances in medicine where, because we had no precedent, no protocols, no gold standards, and with almost nothing in the medical literature on massive acute arsenic overdose—we were making history.

Poison control was involved, of course, but they had no exact instructions either, so the pharmacist, dialysis nursing staff, and I experimented using different lengths of dialysis and different doses of chelation drugs. With no manual for treatment, we had to go on adjustment by observation and experimentation to try to work out which was the best way to remove the arsenic from these people. We were winging it, based on what we knew about the body and kidneys, and what we thought might work.

After a day of constantly measuring the amount of arsenic in the body and dialysis fluid, it became obvious that frequent dialysis and frequent chelation was key. So we just kept going for as long as necessary. The dialysis nursing staff were the unsung heroes, because they were constantly moving between different bedsides conducting whatever ongoing experimental treatments I asked them to.

Never once was there an eye-roll or complaint from these amazing nurses, who were always a pleasure to work with. They were there to save lives, and put their own lives on hold, often working overtime and missing family functions to do so. By the end of the weekend, we were all drained and ready for some relief.

On Tuesday, poison control decided to stage a news conference, but I tried to remain anonymous, preferring to do my job. After the first death was ruled a homicide on Thursday, every TV and media outlet had reporters crawling all over the state. The news was printed all over the world. One of my medical partners, who was on holiday in England, sent a clipping of a report from London's *The Times*, along with a chuckle that he was across the Atlantic.

Fortunately for us, most of media either annoyed the Maine Department of Public Safety at Augusta, or haunted New Sweden and annoyed the church members, instead of us. The one time that media cameras did show up at the hospital, all of the attending doctors were called to the conference room. I was late and took one look in. Seeing the mass of white coats—most of whom had little to do with any of these patients—vying for camera shots, I walked away. Dr. Toby Atkins, a natural in front of an audience, was happy to be the talking head for all of us—so I left him to it.

In a matter of days, we became 'experts', and continued gathering more data over the successive weeks. To me, this type of experimentation had already become second nature. Nephrology is a field where patients on death's door often require desperate measures, so my career to this point had contained many instances of trying new protocols that I had tailor-made, because all too often there were no pathways, or best practice sequence diagrams for the situations that arose.

During my fellowship, I devised a dialysis protocol to anticoagulate the dialysis circuit and then neutralize it with protamine sulphate, before the blood went back into the patient. This was refinement of a technique use since the 1950s that was abandoned due to potential complications. Some patients, like postoperative, hemorrhagic stroke, or trauma patients, have a high risk of bleeding if given heparin. But if you don't anticoagulate the dialysis circuit, enough blood can be lost in the tiny capillaries of the dialysis filter to lead to severe anemia and transfusion requirement. My attending physician had said, "Try it." It worked great on dozens of desperate patients, but I've never seen anyone do it that way since then. Medical opinion says it is too dangerous a method, due to possible protamine reactions or bleeding, but our experience was 100% successful.

Today there is a protocol for using citrate in the dialysis circuit instead, which is far more cumbersome and unpredictable and has its own set of potentially serious complications. The point is that nephrologists are very comfortable with testing new treatments and techniques, and flying by the seat of their pants, because it is a part of everyday practice.

Here I was again, in a situation where thinking outside the box, and initiative was required, because we could only guess by the decline in how much arsenic was coming out after chelation, how much might be left trapped in flesh and bone. But that was okay with me. Perhaps more chelation, minerals, and IV vitamin C would have improved the outcome even quicker but, back then, I didn't know what I know now.

All hospital arsenic patients survived and regained kidney function, though some did suffer long-term neuropathic pain. Ironically, while everyone's kidney function was restored to a point where they could live without dialysis, one man came back into the hospital in 2010 with an unrelated problem. He had nearly normal kidneys when admitted to the hospital. However, he was given the swine flu vaccine and his kidneys shut down within 24 hours, landing him back in my care. I'd saved him from arsenic, only for him to be done in by a vaccine.

While we talked long and hard about putting together a medical journal article, what we did was way too complicated, and individualized, to be reduced down to a set of formulas, and the work involved in trying to do that, isn't something that clinicians view with enthusiasm. There were several multidisciplinary meetings, but we never published a summary from the mass of data papers that we had collected. To do that properly involved time and energy that we simply didn't have.

However, in the years that followed I received many phone calls from clinicians, in the USA and overseas, wanting to benefit from my experience, asking how we did the dialysis and removed the poison in conjunction with the chelating agents. The only literature that existed before that was in using peritoneal dialysis.

Chelation is a valuable tool that is vastly underused. When my office patients had seriously high blood pressure and gout, I wanted to do heavy metal challenge tests on them for lead and other heavy metals, but was told that insurance carriers would not pay for it unless there were signs of acute lead poisoning. Only a whole blood lead level without provocation is acceptable to the insurance industry as a way to check. Part of the 'well-child' visit in pediatric offices is an unprovoked blood lead level.

Anyone who knows about chelation will tell you that unprovoked blood levels looking for heavy metal overload are meaningless, because the body sequesters heavy metals. You only see them in the blood for a few weeks after an acute exposure; after which, they are stored in organs such as the brain, bones, heart, and kidneys. Medical literature describes hypertension associated with chronic lead (and other toxic metals) exposure, and shows that chelation helps. However it is just not done in conventional medicine due to reimbursement restrictions, and lack of understanding of physiology of chronic metal poisoning. If you want chelation done, you have to find a quack who is doing it.

It is interesting to look back on this, because I had a sum total of 15 cases of arsenic poisoning; at least four of whom had to be chelated and dialyzed. Doctors called for my opinion and assistance.

Experimental medicine and exchanging recipes is acceptable within the confines of subspecialty practice. Nephrologists do it with each other regularly, over stubborn autoimmune diseases, protein-losing kidney problems, and various difficult unique situations.

I began using high-dose oral sodium ascorbate on infants and children with whooping cough in 2011, got great results, and then wrote about it in a detailed blog. Hundreds of families have benefitted from the protocol under my supervision, and thousands more have used the protocol on their own. The results are always an immediate decrease in cough severity, and eventual recovery even in very young infants. In contrast to the arsenic situation, not one doctor has called me wanting to use sodium ascorbate on their infected patients. Not one doctor, upon seeing the results, was curious when the parents went back to them and told them what they had done. Since then, I have amassed a large number of successful treatments of whooping cough with vitamin C in infants as young as two weeks of age, commonly two months, older children, and adults.

Instead of being asked about this protocol, I have been harassed and verbally abused online by several ignorant doctors who have totally incorrect and uneducated ideas about vitamin C, its action upon the gut and kidneys, and its toxin-neutralizing potential.

You would think the potential of vitamin C to neutralize toxins would be of interest to the medical profession. However, instead of offering a treatment that quickly reduces whooping cough toxin levels in the body and reduces the intensity of the cough to something manageable, the system insists on using antibiotics. Their shoot-from-the-hip approach invariably makes the clinical picture worse and disrupts the microbiome of the children, resulting in potential long-term complications. Those complications are totally unnecessary. Five years has taught me that whooping cough can usually be managed solely with vitamin C, by parents at home, with support from doctors who know how to use it.

Why the refusal to consider vitamin C as an anti-toxin, a reactive oxidative stress reducer, and as support for the immune system? That's the question the system refuses to adequately and intelligently answer. Yet, when the system had nothing to offer people who would otherwise have died from arsenic poisoning, I had the green light to experiment whichever way I wanted.

What You Don't Know, Can Hurt You

Taking a mixed academic/private practice nephrology position in Maine, and helping people in a really constructive way, was awesome. I loved the freedom that came with having money, and the student loan payoff became a focus of reality rather than a 30-year pipe dream. I loved my partners, my office staff, the nurses, and the work. I couldn't believe my good fortune in all ways, and had a few amazingly happy years at work.

There were some noteworthy times in Maine's hospital. Once I felt competent to deal with just about anything medical that came along, I was able to sit back and take in the bigger picture, and the impact of some details on my patients. I started to really listen to them. As a result, I became more of a patient advocate than I had previously been, because I started to see the creation of unnecessary damage that could easily be avoided.

Drive-by renal angiograms

Cardiologists were once intellectuals who could be consulted for assistance in managing the physiology of the cardiovascular system. But somewhere along the line, they became more interested in getting patients to the catheterization laboratory for invasive procedures, rather than analyzing the big picture of working on nutrition, physiology, maximizing medication efficacy, talking to patients about stressors, and getting a really detailed history and physical examination. I saw the outworking of this problem with my father's sickness, and got a bigger dose of it in Maine.

Nephrologists and cardiologists work closely together because kidney and heart disease often co-exist in the same people. Those invasive heart tests all too commonly lead to kidney failure, which can be temporary or permanent. Commonly, the dye used to light up the arteries when looking at the heart vessels will cause something called acute tubular necrosis or damage to the cells in the kidneys. When that happens, everyone waits it out and supports the body in the absence of normal-functioning kidneys. Because kidneys have so many functions including blood pressure maintenance, fluid control, hormone production for red blood cell genesis, bone health, and mineral and electrolyte control, these people need to be paid attention to, until the kidney function returns.

In order to get a catheter up to the heart and squirt dye directly into the heart arteries, the interventional cardiologist usually goes in through the groin, up the femoral artery, and then heads farther north to the heart.

A less common, but far more troubling outcome of any angiogram is the loosening of plaque from inside any artery, which can float away if the arterial catheter hits an unstable plaque just the right way. On the way from the groin to the heart, some interventional cardiologists can't resist doing a 'drive-by' squirt of dye into the kidney arteries. When they do, the potential for bumping off an unstable arterial plaque, which can float into a kidney, means that kidney will likely never work properly again. If it happens to both kidneys it is even worse. If the plaque floats down to the feet or legs, the result can be toes and limbs losing the blood supply, after which gangrene of variable severity sets in.

The idea that motivates the cardiologist is that if there is significant narrowing of one or both kidney arteries, blood pressure can rise. Even though opening those arteries rarely leads to any long-term improvement in blood pressure or kidney function, the cardiologists insist on the chance to squirt dye in there and even place a stent, or balloon blast a plaque-narrowed area.

A nephrologist should be consulted for an opinion because, as the medical literature says, the drive-by kidney test is not warranted. Prospective, randomized treatment trials suggest that little additional benefit is gained from renal revascularization if blood pressure is well controlled and kidney function remains stable. Because of the potential for harm from invasive procedures, we test only those patients who are thought to have a high likelihood of benefiting from the procedure.

One cardiologist in particular used to do angiograms on patients without consulting us. Although those procedures were not necessary and revealed no helpful information, they sometimes led to long-term negative outcomes for the patient, which nephrologists then had to deal with. The patients, of course, were none too happy either. I had more than one stoush with this particular cardiologist over the years. He finally started asking for our opinion before racing into the kidney arteries, but he sometimes still went ahead, even if I said not to do it. After a while he stopped asking again.

These were the kinds of things that really infuriated me. The patient had no idea that these complications could happen to them after a coronary angiogram. I know this because when they landed in my office, they told me that nobody told them this was any risk at all. Go online and read the sample consent forms for cardiac catheterization. Nowhere will you see any warning that the kidneys could shut down for any reason. If patients were told the whole story, I think many more people would refuse consent and opt for medical management. Just like with vaccines and other medical procedures, uninformed consent seems to be more of the rule than the exception.

Keystone cops in ICU

In 2007, one of our patients received a close inspection and treatment from Tufts Medical Center in Boston, and was sent back to our intensive care unit with kidney failure, on chronic dialysis, so our service was called to continue dialysis after her arrival. It turned out that Tufts did not do anything for her. They just examined her, continued dialysis, and vaccinated her. That came as no surprise; it is a rare exception that the upper echelons of academia ever have anything more to offer than those of us in the major city hospitals, yet families often believe that an esteemed hospital with a name will come up with some miracle cure. Patients return home and report that dozens of young doctors evaluated them and the head honcho walked in for three minutes, didn't even talk to the patient, discussed the patient as if she/he was not there, and then left. They are glad to return to their regular doctor and often come back with renewed satisfaction with their local care, after these vaunted second opinions.

This particular patient was delivered back to us with a warning for "full contact precautions" meaning touch and airborne transmission barriers must be used. The reason? She had a very bad case of shingles, which is caused by the varicella virus responsible for chicken pox and shingles. Several of us were going through her medication list from Tufts and we noticed that a shingles vaccine had been given to her about one week prior. We all looked at each other and said, "Can shingles vaccine give a person shingles?" Completely clueless, we did an online search and determined that yes—indeed—many people report getting shingles a week after the shingles vaccine. CDC website[26] states, "Some people who get the shingles vaccine will develop a chickenpox-like rash near the place where they were vaccinated. As a precaution, this rash should be covered until it disappears." Her rash was not where she was

---

[26] http://www.cdc.gov/vaccines/vpd-vac/shingles/vacc-need-know.htm

vaccinated. The manufacturer's product insert[27] states, "Transmission of vaccine virus may occur between vaccinees and susceptible contacts." Reported vaccine adverse events in clinical trials or post-marketing include, among other things, "zoster-like skin rash". I wondered why they called it "zoster-like."

Even though our patient got shingles one week after her shingles vaccine, we just shrugged and carried on. None of us knew about the Vaccine Adverse Event Reporting System (VAERS).

Such was everyday life in the country's best institutions. Most department heads at Eastern Maine Medical Center were graduates of the world's finest medical schools and hospitals. The hospitalists and consultants were top notch, so it wasn't a question of lack of training or education; doctors don't know a lot of things and often scramble to figure out what is happening in front of them. And as illustrated above, even when they do see a problem with a drug or vaccine, they just carry on and don't give it another thought.

Biopsy bloopers

Kidney biopsies are considered to be necessary for some people who have sudden onset of severe kidney disease or even long-smoldering disease of unknown origin. Obtaining some kidney tissue to look at under the microscope can yield valuable information as to which microscopic component of the kidney is suffering, and how. Then there is a chance to figure out how kidney failure may have occurred, and possibly use an effective treatment. Most of the time those drugs provide some remission, but rarely do they yield life-long cures. Unfortunately, nephrology is still a bit like playing in the dark. We still know so little and our tools are quite blunt and limited.

---

[27]http://www.fda.gov/downloads/BiologicsBloodVaccines/Vaccines/Approved Products/UCM132831.pdf

During my fellowship and academic years, we attending physicians and fellows in training did our own kidney biopsies under ultrasound guidance. When carefully done, it was a relatively precise way to obtain tissue. We would look at what was removed under a light microscope to verify that we had indeed retrieved kidney tissue with adequate amounts of the tiny glomerular filters in the specimen, rather than just fat, liver, or muscle, which can also happen. Getting a biopsy sample wrong is a complete waste of time, money, and the patient's tolerance of having a large long needle put into their kidney three times, through the wall of their back.

After going into private practice, we were led to believe that sending these patients to radiologists was a much better and more efficient way to have it done, because they were experts in removing small things from narrow passages under direct CT scan guidance. So, all my patients were sent that route. But the radiologists' biopsy results often returned stating "normal liver", "normal colon", "insufficient tissue to perform analysis", "peri-renal fat", or "skeletal muscle", more often than mine did. This meant that in order to get a diagnosis I had to call the patient, explain what had happened, and that we would have to bring them back in to repeat the procedure.

Being the deliverer of this news to a patient was no fun. In retrospect, I wonder if the procedures would have gone better if I made the radiologist tell patients the bad news when the bloopers happened. I could imagine being the patient on the other end and thus was quite distraught, because this happened far too often. In addition to the radiologists not looking under a light microscope to insure they had actual renal tissue, the patients also hemorrhaged more often after radiologists biopsied using CT, than when we nephrologists did the procedure half-blind under ultrasound. It just goes to show that technology doesn't necessarily give better results than cautious planning, experience, and skill gained through repetition.

I wanted to go back to doing kidney biopsies myself, but it was argued that this wasn't possible. I lodged a complaint to the radiology department with a list of patient names, yet the problem still continued. Then one day, frustrated almost to the point of tears, I spoke to the head of the interventional radiology department who assured me that he would perform all the future biopsies on my patients and that problems would occur no more. Things improved after that, but not 100% because he was not always the radiologist on call when stat biopsies needed to be done.

Such is the buffoonery that occurs behind the scenes of the 'most advanced medicine' on earth.

27

Doctors Are Sick

I am not being derogatory. I mean this literally.

I never saw a drop of breast milk, was fed antibiotics like candy, and vaccinated as per the very light schedule that existed while I was growing up. At some point, my mother realized that medical doctors often didn't have useful answers and she went searching for something more holistic. Growing up under chiropractic care in the latter part of my childhood probably saved me from some of the ravages of my early life, if for no other reason than what was NOT done to my already-weakened constitution, by conventional medicine.

My mother's changed attitude might have been part of her surprise at me wanting to become a medical doctor.

However, many of my fellow medical students had parents who worshipped all new medical advances and some wanted to be doctors because they thought doctors could walk on water. Many had parents or family members who encouraged them to follow in their footsteps and most students had never seen any other way to do anything, so believed that the medical system's way was the only way. All around me at medical school, many students had health problems—some of which were significant—and which often couldn't be fixed by the very people who were training them.

In my own medical office, things weren't much different. One of my medical partners was a true believer in vaccines and prescriptions. I always knew when he was around by the smell in the office the minute I walked in: the breath of a body attempting to offload toxic waste. Once, we were out at dinner and he said "Oh shit." I said "What?" His hamburger and fries had just arrived and he was upset that he forgot to bring his statin to take before he ate. Vaccinations held a god-like status to him. While most of us were celebrating the fact that we were not being harassed to getting the H1N1 flu shot, because there was a shortage of vaccine (yes, go ahead and give it to the needy), this partner stressed out, lamenting that he could not get his hands on one. Never mind that winding oneself up into a fearful lather is like throwing the immune system's door wide open and saying, "Come on in, and make your home here!" When he heard there was a supply at another hospital, he went and got a jab, and probably the placebo effect of believing he was protected, relaxed him. He had more health issues that I will not mention, but will just say that every winter there was at least one severe viral illness in this vaccine believer. It would be explained as something that was not covered by the vaccine, yet my attempts to explain the downside to flu shot effectiveness and mercury toxicity fell on deaf ears.

In 2010, I accidentally walked into the wrong room when going to a nephrology consult in my hospital. I was horrified to see a friend I really liked working with, and who was one of the youngest ICU doctors on staff. We used to share movie recommendations from Netflix. He was a gentle soul, in his 30s, who stood about 6 feet 4 inches, looked like a hippie, and had long hair sometimes pulled into a ponytail. I explained that my pager directed me to that very room and showed him the message, and apologized for walking in on what seemed like a dire situation. His wife was there and I introduced myself, said I was a friend and asked her to call upon me if she needed anything.

A few weeks later, I got an email stating that my friend had died. Shock filled my bones. His wife and I talked more and she told me that she agreed with me on vaccines and that it was a huge bone of contention between the two of them and, if there was a silver lining to his death, at least their child would no longer have to suffer any further jabs. Her grief was real and apparent, but so was her upset over the vaccine issue.

He died of colon cancer after accepting all the bells and whistles the medical profession had to offer. His lifetime of indoctrination into the medical model, and undoubtedly the food pyramid, compliance with vaccines, and treating every fever and runny nose with OTC drugs, likely contributed to his demise. Doctors can be blind, because on some of the really important issues surrounding health and the immune system, we are taught by the blind and led by the blind, so later we also blindly stumble along.

I had regular run-ins with the angiogram-happy cardiologist who, without asking me my opinion, did drive-by angiograms on my patients' kidney arteries that shut down their kidneys—mostly temporarily but sometimes permanently. His cavalier stupidity made me livid. He was a true believer that the more interventions of all sorts, the better. One day on medical rounds, I was told that he had consulted the nephrology team who were about to sign his case off as his kidneys had recovered. It turned out that even though he was only 50 years old, he had survived treatment of lymphoma in the past, and now it was recurring.

Another young colleague, a surgeon aged around 40 years old, dropped out of the medical service abruptly. I was initially told it was a terrible tragedy and that he and his family did not want any discussion of it. He was not expected to return to work, due to an aggressive sarcoma cancer. Surprisingly, about one year later, I saw him back at work, albeit much thinner and looking very frail. We never discussed the issue and I am not sure where he is today.

Working in mainstream medicine, I saw doctor after doctor taken out by cancer or serious medical issues, at seemingly higher rates than the general public. Recent medical literature shows that **overall**, physicians are at lower risk of cancer but at least Taiwanese physicians are at a significantly higher risk of thyroid cancer (HR=1.75, 95% CI=1.14, 2.68), prostate cancer (HR=1.54, 95% CI=1.21, 1.97), breast cancer (HR=1.45, 95% CI=1.00, 2.09), and non-cervical gynecological cancer (HR=4.03, 95% CI=1.77, 9.17), compared with the general population[28]. Those are huge differences in rates. Could this increased mortality be from the high stress of being a physician or might it be due to easy access, and lifelong dedication, to treating all things medical with toxic drugs?

As I write this, more and more memories of sick and dying colleagues flood back to memory. I once dialyzed a trauma surgeon after he had cardiovascular collapse, and sepsis. He was obese and under a doctor's care for years before his illness.

Isn't continuing to do the same thing, even when it's not working, the definition of insanity?

Eventually he left surgery and went to get another education, apparently an MBA. Hopefully he woke up too.

As mentioned previously, doctors are definitely at higher risk for depression and suicide, which is thought to be the result of inadequately treated depression. On average, the United States loses as many as 400 physicians to suicide each year[29]. Within my own sphere in Maine, to everyone's surprise, a successful and well-liked orthopedic surgeon shot himself at home. The success rate for doctors' suicide attempts is also higher than the general population. The most common route is intentional drug overdose.

Today, I know a young man of about 17 who has his sights set on medical school. All through his childhood, he has been plagued with many allergies, with total dependence on OTC and prescription

---

[28] Lin S. Y., et al., 2013 "A comparison of cancer incidence among physician specialists and the general population: a Taiwanese cohort study," *Journal of Occupational Health*, 2013;55(3):158-66. PMID: 23574776

[29] Andrew L. B., et al., 2015 "Physicians and Suicide," *Medscape*, July 9. http://emedicine.medscape.com/article/806779-overview

drugs. He actually thinks the medical profession is the reason why he is alive, but hasn't the slightest notion what started his health problems, or that there might be other, more fundamental, answers that could have solved his problems.

It isn't just doctors who are sick. So are their families. Someone I went to medical school with is now a neonatologist. Her previously healthy spouse tragically died of a mysterious neuromuscular disease around the age of 40. Every cabinet in that house was filled with drugs and everyone was always vaccinated up-to-date for every recommended vaccine. Her daughter has always been on several regular 'meds' and is emotionally dysregulated.

Everywhere I looked, I saw doctors' kids that were sick with emotional and health issues. I have treated sick doctors and their sick children for kidney disease. One of the more memorable was the daughter of an orthopedic surgeon and a RN who had bipolar disorder and was on lithium most of her life. The daughter presented to me at the age of 18 with renal failure and small kidneys. She had had all the gold standard bells and whistles of medicine since birth.

The doctor's cure is all too often part of the disease and, strangely enough, that applies to doctors as well as patients. This might be why people who look at their sick doctors have low expectations for their own health as well.

Lame Ducks

Up the food chain: the VAERS reports

Even though medical journals[30] publish information about reporting vaccine reactions to VAERS, I had never read it, or heard of it. Not only that, but I didn't think of vaccine reactions at all prior to 2009. Even though I got really sick after being coerced into getting a flu shot in winter of 1992, I never considered why, or what, could be in the vaccine or what it did to my immune system. I had just got sick and thought, "Hmm that was a weird coincidence. Won't be going back for more . . . just in case it was not a coincidence," and I never had another flu shot. Nobody asked me to and I just never thought about it afterwards. However, the few times I said how sick I had become after the shot, my hypothesis was immediately shot down. It's not just mothers whose instincts get vaporized by the 'experts', but it happens to doctors-in-training too.

Today there is a copious amount of literature, describing exactly how and why I got sick after that vaccine, which most doctors have neither read, nor have any idea it exists. The cycle of ignorance continues.

If doctors can't even work out when or why **they** have a problem with a vaccine, they are hardly likely to work out when someone else does, particularly if they are the ones who put the needle in.

---

[30] Singleton, J. A., et al., 1999 "An overview of the vaccine adverse event reporting system (VAERS) as a surveillance system. VAERS Working Group," *Vaccine*, Jul 16;17(22):2908-17. PMID:10438063

Back when I had my flu shot, I knew nothing about the children who were damaged by vaccines in the decades following the introduction of the inactivated polio vaccines, or any other vaccine. I didn't know about the many parents who regret vaccinating and not listening to the little voice of alarm inside them, which knew better than their fear-based reasoning. Many parents have won court hearings against vaccine companies, but not as many as should have. There have been enough successful lawsuits to seriously erode public confidence about vaccines.

While all that was brewing away in the 1980s and earlier, none of it reached my ears. I had no idea that vaccine manufacturers had threatened to stop providing vaccines because they were scared of going bankrupt. Such information was never discussed.

The National Childhood Vaccine Injury Act of 1986 and the Vaccine Adverse Event Reporting System (VAERS) was voted into existence just three years before I entered medical school. It was never mentioned during medical school, residency, fellowship, or anywhere in my midst. I never saw VAERS posters on walls in hospitals, waiting rooms, or practices.

After I saw my first vaccine injury around 2006, I mentioned it to a friend outside medicine, and was shocked to be informed that a system encouraging voluntary reporting of any adverse vaccine event had long existed. Why was this not widespread knowledge?

So when people developed problems that THEY considered were due to the vaccines in 2009, and I could find no other cause, I reported the reactions to VAERS.

The response by the CDC was nothing short of bizarre and actually intimidating. Isn't it strange that a doctor, who did as the medical literature advises, was suddenly treated like a pariah? Looking back on things now, I wonder how I would have been treated if I had also reported every drug reaction I saw. That certainly would have kept me busy, since so much of what nephrologists do from day-to-day is stop 'appropriately' prescribed drugs and pick up the pieces of people who have been wounded by obediently taking them in the belief they would make them better. It also never occurred to me to report any drug reactions until 2010. Nobody else did it, because such a concept simply wasn't on the radar of medical professionals. Why would it be? Drug reactions are so commonplace; we see them every day, and eventually they just become a daily part of practicing medicine.

My first adverse drug event report

Mrs. H. was a patient I was very fond of, and had followed for years in Northern Maine. She had mild kidney impairment and was a breast-cancer-treatment survivor: mastectomy, radiation, and long-term estrogen blocking therapy with Tamoxifen. She remained quite stable in the years we worked together but, around 2010, her oncologist decided to switch her over to a new drug called Aromasin (exemestane). Her kidney function dropped immediately from around 50% to 30%, so I called the oncologist who agreed to switch her back to Tamoxifen. The kidneys went back up to her old level of 50%. Then he wanted to do one more trial of Aromasin just to be sure it was not coincidence. I agreed and the same thing happened.

This time I called Pfizer and got an Indian gentleman on the phone. The reception quality was poor and on three separate occasions, I described to him what had happened. He kept calling back asking for further clarification and to see how Mrs. H. was doing. His response was one of wonder and disbelief. He insisted that my patient was the first to have such a report, but the company would keep an eye out for other problems. Even though I had been working alongside doctors from India as long as I could remember, his thick accent stretched my accent-listening capabilities to the limit.

I searched various databases recently for Aromasin's complications, and all I could find was a comment to "Tell your doctor if you have any kidney problems." Is that the result of my report? Nowhere is there any information for the doctor to figure out what to do after finding their patients have drug-induced kidney problems, or whether or not to start the drug in a patient with pre-existing kidney problems. There are no potential adverse events listed for kidneys.

This is actually worse than VAERS, because while VAERS is a system meant to placate parents, rather than have any effect on vaccine safety, VAERS at least anonymously lists the adverse events publicly, while the drug adverse event reporting seems to not even list the events at all. I think that numerous proven-related events must have to occur in order to be put on the adverse event list on the package inserts, but what about the events that were never reported in the first place?

The most important question is, "Are most doctors still not reporting reactions and just going on, as if nothing has happened?"

Drugs And Dominos

What kept me sane in my job, in Maine, was the good I could do for the people that I was dealing with, sometimes just by listening in the extra time in the office, and chatting with Henry present. It wasn't just for the 'skills' that I had been honing medically over 12 years as a nephrologist.

I loved the people I worked with and for the first few years, I really enjoyed the job. But as more time went by, it became painfully obvious that my main qualification had become writing prescriptions. Being a highly trained agent for the pharmaceutical industry felt limiting, but I stuck to it anyway because there were people who still needed those prescriptions and I hadn't yet paid off the loans or saved any money. I call it, the golden handcuffs.

I started to realize that many of the kidney-failure patients were there BECAUSE of the drugs prescribed to them by general practitioners and internal medicine specialists. As a nephrologist, I'd reason, "That statin or that non-steroidal anti-inflammatory, or that lithium, or that antibiotic (which were the main culprits when it came to kidney failure) caused this kidney problem. Stop that drug and we'll look at an alternative." Nobody batted an eyelash, tried to argue with me, or dared to contradict me. They just stopped the drug. Why? I was the expert, and there was usually a smorgasbord of alternative drugs that could be prescribed instead.

In conventional medicine, doctors use that smorgasbord to the fullest. Any patient on six or more medications, is always thinking,

"Do I really need all of these drugs?" It was not uncommon for patients referred to me to be taking upwards of 12 different drugs per day.

As time went on, some primary care doctors sent their patients to me, specifically, because I had some success at getting people OFF their drugs. Patients referred each other to me in the hopes that their drug lists could be shortened, and often it could be. After all, when a patient sees four different practitioners who can only spend 15 minutes with them, the drug list just grows and grows. That's how you get them out of the office: new complaint equals new drug and the left hand rarely notices what the right hand has done.

I tried to make the most of the fact that I was primarily a glorified technician stuck within 'gold standard protocols', doing pretty much the same thing, day in and day out, prescribing the same drugs and putting the same hammer to the same nail, with similarly disappointing outcomes for most patients.

In the meantime, I began studying conventional medical literature and alternative sources on probiotics, because it is well known and accepted that antibiotics cause microbiome damage even when effective against a specific target. So, probiotic prescribing became a regular practice of mine, both in and out of the hospital, to try to limit collateral damage. I was always trying to find anything in the literature that could make a difference to basic health, beyond just doling out lifelong drugs. Vitamin D and nutrition made some minor positive changes in my hypertensive population who did not have kidney failure. I knew there were better and more effective ways to handle the most common referral issues like high cholesterol, gout, hyperglycemia, and urinary infections. I also knew that anything outside what hospital nephrologists were doing would be considered either quackery or 'unstudied'. CoQ-10 was another supplement I felt all practitioners should be giving if they insist on drugging with statins. There certainly was enough evidence that it helps counter the brain effects. Many patients figured it out themselves, but most primary doctors and specialists told them it was just giving them 'expensive urine'.

After years of following the same patients, it was obvious that although antibiotics might temporarily fix a urinary infection, the patient might then have to be treated for an antibiotic-induced clostridium difficile, methicillin-resistant staph aureus (MRSA) or vancomycin-resistant enterococci (VRE) infection. Antibiotic resistance in general is on the rise worldwide, but one especially troubling example is the rise in resistant strains of E. coli, the bacteria that cause more than 80% of UTIs. They are becoming resistant to the most common empirically prescribed drugs; Ciprofloxacin and trimethoprim/sulfamethoxazole.

I didn't know back then, the long-term and profound effects of changing the non-pathogenic microbial flora with antibiotics, or how that affected all other organs including the brain. Nor did I know any other means to rid the body of infection. But I knew that before 1940 people dealt with infections somehow, and they didn't always die or have kidney failure from too many infections.

The kidney failure population is bigger today than it has ever been. Since 2011, I've gotten some of the answers I sought and, as a result, my drug prescribing has gone way down. There are better interventions than always attacking the symptoms with drugs. For instance, I was floored to discover that uric acid, the culprit of gout, is a powerful antioxidant. Same for bilirubin. Might gout be a cry for change in oxidative stress? Can we alleviate gout symptoms and shift the underlying pathology with more than just drugs and limiting certain foods? Yes, of course. Today I can alleviate gout symptoms while improving overall health, whereas in the past I could only 'treat' gout symptoms with drugs that had their own symptoms. Now I know that, but then I didn't.

The body has many calls for help and conventional medicine can find a drug to silence every last one of them. The problem is that while each drug silences the first distress call, it often sets off another.

In conventional medicine, we have a saying: "When you hear hoof beats, look for horses and not zebras." A zebra is another term for a very unlikely diagnostic possibility. Looking back over 23 years of being a medical doctor, I can say with confidence that cures are the rarest WHITE zebras in conventional medicine.

However, even worse than realizing the fact that conventional medicine cures were somewhat of a mirage, were the occasions when I made the health of my patients worse. It's all very well for some in the medical system to say it's inevitable, but I took it badly and personally.

Preventable Harm

There is a saying in surgery that goes, "If you haven't ever dropped [punctured] a lung putting in a central line, you haven't inserted enough central lines." It is true that most doctors will, at some time in their careers, make a choice or be in a position where something goes wrong with a patient under their treatment.

I was not exempt from such undesirable outcomes and mishaps, and every one of them smacked me in the guts.

Around 2003, a 40-year-old auto mechanic presented to me with nephrotic-range proteinuria. He was a large man, probably around 80 kg, and, after a kidney biopsy, was diagnosed with focal and segmental glomerulosclerosis; a nasty problem at the best of times. Primary treatment in his particular case involved corticosteroids at 1 mg/kg/day.

He already had borderline type II diabetes so I decided to initiate an every-other-day dose of 2 mg/kg/day, which is generally accepted as a risk-reducing treatment for those at risk of steroid complications. I took out my prescription pad and sent him off to begin treatment.

A month later, he returned with morbid fluid accumulation and hypertension. I asked him what dose he was taking and he told me he took what was on the bottle. I said, "But what dose was it?" He replied, "150 mg per day."

I thought the pharmacist must have made a mistake so I requested my prescription be copied and faxed to me for inspection. Fifteen minutes later it came through the office with my writing stating 150 mg prednisone QD, which means daily. I did not write QOD, which would have meant every other day.

It didn't matter that I told the patient to take it every other day. He did what the prescription said. It was my fault.

I was mortified and told him that I had overdosed him on prednisone and most of the swelling was because I had written the prescription incorrectly. I told him how sorry I was and that he could make a report if he wanted to. He declined and carried on being my patient. The swelling decreased and the side effects wore off after putting him on the appropriate dose.

I took care of him for several more years, trying different drugs to slow the disease but none of them worked.

He eventually wound up on dialysis and succumbed to depression and failure to thrive after many cardiac and vascular procedures. He was only 46 at the time of his death.

While that first case might not seem like a big deal, I took all of my errors very much to heart. This one was made worse by the fact that yet again, there was nothing in my toolbox to help fix him.

But the next one would trouble me even more.

A young, fit athlete was referred to me for a rash, slight decrease in kidney function, and hematuria (blood in the urine). He otherwise felt fine and I could not elicit any obvious cause on interview, so did the shotgun approach of testing for just about everything including the garden gate. After a battery of tests, the patient called for his results while I was up north in Presque Isle. I called my secretary in Bangor and asked her to read me off the results, and I wrote them down. One of the tests for vasculitis was positive according to her reading to me. It was so high that I kept asking her if it was really this patient and to check the name, date of birth, and medical record number. I called the patient and explained the test result to him and, that in order to preserve his kidney function, the recommendations are to put a catheter into his neck and begin a toxic immune-suppressing drug and prednisone. I had the whole thing arranged in my absence because I was a four-hour drive away.

After witnessed verbal information was given and consent obtained by phone from the patient, the catheter was placed, and the first infusion was given.

When I returned to the office two days later, a copy of the lab report was sitting on my desk. I picked it up to tick it off manually and, straight away, felt weak at the knees and my heart pounded. The secretary had read the report wrong and had read me the range of abnormal results, not the patient's actual result, which fell well within the range of normal. I had just given a highly toxic drug to a patient who didn't need it. It was my fault for not having the lab result emailed or faxed directly to myself, and believing the reading from my secretary instead.

I immediately called the patient and told him that I was given erroneous information that I did not see firsthand and that he did not require either the drugs or the catheter. Strangely, he was so elated at not having a disease requiring the drug and catheter that he never complained about the dose of cyclophosphamide.

A young woman of about 20 years of age was the last and most tragic death on record in my hospital years. She was under the care of one of my nephrology partners for about one year. She lived alone, worked full time, and was able to maintain a normal life even with her illness. The diagnosis was lupus, with kidney involvement. Because of the aggressive nature of the lupus, she was treated with powerful immune-suppressing drugs; cyclophosphamide and prednisone, which seemed to be relatively well tolerated.

I was on call the weekend she was admitted to the hospitalist service, and thus my opinion was requested. The main problem was anemia, which was quite severe with a hemoglobin of 5.0 g/dL (normal being 12-15.5) for women. The hospitalists had given two units of packed red blood cells and were evaluating possible causes of the anemia. I suggested the cyclophosphamide be discontinued, the prednisone continued as she was dependent upon it by that point, and a hematology consultation. Her kidneys were stable.

When I arrived on Sunday to see her, the room was empty. I inquired with the nurse in charge of the room, who told me she had passed away in the night. I was speechless because she did not seem very ill, had no fever, was conversant and only complained of a weakness. The autopsy revealed a wide spread fungal infection that had rapidly taken over and killed her.

There was never a complaint or phone call from the family. Why? Because they knew she had a serious illness, and it is well known that these powerful immune suppressing drugs can lead to fatal infections. In a court of law there would have been no case against any of the doctors. What strikes me today about this case is the fact that if you hit the hammer to the nail in the manner that conventional medicine approves of and a patient dies, there are no consequences. Consent was signed by this lady for the drugs and it was considered her best bet to maintain any sort of remission.

This is all part of the drugs, dominoes, and failures. When I look back on my life, both as a person and a doctor, most of the problems detailed in this book were as a result of over-trusting myself or someone else, or going too fast and not paying close enough attention. Having a drink spiked could be considered naïvety, but the lesson I learned was NEVER to trust anyone else when it came to alcohol. I've worked in places, and seen that all anyone has to do is turn their head to one side, and their drink can be altered in a flash.

When I was doing my trauma rotation, several years after the PCP episode, one of the surgeons said something to me I will never forget: "Suzanne, these people almost always get here by doing something they shouldn't have been doing, and not taking good care." At the time, I thought, "Right, like drunk driving or taking hard drugs or being in a gang." But the reality is that it takes much less than that to lead to big trouble; much of which could be avoided, with a little more attention and care.

I learned as a doctor that a person's life is so precious that my responsibility, always, is to slow down, be careful what I write, double check any tests results with my own eyes, and never be hasty to make decisions that could have serious ramifications.

Sometimes that is hard, because there are times when doctors need to move fast in order to save a life. Sometimes doctors want to get home at a certain hour and there is a mountain of administrative paperwork or electronic medical records to deal with. Sometimes the pager is going off, five people are in line requiring questions answered, and there are still three more consults to be done. So it's a balance, and sometimes that balance is lost, which can result in the doctor bearing a weight that truly feels like helplessness.

For false Christs and false prophets will appear and perform great signs and miracles to deceive even the elect.

~ Matthew 24:24

The Weight Of Helplessness

One of the other reasons I had moved to Maine to start a new life, was because a change of scenery sometimes helped stave off my years-long struggle with subclinical depression, which can and does afflict many new doctors who see that reality doesn't match their long-held dreams.

I'd managed to keep away from the quicksand pit, which dogged me in my residency, and most of the time the doldrums were kept at a low hum, with enough variety, challenge, and adventure in my schedule to reduce the clinical-level heart sickness, down to the occasional bounce back. My job in New Jersey, and the death of my father, had flung me to a low place. Being in Maine had initially taken me to a high place, because Maine was exciting and left my heart fluttering for quite a while. Having a dream job and money to start paying off my loans lifted me up.

But my depression was simply buried beneath the freshness and regalement. When the weekends off arrived, and I was alone with no adventure to chase, the gray low-frequency landscape in the recesses of my heart could quickly re-emerge. As I started to see the drug and treatment problems mentioned in the previous two chapters more clearly, and realized that I was part of problem with seemingly few answers, I felt the burden within start to grow again.

I knew I needed to reach out for help. Out of desperation during residency, I had tried a couple of different SSRIs and bupropion. All they did was pile side effects onto my helplessness. During the worst times in New York and Philadelphia, I'd also attended years of expensive psychotherapy recommended by others in this situation, which, at best, sanded the sharp points off stalactites inside the dark cave of my dysphoria.

Now that I had confidence, career success, more time and more money to do whatever I wanted, I chose to go back into psychotherapy. But this time, it was going to be different to the more conventional PhDs, MSWs, and MDs I'd consulted in the past.

Something in me suspected that part of my problem also had spiritual roots, so I chose a psychotherapist who was using unconventional means to (hopefully) help people heal. Eastern Maine Medical Center was also welcoming Reiki to their sickest hospital patients, through volunteers that were permitted entrance to the hospital with patient access. There was also an excellent trauma surgeon in Maine, whom everyone loved. He did Reiki on his patients as a matter of course, and his patients had seen unexplained improvement. It seems that 'Reiki masters' are a dime a dozen today. It was also understandable that certain sections of the alternative medical profession were enthusiastically embracing aspects of shamanism. Another well-known health center in Portland Maine had MDs openly working alongside Reiki masters and shamanic practitioners.

In asking around, I was recommended a psychologist who was not like the rest. I will refer to him as 'Medicine Man.' His personal statement went something like this:

Integrating psychology and spirituality, I provide a heart-centered transformational process to awaken people to their true nature and purpose. I have found that "diagnosis" and "treatment" are concepts too narrow to understand the depth and richness of our experience, heal the wounds of our history, and allow us to embody our fullness . . . My approach is deep and soulful, rather than simply psychological. I provide a heart-centered transformational process to awaken people to their Essence. Once a person opens to their true nature and life purpose they become grounded, centered, and naturally happy.

I was really happy to have found a potential solution to my emptiness and deadness. Our first meeting gave me even more hope because Medicine Man was happy to be working with a doctor who he thought might find some of the shamanic healing traditions useful.

After our first meeting, I drove the 75 minutes home with a kind of hope I'd never felt before. Opening the door to the house that winter's night, I was met with a leafless fig tree. So I called Mary and asked her to take it back, which she did. At their house, it was instantly revived once again. Figgie's offspring was happy to live on, but not under my care.

Medicine Man held group classes, so I signed onto one, and decided to sit back and see whether something useful could be learned from him, outside of his psychotherapy training. I rarely missed a class in 10 years.

After four years, the group decided that to make life easier, we would meet at my home. It was in these day- and weekend-long meetings, that I discovered how spiritually eclectic this conventionally trained psychotherapist was. He started introducing concepts that had to do with breaking undesirable mental and spiritual bonds, which he maintained undergirded everyone's helplessness. Our limitations and problems were supposedly created by the teaching systems of the dense, conformed world, living in 'ordinary reality', spiritual 'entities' that needed to be expelled, and partial loss of our souls from past-life trauma. These issues, he said, all contributed to the burying of our 'Essences' and veiled our natural vision that could perceive spiritual reality beyond the third dimension.

In addition, there was great consideration given to human soul progression over thousands of lifetimes, in which we needed to learn karmic lessons as we advanced, or in some cases regressed. Naturally, this raised some questions with people who said they were Jews, or Christians, but we were told that no one need put aside their religious preferences, because shamanism was quite different to religion.

Knowing that there were other MDs happily working with these types of practitioners, I settled in and took everything he said seriously, and started working hard at whatever challenge he set before me.

However, before I really started to see through Medicine Man's facade, and identify the emptiness of his words, there was a cardinal event that opened my mind to the power of Christ.

Each of you is to take up a stone on his shoulder, according to the number of the tribes of the Israelites, to serve as a sign among you. In the future, when your children ask you, 'What do these stones mean?' tell them that the flow of the Jordan was cut off before the ark of the covenant of the Lord.

~Joshua 4:5-7

32

Oh, Jesus!

A consult, which came late in the day, held me at work longer than usual, and turned out to be the beginning of one of the most amazing things I had yet seen, or experienced. If someone had just told me such a thing would happen, I would have laughed. I had not long been consulting with Medicine Man at this point, but perhaps my own desperation allowed a tiny chink to open in my mind, towards any miracle, no matter where it came from, and hear what this patient was about to tell me. Mr. LeJoy gave me hope.

Mr. C. LeJoy was an 80-something-year-old farmer from up in the northern regions of Maine. His baseline kidney function, noted on months of records, was around 50%. He had got a thorn in his hand, which had become infected and later extended deeper into the tendons, forming an abscess. He was transferred to Eastern Maine Medical Center after the local hospital up north became concerned that his left palmar cellulitis was not responding to antibiotic treatment. It looked very bad for the hand, but after two surgeries for debridement and more antibiotics, he turned the corner for the better and was sent home with an open wound to drain, and oral antibiotics. His kidney function had declined since admission and by the time I saw him, his kidney function was down to about 25% and he still needed high doses of antibiotics.

Upon discharge from the hospital, Mr. LeJoy's kidney function had only improved slightly, so I scheduled him in my clinic the next time I was going to be up north.

Two weeks later, he met me in the office in Presque Isle. I examined him and noted the palm was healed. But his kidney function decline from baseline had not improved much at all. His underlying type II diabetes had been out of control for a long time. His moderate obesity and now the insult from the sepsis may have been too much for his already diseased kidneys.

When I looked at his urine in my lab, there was a large amount of protein, which is a bad sign in terms of risk for progression to dialysis. I put him on a drug that decreases the protein in the urine but also decreases kidney function. It is the standard of care for diabetics in nephrology. Then I told him that barring a miracle, which I couldn't supply, his kidneys would likely continue to decline over time. "How long?" he asked. My honest reply was, "I can't say exactly, But if you follow the usual trend, maybe a year or so before needing to think about dialysis."

To make things worse for him, he was the devoted, sole-caregiver for his wife, who had dementia. He simply couldn't afford to be sick.

On follow-up, a few weeks later, not much had changed. He agreed to keep on working towards weight loss and blood pressure control and to take the new drug. When he didn't show for his next couple of visits and I thought that meant he had either died, progressed to worsening kidney status, or was just going to be one of those people who goes into denial, stops all their drugs, and returns to the hospital on death's door needing dialysis.

Mr. LeJoy was none of those patients.

He returned to see me nearly a year later and looking to be the same weight, but not very sick at all. Thinking the drug I gave him for his blood pressure must have been key to his health, I started asking him questions. He told me that he stopped all his drugs. Incredulous and worried, I asked why. He said he didn't think he needed them anymore.

I picked up his test results to show him why he needed them, and looked at his kidney function and urine protein from the week before. Then I checked the name again. Yes, same name. Oh well . . . in Presque Isle lots of people had the same name. Date of birth and address were the same too. But . . . his kidney function was now totally normal, and far better than his long-term baseline. There was no protein in his urine, and he had not lost a pound of weight. In fact he may have even gained. Even stranger, his hemoglobin A1C was normal, showing that there was no more diabetes.

He watched me and waited as I looked over the papers, and when I told him the results he began to cry. Mr. LeJoy had a handsome face despite his age and wrinkled skin, and a very sincere, gentle mannerism. I asked him why he was crying and he said, "My Jesus is the most wonderful, beautiful savior."

Back then, I imagined that all spiritual healings were probably the same, and equally rare. So being ultra-liberal and inclusive, I said, "Yes, he surely must be. What did you do?" To which he replied that he had his church pray for him and afterwards he knew deep inside, that he had been healed.

Harboring quite a bit of doubt, I had him back one month later and repeated the tests just to make sure it was not a switch up in the lab.

Four weeks later, everything was still the same. Normal blood pressure, normal urine both in my lab and the hospital lab, and normal kidney function.

After that, I brought him back every six months just because I wanted to be reminded of the miracle, and of course check his lab numbers to make sure the miracle stuck.

He humored me and came dutifully to each visit, if for nothing else than to pet my dog Henry and let me sit with a man who had been the recipient of a miracle. Every time he would cry with joy and gratitude. He was the first patient I ever knew who claimed their miraculous healing was from the grace of Jesus' work.

I am so glad to have known Mr. LeJoy because nearly a decade later, when needing just such a healing for myself, he would become a 'cairn in the River Jordan', as I looked back. The tangible laboratory evidence of success, piling up in his file, planted a seed in me that was to lie dormant for a few more years.

33

The Quinine Quandary

Many years after graduating medical school, the limitations I saw in my training had become a reality in my practice, and nagged me more than ever. Around six years after I arrived in Maine, I encountered another crossroads. Where to from here? There were so many quandaries. For example, although the question might sound simple, what do you do about dialysis muscle cramps?

Quinine is one of the oldest drugs ever used. Even before the Spanish discovered their New World, native healers in Peru were using the bark of the Cinchona tree to treat fever, malaria, and indigestion. To this day, the exact mechanism of action remains a mystery. It is still used in medicine for its anti-malarial, anti-arrhythmic, and anti-inflammatory effects. In dialysis, low doses were extremely effective in preventing leg cramps, which are the bane of hemodialysis-dependent kidney-failure patients. In 2007, the FDA restricted the use of quinine for leg cramps, maintaining that leg cramps are not a serious health problem, while quinine can be lethal. Try telling that to a dialysis patient who had been safely using quinine for years, and then all of a sudden their remedy is pulled from the market. Millions of Americans had been using quinine daily for restless legs and cramps until then. After the ban, other expensive new drugs were proposed for the leg cramps, but none of them worked and they all carried side effects. I was totally frustrated and the patients were beyond upset.

After a long day in our Northern Maine dialysis unit in Presque Isle, I was in the market shopping for some dinner. I wandered into the natural section of the store, looked up, and saw a homeopathic remedy for cramps. I had no idea at that time that Dr. Samuel Hahnemann also had a eureka moment about quinine back when he became a medical translator after giving up on the conventional medicine of his time, over much the same frustrations I was having. With an urge to consider other concepts of disease, in my spare hours, I decided to study homeopathy. After all, Dr. Samuel Hahnemann, the father of homeopathy, had been a medical doctor too, and I knew that in the early-1900s most medical doctors and pharmacists reported using homeopathic remedies with success. Maybe homeopathy would be a valuable addition to my limited repertoire. Another attraction was that homeopathy didn't create the sort of metabolic havoc I saw every day from the drugs I was prescribing. The question was, however, could homeopathy be a tool in my bag today? The results, which today's homeopaths took credit for, often seemed more promising than the results I saw in my conventional medical career.

After some searching around for a distance-learning course, I enrolled in the School of Homeopathy in Devon, UK with Misha Norland. I studied diligently at home; learning scientific facts about the plant and mineral kingdoms that I never knew before. Besides the requisite anatomy and pathology, homeopathic philosophy was totally different to what I learned at medical school. During my studies, several homeopaths talked about how many cures they had and how wonderful the effects were, and I thought, "That would be really nice."

During the third-year clinical curriculum, I can remember my supervisor saying, "Suzanne, every day, I get paid to watch miracles happen." And I thought, "Yes! Any patient would want that, and so do I!" So for about three-and-a-half years, I was a nephrologist during the day and studied homeopathy at night and on weekends, and attended mandatory seminars in the UK during my vacation weeks.

One area of homeopathy study, which hit me as being so true, was the progression of illnesses as a result of suppressively treating the symptoms of one small superficial complaint. The end result was something bigger and deeper inside the body. I had seen this so often in the medical system yet I had never really thought about it. The homeopathic teaching of how diseases enter and leave the body inspired me to look closer at what is really known about the complexity of the immune system. I began asking patients about their illnesses as a child—how they were treated and what happened next—and linking some new dots. I noted that, even in my conventional patients, Constantine Hering's Law of Cure was exactly spot on.

I was also amused by the history of Dr. Hering.

Hering attended Leipzig University in Germany, where he was the favorite student of a famous surgeon named Dr. Henrich Robbi, who happened to be a critic of Hahnemann. In 1821, while a campaign against Hahnemann was raging. The founder of a publishing house in Leipzig, C. Baumgartner, wanted to publish a book against homeopathy to quash the practice for good. Dr. Robbi was asked to write it but he was too busy, so suggested that Dr. Hering do it.

Dr. Hering read Hahnemann's philosophy, tried out the remedies out on different conditions and was surprised to see that they were effective. But what removed all his initial doubt was when Hering cut the forefinger on his right hand while making a dissection on a dead body. The wound rapidly became gangrenous. After normal orthodox medical treatment made no difference, a student of Hahnemann persuaded Hering to take the homeopathic remedy, arsenicum album. What did he have to lose? After a few doses he felt better and the gangrene had gone completely. Hering still managed to graduate medical college with the highest honors, but never completed the book for Dr. Robbi. After graduation, he went to Philadelphia, PA in the USA, and started a homeopathic medical school.

While I realized that Hering's Law of Cure was true, all I really ever saw in conventional practice was disease going from minor, to major. Only later, when talking to parents of previously autistic children, did it become obvious that Hering's laws of reversal of disease were what these parents saw. Most of them described how their children's eczema or skin troubles would resurface when the brain started getting better, and their child started to relate to the world again. Such a phenomenon is not part of conventional medical thinking, probably because true cure rarely happens in conventional medicine, so symptom reversal wasn't there to study.

And nobody wants to admit that everyday treatments, given in sanctioned medical facilities all over the world, might seem to fix a simple surface problem, but as a result create another deeper problem.

I saw many people brought to higher levels of 'cure' through the treatment of other homeopathic practitioners, but in my hands, homeopathy was not giving the results I hoped for. By then, two-hour interviews and several hours of hunting down the right remedy at the right dose were too time consuming for my life. Even though I didn't complete my homeopathic studies and or become a homeopath, the educational experience enriched my overall fund of knowledge. I still refer patients to homeopaths when I think it could help.

In 2009, the vaccine issue became my primary focus. Everything besides vaccines was relegated to the sidelines. It got to the point where there was nothing more important to me than getting to the truth about what was going on, and answering my own lingering questions about medicine, history, and vaccination.

34

The Final Straw

During the time I was studying homeopathy, I came into contact with a Steiner[31] educational community and noticed a huge difference between those children, and children who were at public school, and . . . me as a child. Steiner's philosophy is manifested in the Waldorf education system. The schools are not formally opposed to vaccination, but the philosophy lends itself to non-vaccination. At least back then, most pupils did not have the full vaccine schedule and a large number had no vaccines at all. Antibiotic usage also tends to be very low.

The Steiner schoolchildren may as well have been a different species. In general, they were very alert, bright, happy, and well-adjusted, and almost never sick with the usual colds etc. When they got sick, it was quick, strong, and then over in a day or two at most. This further confirmed much of Samuel Hahnemann's writings on the vital force. Many of these children had never taken antibiotics their whole lives. Among the students I saw, it was often easy to pick out the children who had had their full vaccine schedule and whose parents had listened to the doctor instead of following the Steiner theory.

---

[31] Waldorf (Steiner) education is based on the educational philosophy of Rudolf Steiner, the founder of Anthroposophy. The pedagogy emphasizes the role of imagination in learning, striving to integrate holistically the intellectual, practical, and artistic development of pupils.
http://www.anthromed.org/Article.aspx?artpk=764

Then, the day came when I got to hear my own ignorance while watching a child play with a hammer and nails. I said, *"That child shouldn't be doing that. They've not even had a tetanus vaccine!"* Someone asked me, *"What do you know about tetanus?"* to which I replied, *"It's not a disease you want to have. You can get lockjaw and die, so you don't want to get it."*

A voice in my head said, *"You don't know squat about tetanus or the vaccine, Suzanne."* Hearing the ignorance from my own mouth led me to think . . . Why do I know so little about tetanus? My colleagues would all parrot, "Tetanus vaccine is a victim of its own success. You don't see tetanus anymore because of the vaccine." Same with diphtheria. Doctors are pretty much taught that the vaccine did away with it, and that's all we needed to know. It wasn't until years later that I studied a slew of literature on tetanus in the vaccinated and found out the important details on the disease that parroting medical doctors, including my former self, had no clue about. There is a video from my talks in Sweden, on YouTube, where I detailed some of my research findings. Since then, I've helped several people treat their clinical tetanus as an outpatient, AFTER the medical system denied the diagnosis.

Once the gaping holes in my knowledge became obvious, I started reading even more about the immune system, diseases, and vaccines, which are actually fascinating topics that doctors are taught very little of at medical school — during residency, or afterwards. Whatever doctors pick up is usually on a need-to-know basis. Most infectious disease specialists do not read to the breadth that I have since 2009. I know this because I used to discuss different topics with the infectious disease doctors on call, and their knowledge base was clearly superficial and targeted at dealing with common hospital infections.

In 2009, because of the predicted 'Swine Flu Epidemic', the hospital that my practice was attached to changed its vaccine policy, and started vaccinating every willing non-vaccinated person with seasonal flu vaccines, swine flu vaccines, and pneumococcal vaccines as soon as they were admitted to the hospital. I saw people with active congestive heart failure, active cancer on IV chemotherapy, peritonitis, and more, getting vaccinated on their first or second hospital day. Patients could have been on death's door for all the vaccinators cared. All the patient or family had to do was agree to it after a cursory summary of the supposed benefits and lack of any likely harm. Even worse, they would put my name on the orders even though a vaccine was last on my list of priorities and I never ordered it. My first priority, like any doctor, was to figure out the clinical problem.

One of my patients had worsening inflammatory kidney disease and was admitted to the hospital by me, for a kidney biopsy. Before I even saw her or wrote the admission orders, she received a flu shot, with my name on the order.

Because I had just been reading about inflammation and the potential hematological risks of vaccines, I knew that flu shots could alter the blood clotting and bleeding patterns. Therefore, I was concerned that her kidney disease could worsen and that she was at higher risk of bleeding after the biopsy. The kidney is a heavily immunogenic and vascularized organ, rich with all-sized arterioles, capillaries, dendritic cells, and macrophages. Her kidney disease remained stable, but she did hemorrhage after the biopsy and required a blood transfusion. This was just considered coincidence and nothing to do with the vaccine.

Before the hospital decided to vaccinate on admission with seasonal flu, epidemic flu, and pneumonia vaccines, the clinical picture was usually relatively clear.

After the vaccine policy changed, working out what the real problem was, in the kidney failure patients I was consulted on, became much more challenging. The neurosurgery department had a standing order to NOT vaccinate their patients during hospitalization, because they didn't want to have to guess what could be causing a fever after surgery. When I questioned one of the neurosurgeons he told me they tried to make sure vaccines were given well in advance of elective surgeries. Apparently the rest of the doctors were not afforded the luxury of not having a cluster bomb tossed into sick patients before their medical work-up or intervention.

During this time, two patients who came into the hospital both said to me that they were fine until their outside doctor vaccinated them for seasonal and swine flu at which point they became violently ill and were diagnosed with acute kidney failure. Then came a third patient who said nearly the same thing and I noted that his kidneys went from moderately impaired to total shutdown, after being vaccinated.

After reviewing all of my inpatient and outpatient files, it was clear to me that unintended illness effects from vaccines, like sudden deterioration in kidneys or blood pressure after a vaccine had been administered, were far more common than the proverbial 'one in a million'. With patients in the hospital, the vaccine effect was easier to see because the injection was noted and the fall in kidney function was right there in the chart within 24-48 hours.

As the nephrology 'expert', when my chief of medicine stopped me in the corridor and said, "How are things going?" I replied, "Oh, funny you should ask, something really interesting has happened," and I mentioned the new dialysis patient who adamantly told me he was fine until he got the flu shot. Then I told him about the other man with a nearly identical history. He immediately retorted, "Well, the flu shot just didn't have time to work and they got the flu." I was shocked. My problem, with that immediate, curt brush off, was that those patients didn't have flu symptoms. He wouldn't even consider the possibility that the shots could have contributed to the kidney failure.

It was bizarre how he just turned cold. This was someone I had known for years—a person who was normally clinically thoughtful. I liked him. He liked me. We were always friendly. My life in Maine was idyllic. I loved working in this hospital—it was very different to working in a Philadelphia or New York hospital. While the medical center in Maine was a big deal hospital, it was also a community hospital. My office overlooked a large tidal river with eagles flying overhead and nesting on the trees of the uninhabited far bank. During the years that I was enjoying working with my patients, and my amazing staff, I used to pinch myself and think, *"This is paradise! This job is awesome!"* My medical partners were the best. We were like blood siblings . . . and would hang out with each other and get together on holidays—it was really warm—really nice.

Then the final nightmare started.

The hospital's vaccine policy was permanently ratified, and my discussion of patients who deteriorated after vaccines, highlighted the integrity or lack thereof, of hospital staff. If I suggested there was a kidney problem from any other drug, I was seriously listened to. There were even group meetings with all sorts of solutions discussed. But because I said, "Something is going on here with vaccines, and that needs attention," the shutters slammed down. Colleagues, who were normally clinically astute and assertive, became invisible wimps; hiding in the shadows as if their jobs or reputations could be lynched.

The more they ignored the science I presented, the more passionate I became.

Again, my medical chief stopped me again in the corridor, this time to discuss the rising numbers of patients with kidney problems after taking ACE inhibitors (blood pressure drugs that can shut down kidneys). I said to him, "I find it really interesting that you are passionate about patients with ACE inhibitor-injured kidneys, yet you have no time when it comes to kidney failure after vaccines. Why is that?"

Once again, the blinds slammed down and his response was very negative.

I wasn't being confrontational. It was just an opportunity to tell him that I'd witnessed even more cases since the last time we discussed kidney failure after vaccines. But he wouldn't go there. Perhaps he was bound by hospital policy to vaccinate regardless of how sick a person was. Maybe there was a directive from above to keep the vaccination rates high. But still, I had thought more of him than that—I thought he was someone who would look with deep concern at a situation, and be a patient advocate.

After hearing the proverbial *"But Suzanne, vaccines are very safe!"* I replied with, *"What studies do you know of, which have been done with regard to vaccines and kidneys?"* There was silence.

More research was undertaken on my part. It was around this point that I finally became aware that there was actually a reporting system for vaccine reactions.

While readers might struggle with this, the fact was that at this point I had only just become aware that vaccine reactions should be reported. Even though I was 'the expert', I never considered reporting adverse drug events to any authority, either. No other doctors reported such reactions because they are so common. Since we didn't even report the common drug reactions, why report vaccine reactions? There wasn't much point in reporting ACE inhibitors, statins, non-steroidal anti-inflammatories, antibiotics, and diuretics, because side effects were so common, that of course the FDA knew about them. Drug histories, on the other hand, are part of the normal evaluation because patients often notice a difference in health after taking or changing drugs, and are apt to report it to the doctor. Those side effects and reactions are poorly quantified, but the effects are well-known and accepted as a necessary evil. But vaccines? That was different. Initially, I was surprised that no one else knew about this, so I wanted to know what they did know. Answer? ZILCH. But then, if I didn't know, why should they know either? With vaccines, because nobody bothers to get a history, they usually don't connect a reaction with the vaccine.

Ironically, what got me deeper into the medical literature was the refusal of the hospital administration and other doctors to even **consider** that vaccines could have done anything negative to my patients, or that vulnerable patients should be protected from vaccines. First, I started looking for studies of vaccines tested in kidney patients and then looked at the ingredients in vaccines, how they were made, and what was in them.

People march off after getting vaccinated, thinking they got something injected that was good for them. However, my research showed that there is almost nothing nutritive in a vaccine ingredient list. The animal and human tissue—both diseased and healthy—used in vaccine cultures, was revolting to me. I was not reassured by the purification methods either. One of my patients was a hospital staff member who suffered kidney failure after MMR vaccination. As part of my research, I read a 2006[32] document from the European Medicines Agency that said, *"**Measles vaccine bulk is an unpurified product whose potency was measured through a biological assay for the active substance rather than through evaluation of integrity of the physical form. Degradation products are neither identified nor quantified.**"*

The same statement was repeated in the mumps and rubella component sections. Interestingly, I'd never seen such information

---

[32] MMR VAXPRO scientific discussion.
http://www.ema.europa.eu/docs/en_GB/document_library/EPAR_-
_Scientific_Discussion/human/000604/WC500030167. Pdf accessed February 14, 2016.

in patient consent information, or the data sheets provided to doctors. Not that many doctors read the data sheets anyway. I didn't, until vaccines became an issue to my clinical practice.

I found that there had never been any studies on the effects of seasonal flu vaccines on the kidneys. Few, if any, reactions were reported in the vast body of medical literature. Because the correlation was clear to me, I decided that reactions should be reported to VAERS. Within a few weeks, I had reported four potential adverse events, and that was more than the VAERS system usually hears from one doctor.

They must have thought, 'There's either a bad lot of vaccines going around, or there is a crazy doctor.' They ruled out the bad lot, so they wanted to know why I, compared to all the other nephrologists (who probably like me, didn't know there was a reporting system!), was officially reporting all these reactions. For the first four reports, I just got the regular phone call to make sure you are who you say you are: you work at the hospital, the patient exists, and you're not a crank.

Then, one dialysis tech had new onset seizures after his flu vaccine, but didn't want to report it, because he didn't think anyone would believe him, and he thought he would be penalized if he did. After I explained the system to him and that he would not be penalized, he filed the report.

In a four-person medical practice, you share a lot of patients and cover for each other. Some of my partners' patients also had vaccine reactions, which they told me about, knowing I would report to VAERS and spare them the trouble. So I reported for them as well.

At this point, the CDC decided to follow up more intensely. It would usually start with a young woman who would confirm who I was, and then say, "Well, okay, somebody else will be calling you." Then I would get several calls, and each time I was told, *"Someone else will call you,"* as if I was being transferred up the CDC hierarchy.

Finally, the CDC director for the state of Maine called me, and kept saying, *"What made you change and be different to what you used to be?"* Quite apart from the fact that he couldn't believe my cases were real, he was only really interested in sticking it to me. The conversation really degenerated when I asked him, *"What do you think about the fact that we're vaccinating kids up the nose with a live attenuated flu virus when the package insert says that recipients shouldn't be around the immunosuppressed or elderly? Does that tell you that vaccinated children might be contagious and spreading the virus?"* He said, *"I can tell you that this is an area of study for me, and I assure you nasal flu vaccines do not spread the virus and this is absolutely false."* I responded, *"Then why does it say that on the package insert? Did you read the symptoms, 'sore throat, fever, runny nose' after getting the vaccine and don't be around immuno-compromised people? To me that says we're giving these kids the flu and they have capacity to spread it around. I have a problem with that."* Then I said, *"And I've seen people getting kidney failure after their vaccines, and I've reported it. What's your problem?"*

Completely ignoring any science I put to him, he just wanted to compare me to everyone else who never reported reactions. I told him that there may come a time when the same truths that hit me between the eyes will hit other doctors, and he may be getting more reports. After the phone call, which certainly seemed slanted to shut me up, I kept on reporting reactions. But after that, I only got the usual CDC phone calls to verify the case was real.

The fact was that in 2009, not one doctor in my midst, other than my partners whom I had informed, and the Maine CDC director, appeared to know that the VAERS reporting system existed and what it was. Nowhere in the hospital was there the VAERS information posters put out by the CDC. In all my years as a doctor,

I have NEVER seen posters or any relevant VAERS information anywhere in the hospital.

Yet, the CDC is supposed to be relying on doctors to report vaccine reactions so that they can study VAERS to try to discern vaccine reaction trends. I wonder how the CDC think their ongoing risk assessment has any validity, given the mass ignorance among health care practitioners and the fact that few ever report anything, and most people never think to take a vaccine history when a new problem arises.

Because I was taking vaccine histories, I was seeing the vaccine reactions, had them in my differential diagnoses, and was prepared to record and report them, because the appropriate tests constantly showed a correlation. What were the others seeing? Were they even looking? I guess they were seeing 'coincidences' or 'idiopathic' diseases, and were mesmerized into inaction by the 'safe, effective, and necessary' mantra.

Even after I informed hospital doctors about VAERS, most refused to use the system.

Despite all but one of the doctors in my practice disagreeing with the flu vaccines for themselves or their kids, they still said that most other vaccines are really necessary. One of my associates was upset that his daughter was told she needed Gardasil at age 11. He did some cursory research and said no. When I asked him why, he volunteered, "I followed the money trail." To him, Gardasil was a 'bad vaccine', and so was influenza, but most of the other ones were still ok. In hindsight, I wish I had asked him to follow the money trail for the polio vaccines in 1955, and many other vaccines since then.

Most of my medical partners signed their own flu vaccine waivers, but they didn't want to have much to do with the stand I was taking. They would come up to me with questions like, *"Well what about pneumococcal vaccine for children? The incidence of invasive bacterial infections has gone down . . . "* Or they would say things like, *"What about smallpox? What about polio?"* . . . as if those vaccines had any relevance to vaccinating acutely sick people with two or three different vaccines on admission to the hospital.

It is strange that, since 2009, whenever I have questioned the safety of a vaccine that clearly caused harm to a patient, like a flu shot or HPV vaccine, I have been met with challenges about the success of other vaccines, sometimes from a very long time ago. The questions usually come at me as if the two are related. Why is a flu shot today the same as a smallpox vaccine 60 years ago? Why is giving a pneumococcal vaccine to a newly admitted, acutely sick patient, even discussed in the same breath as neonatal vaccines? I never claim that vaccines have no preventive effect. Clearly they do, at least for a short time, for most patients.

My question is, are all these vaccines worth the largely unknown and unstudied risks? And shouldn't the recipients be given all the facts? None of my patients had a clue that there was even the slightest potential for kidney disease—or anything else for that matter—as a result of accepting the vaccine while they were sick.

Meanwhile, another medical associate's two children were coming into the hospital to have ear grommets placed, and were frequently on antibiotics and looking a little 'strange', with obvious temperament issues. The younger child was inconsolable most of the time, which in hindsight is no big surprise.

Our group was caring for a patient that was signed out to me for the weekend. He had acute Guillain-Barré syndrome, and hospital policy was to give him the flu vaccine regardless. I argued against it over the weekend, and on Monday said to my partner, *"Do you agree?"* He also thought it was outrageous, but the doctor who consulted our group decided to just call in an infectious disease specialist, who said that they should wait and give him the flu shot AFTER he had got over his acute episode of Guillain-Barré syndrome.

Just this year, a medical secretary that I have stayed in touch with, volunteered to me that her husband was in the hospital with Guillain-Barré syndrome. I asked her when the last flu shot was, as no other doctor asked that question. The answer was, "One week prior to symptoms." That further cemented for me, that the proverbial 'one in a million' vaccine reaction only applies to a population that is never asked any questions and where reactions are rarely reported.

Today, I get many letters from patients telling me how sick they became after their vaccines, either immediately or a few weeks later. Some report the death of their children, parents, or spouse.

I also get letters from doctors who have seen their patients deteriorate after vaccines, to thank me for speaking out. My question to those doctors is, "Why don't you speak out?"

Just about all patients say nobody in the medical system will validate the association. Worldwide, this continues to be the trend. Even when numerous children get morbidly sick or die after vaccines in a cluster, the authorities report to the media that the vaccine was not the cause. We hear statements like: 'The cause is unknown: idiopathic. Background noise . . . because the denominator is so high.' The excuses would be amusing were they not so common and fueled by such arrogance.

So the vast majority of doctors see nothing, hear nothing, and report nothing, because they believe that everything they are hearing is a coincidence disorder dreamed up by people incapable of complex cognitive thinking, who just want to play the blame game.

But what really frightens doctors is when they see what happens to doctors like me when we follow a scientific process and actually do what the CDC recommends that we do—report vaccine reactions accurately. We are shafted.

*"The world is a dangerous place, not because of those who do evil,
but because of those who look on and do nothing."*

~ Dr. Albert Einstein

Flying The Coop

It's distressing for any doctor to question the dogma they have been so comfortable with. I was very unhappy with the splay between what I saw, and what I was told to think. Evidence-based medicine is actually important to me. Most doctors, even the most conservative of my medical partners, could see the point to not vaccinating sick patients on admission, but ultimately they slammed the door shut. I chose to keep moving through new doorways. The treatment I received as a result of my informed opinion was definitely difficult, but standing up for what is right for patients made it all worthwhile. Doctors who slam the door can refuse to look at what lies beyond the threshold, but they can't say there is nothing there. They can carry on signing their own waivers, while staying under the radar, but should the day come when no waivers are allowed, where will they be then? Many hospital staff are having to face that reality today, and even the pro-vaccine among them are displeased.

I gave my notice around February of 2010. My partners were in disbelief that I was leaving. To them, my issue with the vaccines was not such a huge thing and they didn't see it as a barrier. They said, "Why not do some research, like a case series using medical charts, and prove what you are saying is demonstrable?" I should have asked them, "Will you co-author it with me, using some of your patients that I reported for you?" The same administration that was giving me the helicopter treatment said a similar thing,

"Conduct your own research— get IRB approval, do a retrospective analysis, and publish the findings."

The array of problems with that suggestion was that it would have required ethics approval, funding, time, and a huge group of patients. Standardizing everything to the satisfaction of vaccine critics, and dealing with 'healthy user bias'[33] would be difficult. In that environment, doing such a study would be fraught with conflict and stress, let alone finding a journal prepared to publish it. The environment, at the moment (2016), is such that journals like the Lancet, JAMA, or NEJM will not even touch that kind of a study if it shows the vaccines are indeed a problem. Elsevier's policy, for instance, is explained as follows[34]:

Article Removal: Legal limitations

*In an extremely limited number of cases, it may be necessary to remove an article from the online database. This will only occur where the article is clearly defamatory, or infringes others' legal rights, or where the article is, or we have good reason to expect it will be, the subject of a court order, or where the article, **if acted upon, might pose a serious health risk**. In these circumstances, while the metadata (Title and Authors) will be retained, the text will be replaced with a screen indicating the article has been removed for legal reasons.*

So if my research were to show high levels of kidney problems in vaccinated patients, would an editor argue that stopping admission-

---

[33] "Healthy User Bias: Why Most Vaccine Safety Studies Are Wrong," *Vaccine Papers*. http://vaccinepapers.org/healthy-user-bias-why-most-vaccine-safety-studies-are-wrong/

[34] Elsevier's website. Policy on article withdrawal. https://www.elsevier.com/about/company-information/policies/article-withdrawal#. Article accessed February 24, 2016.

vaccinating might pose a serious health risk, and refuse the article for that reason? Or that any doubts whether or not well-founded, must not be allowed to exist?

And even if they did accept it, would I be forced to water it down? Or would I be told, "Oh, this is a 'lone ranger' outlier study and we need at least six more studies with long-term follow up before we can give the results any real consideration." The fact is, questioning vaccines is career suicide. Who would be willing to join the ranks of the shunned? Even if one study was accepted, how many decades away might follow-up studies be?

But the two biggest factors that prevented me from doing a study, were these: Firstly, if you KNOW something is adversely affecting people, is it even ethical to allow the hospital to vaccinate your patients without your approval, just so that you could document even more damage? How does that sit with the Hippocratic Oath?

Secondly, should clinicians be responsible for doing studies to prove that drugs are safe (on their own unpaid time) in their own patient population, just because the drug companies assumed their drug was okay based on limited or no science?

I was already working really long days and traveling all over Northern Maine to different dialysis units. I should not have the additional task of proving vaccines were safe to these fragile hospital patients, when I had already shown that they were not safe in my own case series. The burden of proof was on the vaccine manufacturers, the hospital, and the advisory committees that said vaccines are safe for all-comers. Why should that burden of proof rest on one busy doctor's shoulders?

By this time, I knew what the self-proclaimed 'skeptic' movement was made of, because they were in charge of public opinion, medical school education, and now, hospital policy. I was told that all patients were to be vaccinated, and to stop confusing nurses. Dr. Lawrence D. Ramunno told me point blank in writing, (after the hospital administration consulted him in order to reply to my well-documented concerns) that it was "going to become a global measure to vaccinate all hospital patients by 2010".

Was spending a few years doing research that would be criticized every different way to Sunday, even be worth my while? All the time this was going on, I was being watched, and everything I wrote in my records was monitored as if I was on probation. There was no case against my ethics, or my work, whatsoever. I knew that the chief of medicine was constantly looking at my orders, and reviewing my hospital patient records. He actually stopped me one day because of a note I had written in a chart saying, *"This is why vaccines shouldn't be given to sick patients."* I had put it in alongside a graph denoting the fall in kidney function that occurred after a flu shot was given in the hospital, yet all the other doctors had denied the relationship and called the kidney failure 'idiopathic'.

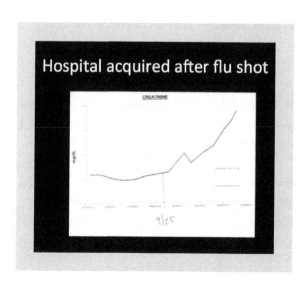

Graph from chart described

He pulled me up and said *"You can't say things like that in the charts."* The note was then removed. I found this interesting as I'm pretty certain patient charts are legal documents, which should not be altered.

I had read about the wasted years when Bernice Eddy

was silenced, along with others, and how hard it was for Dr. Anthony Morris to sit around for nearly a decade, while the Division of Biologic Sciences (precursor to the FDA) ignored his repeated evidence that flu vaccines were not only useless, but also dangerous. Dr. Morris also chose to bring his message to the public directly, and bypass the DBS because they had literally shut him away in a back room and told him not to speak to anyone. Nothing has changed and in fact, it has only gotten worse.

Who, within the ivory tower's walls, was going to listen to me, particularly with the adversarial way they were now treating me? Precious few. There was no academic tolerance, acceptance, or friendly civility. Every day, I would leave the hospital, get into my car bone-weary, and have to sleep for half an hour, just to find the energy to drive home.

After serious consideration, I decided my time was better spent continuing my research to understand more of the full history, immunology, toxicology, and politics in relation to vaccination, and to bring my findings to the public, and let them decide for themselves.

Even my cello playing stopped. After years of lessons and hours of cello playing each day, I eventually sold my entire instrument collection due to lack of use and the need for money after I left my job. That saddens me and I hold hope that I will pick up a cello, and once again play seriously someday.

My partners were distraught because I was a very hard working smart, reliable nephrologist, and they were going to have to replace me. Because it was rather late in the academic year to hire a new graduate, I agreed to stay until they found a replacement, which took almost two years.

For whatever reason, they slowly disengaged from me after the time I handed in my resignation. I don't know if I looked too crazy to them, or because they watched the way the hospital administration systematically undermined me. In those two years until a replacement was found, it felt like I was walking into enemy territory every day I entered the hospital. I felt that my hospital privileges could be revoked at any time, but fortunately the hospital had no say over my private practice.

The last year was very busy and full of turmoil, particularly as my mother was nearing the end of her life, and I was only able to do a little writing and research. What kept me going in those two years, were my patients, and the nurses, some of whom let me know the things that were said behind my back, but most of whom agreed with my concern for my patients' welfare. Even though I felt at siege, often the nurses and ward clerks who heard these discussions would come up to me in private and whisper things like, "I really agree with you about these vaccines. That's why I had to stop working in NICU [or pediatrics] because I couldn't stand it." Or, "I stopped vaccinating my own kids and I don't take that flu vaccine myself either."

However, they too started to pay the price, as Eastern Maine Medical Center's hospital system made some drastic changes to the nursing staff. By the time I left, every single head nurse of the inpatient and satellite dialysis units had been fired, along with some of the best, most experienced RNs I've ever worked with.

While I am not certain of any link, I did find it very sobering when I realized that these amazing nurses all had one thing in common: they were friends, and sympathizers, of mine.

A Nigerian internist overheard me debating the necessity to vaccinate on the first hospital day, and he said, "I know why they do the vaccines . . . because if it was up to me, I would not give them at all." I'm not sure whether he continued there or not. Plainly, having an opinion was dangerous.

My partners were never contentious with me directly, and gave me everything I asked for when I left the practice. Yet, even though they were all on campus, not one of them showed up to my farewell party to say good-bye on my final work day, and I've not heard from any of them since leaving. I was gutted at how the whole thing ended.

My suspicion that there was a directive from on high to keep vaccination rates as high as possible, was confirmed in 2014. I met up with an old friend, a nurse in high-level hospital management in New Jersey, who told me that hospitals are not reimbursed for the entire admission if a patient is not vaccinated with flu and pneumococcal vaccines, unless there is documentation reporting why they were not given.

Since then, I have seen two nurses on YouTube stating that their hospitals had the same policy. One of them recently said[35] that Medicare and Medicaid orders dictate that, unless elderly ICU heart patients fit specific criteria for exemption, all must be discharged with five different classes of heart drugs including cholesterol and blood pressure medication, or the hospital would not be reimbursed for their stay either.

When hospital reimbursement is dependent on policies reflecting the drug industry's gold standard protocols, doctors and nurses with similar views to me obstruct those aims and objectives. What people need to consider is whether they want their healthcare decisions made by the pharmaceutical industry, or by doctors who have their best interests at heart.

---

[35] https://www.youtube.com/watch?v=7PzlQh38_tI Accessed: 17.6.2016

36 Self-Righteous Indignation

After a few weeks of rest, cleaning house, and thinking, I didn't have time to consider my future because my thoughts had turned to my mother. Much though we loved each other, there was a component of our relationship that could only have been called toxic.

I never doubted whether or not my mother loved me. It was always plainly obvious that she adored and cherished my two siblings and me. I could tell by the way she attended to every detail of my clothing, often making beautiful things from patterns and material I picked out. The lunches that were packed with love and attention, and the meals that were reliably placed on the table, were clearly the product of a woman who considered all palates and wanted to please and nourish everyone. When I was sick, she was there every second, making sure I had anything and everything my heart and body desired. When I was hurt, she hurt too and was a staunch supporter of my alternative medical views. Most of all, what I loved about Mom was her open mind and consideration for all things that made sense to her. She was never bound by what popular opinion dictated. I also remember that when other kids in the neighborhood were injured and bleeding, they would cry out "I want Mrs. Humphries." She had gained a reputation as the ad-hoc nurse wherever we lived, because she was intuitively good at dealing with children's gory messes.

I believe the toxic part of our relationship was a result of things that had nothing to do with me. She had a very rough beginning, back in an era when feelings were not discussed, or considered at all. There was also no spiritual foundation in her childhood, for her to cast her troubles onto. She carried them with weight and was haunted by the abuse and abandonment she endured growing up as a child of two alcoholic parents, one who killed himself in front of her by tossing himself out a window, and the other who slowly drank herself to death. Fortunately, she and her sister were put into foster care with a lovely older woman. When Mom could not contain the resultant venom left over from her abuse and abandonment, it spewed all over those she loved the most at home, leaving the rest of the world usually viewing a seemingly perfectly lovely lady. Her demons often got the best of her, but she did far better for us than her parents did for her.

I never held her volatile and unpredictable temper against her and it never dampened my undying love. But sometimes it made things really, really difficult. Since leaving home, I had grown to love living with no television in a quiet house. Going back to her home with a TV in each room, usually with the news blasting, and her yelling at either the dog or a person, was akin to sensory waterboarding.

Now, she was facing death.

Myelofibrosis is a rare bone-marrow cancer that, in simple terms, replaces the bone marrow with scar tissue. The person most often succumbs to bleeding or infection within a year of diagnosis.

Just about 10 years before her diagnosis, she had radiation for breast cancer. Ionizing radiation is an underlying cause of myelofibrosis. I'd never dealt with myelofibrosis in my career, so understanding how her life would end was a bit of a mystery to me, and created great anxiety in her.

Mom was a worrier and very high-strung at baseline. After starting sedatives, the anxiety was manageable and I could have conversations with her from Maine, near the end of my hospital employment, getting reports from her of what the doctors were thinking. Since she was always open minded to non-conventional treatments, she tried a few things that the oncologists approved of, like alkalizing and juicing, but it didn't make any difference. By June of 2011, the disease had progressed to the point that she was requiring red blood cell and platelet transfusions regularly.

Add to that, the unknown entity of a rare bone marrow failure disease where she expected to bleed to death. The fear she lived with on a good day, spiked up to a 20 out of 10 on the Richter scale after blood blisters appeared in her mouth, horrible bruising on her skin, and hematomas in her muscles. She was convinced she would bleed to death at home or have a massive hemorrhagic stroke. Early on, while Mom obsessed over her anticipated gruesome demise she freaked out on a regular basis. This was all based on her own reading and what she was told by her doctors. Her life didn't end anything like she feared—from infection or bleeding—but with a comfortable death at home. She just seemed to wear out. Her heart was probably weakened from the severe anemia after she stopped getting blood-product infusions. Before she died, I wanted to crawl under the bed as she piqued at the doctor, "You told me I would be dead by now . . . and here I am twelve weeks beyond the six months you gave me!" No one escaped her wrath.

I had just left my nephrology job, so could travel to New Jersey whenever I wanted, for as long as I wanted. Each time I visited, I joined my siblings in donating blood to the Red Cross as often as possible, for direct use to my mother. Regardless, unable to control her own demons, she took every opportunity to spew her Mt. Vesuvius of anger all over anyone in her path.

Though I loved her dearly, sadness and regret were familiar feelings because, over the years, I always wanted to spend more time with her, even when she was well. Because I was always unwilling to stay longer than two nights in her house, I caught the brunt of her anger over her feeling rejected. This was fairly longstanding, at least since I left home at the age of 19. But now, in the face of Mt. Vesuvius, I would find myself launched into flight mode, having to politely leave and making any excuse I needed in order to preserve my equanimity.

Her mood swings and eruptions of irrational anger were always intense but in the months following June 2011, they became worse than ever. I made several trips down to see her, either by car or plane, but could not relax into being there. Each departure filled me with an uneasy emptiness and, as always, questions like "What could I do differently to make this better?"

I took my pop-up camper down in August and stayed for three weeks in a local campground, but I was not able to overcome the claustrophobia that went along with staying longer than my nerve endings could endure. At the close of August's trip, having taken on more abuse than I cared to, I left totally embittered . . . again.

I wanted to be with her until the end, but emotionally it felt impossible. I was disgusted with her growing anger, her increasing possessiveness, exploding nastiness, and inability to deal with her death without constantly lashing out at those who were closest to her.

Various counselors and friends, who knew the situation in detail, including Medicine Man, said that enough was enough. Everyone agreed that I had done my bit, didn't owe her anything, and that since she was behaving like an irrational, threatened mamba[36], I had no obligation to go back. I knew this feeling well, as did my

---

[36] Known as the fastest snake in the world, the black mamba has a reputation for a propensity to chase its prey a distance. It is capable of striking at considerable range and delivering a series of bites in rapid succession. The venom of the black mamba is highly toxic, potentially causing collapse in humans within 45 minutes or less from a single bite.

sister, who had done way more than her share with and for Mom over the years that I was absent. Even she was totally at the end of her saintly tolerance level.

On one hand, my friends' line of reasoning felt like a relief, because it released me from the torture of being at the end of her bite, which could strike at any time, unprovoked. But on the other hand, even though I had abandoned Catholicism, I always felt the Old Testament's Ten Commandments were mostly good things to live by; especially "Honor thy father and thy mother." I had been with Dad at his death and knew how reassuring the doctor/daughter combination can be. In one sense, I knew that was also important for Mom. Not just because I'd been there with Dad, but because Mom was my mother, and in reality who wants to die with strangers around?

At the end of my own resources, never going back felt intellectually justifiable: I had tried, over and over, literally given my blood to her, and anything else she wanted besides my soul, yet I constantly felt skewered. My default mode was now to shield my soul the best I could—and that infuriated her.

Strangers, of course, like her friends from church, thought she was a martyr, and that her children were a bunch of ungrateful cave dwellers. Several people, who had only listened to Mom rant about me, were shocked when they met me during the weeks before she died, because they saw a totally different person than the one Mom had painted. Even through all the abuse, I loved her, and I still do.

But by September, I'd lost the strength to push past my own indignation.

37 Take Two

A new friend, Miriam, who had given me some polio information for a book I was contemplating writing, happened to be a Christian. This was a surprise to me, because I had a broad, more evolved, and eclectic concept of God. I couldn't understand how such a highly intelligent person could ascribe to the narrow backwards religion of Christianity. My own sister Liz, had gotten born again years before, and though I loved her dearly, I thought she was totally daft for believing that the Bible was the literal truth. I was totally unaffected by her devotion to the fairy tale of the Bible. Liz was agreeable to ignoring my yoga, shamanism, and eclecticism.

So my relationship with Miriam ran along the same lines as the relationship with my sister. I would ignore Miriam's shortcomings, because she was ingenious and the information on polio was very good. Let the other sleeping dogs lie.

However, as things heated up with my mother right after I had left my hospital job, the deadness was getting deader, and the depression even deeper. I had seen the emptiness of Medicine Man. I felt like I was looking into a chasm, and I was also in denial about health issues of my own that were dangling over me.

In the depth of my despair, something made me share the situation of my mother with Miriam.

We Skyped. She said, *"Suzanne, if you don't go and be with your mother, you will regret it to the day you die."*
Puzzled, I asked why and listened as she explained.

The truth hit me in the solar plexus, and my brain sent out a distressed scream, which bounced back from outer space. Deep down, my heart groaned, "She's right."

In frustration I snapped, "You don't get it Miriam. Being in the same room as my mother is enough to send every nerve and emotion totally ballistic. Trust me when I say you have never met anyone like her. My brother can barely handle it. After years of dedication to my mother and continuously getting slapped in the face, my sister won't go or bring her family anywhere near her right now, and now you tell me I will regret it? More likely, I'll build up such an internal temperature that I will spontaneously combust!"

Not to be outdone, after hearing the whole sordid story, a quiet voice replied, *"There is a way you could cope."* I snorted, "Really, like how?!" She replied, *"Jesus. You've told me Medicine Man said Jesus was just a shaman—but he's not. He's God's son."*

That made me recoil. I was much more aligned with the idea of God as impersonal, as 'source' of everything, and the many archetypes and gods in Eastern religions like Hinduism. Even though I'd barely read the bible, I thought I knew what the Bible meant and said because I'd been told in school, done lots of independent reading, and come to my own conclusions. I felt my current eclectic shamanic reasoning with the new and improved, expanded version of 'Spirit', courtesy of Medicine Man, which had everyone eventually making it to nirvana by the end . . . was far superior to Miriam's. And the best part was that my own internal moral compass was the only guide I needed, not some rigid Christian set of rules that would turn me into a fire and brimstone believing, dress-wearing, plain Jane, subservient maiden to Jesus, never having any fun at all.

Christianity, to me, was a religion dominated by power-hungry men who spent more time putting women in their places, than actually being like Jesus. Christianity seemed to dismiss the fact that women give birth, grow life within, and have equal ability to be leaders and clergy. The concept of God as a man was bad enough, let alone having a 'son'.

"You have to be joking," I countered. "Why should God be a man?" Miriam replied:

"Suzanne, you're a doctor and have studied genetics. The answer should be obvious to you. You cannot give what you don't have. A woman can't determine the sex of a child, because she doesn't have a Y chromosome. A man has both chromosomes, and it's the man who determines the sex of a child. Remember Genesis? Humans are made in God's likeness. If God was a woman, there would be no men. God has to be, and is, male."

Okay . . . But, "Jesus, God's son"? "A virgin birth"? I'd heard these same nutty things a million times. "God so loved the world that he gave his only begotten son so that we shall not perish." Blah, blah, blah . . . If God is so powerful, she or he could come to Earth any which way he wanted. And he or she could wave a magic wand and have made as many sons as she or he wanted with whatever chromosomes he or she wanted. How could Miriam really believe this? She was so smart and had such an incisive wit. How could she of all people fall for that outrageous mythology?! Anyone with a brain was a women's rights activist. So . . . I sent her an email with some biblical verses in them and requested some explanations . . .

Question: So in Leviticus 12, if a woman gives birth to a male child, she's unclean, but if she gives birth to a female child, she is double filthy?

The answer from Miriam was:

"How would you know why God said that? In one respect it's totally practical. When a woman is pregnant her hormones and body function differently according to the sex of the child.

"God specified a different time frame for a boy or a girl baby. I don't know why. But apparently there are hormonal differences when you bear a boy or a girl. Some people say that healing time is different between sexes too.

"God can call women spiritually unclean if he wants, but as a mother who has had two babies, the last thing I wanted was a man up there even four months after I had had a baby.

"I prefer to look at it this way: God knew that the culture would become abusive towards women, so in order to give women space to heal, and bond with their children, he gave a 'spiritual' reason—knowing that a man thinking about the law, and God's comment about 'uncleanness' might be the only way to overcome the male urges of a rampant wanger.

"To me, this is a sign of God's forethought and love. He doesn't want a woman to be 'forced' by any man, to do something she can't, and the law is to her advantage, because if a man tries to force her, she can quote the law against him:

> *"'And she shall then continue in the blood of her purifying*
> ***three and thirty days****; she shall touch no hallowed thing, nor*

come into the sanctuary, until the days of her purifying be fulfilled.'

"This is actually incredibly gracious IMO. It's around 30 days before the bleeding stops . . . the red blood stops within seven days, but there is a pale pinkish discharge that continues after that similar to what weeps off a skin scrape . . . which I suppose is what it sort of is inside . . . But for the mother, the lining of the uterus takes a long time to heal after the placenta has come away. Consider the size of the placenta: that had 'sinuses'—quite big blood tunnels . . . and many of them going nearly through the whole width of the wall of the uterus, and even though the uterus shrinks afterwards, the whole wall of the uterus is susceptible to problems if a mother, who is stressed, adjusting to hormones, a baby etc., is to be treated as 'normal' and goes places, touches things, and is touched by people who could end her life right there. The last thing a mother needs is sperm and anything at all going up there during healing, and during the time she's bonding with her child.

"And it also takes between 4 and 6 weeks for a woman's hormones to start to come back normal aka the hormonal spots on a baby. During that time, a mother's innate immune system is starting to come back to normal. For the first few weeks a mother can also be very susceptible to lung and other infections. The suppression of the Th1 immune system in order for the baby not to be miscarried in pregnancy, has to come back to normal, and that doesn't happen overnight.

"Think also, of what a temple was back then: A place where all sorts of animals were brought in, with all their excrement and blood of slaughter, on the altar and sprinkled. Do you think there were janitors with disinfectants wiping down all the surfaces obsessively? No. Lots of potentially dangerous microbes were all about, on surfaces, sandals, feet, hands and surely by virtue of touch make it to the penises, which the men handle to urinate. And while it is no danger to a person with intact mucus membranes, or to a man's penis, or to healthy persons, a woman with a freshly open uterus could be in big trouble and so could her infant.

"To me, this law is a God wanting to protect women and infants. The mother is not to touch something other people touch in case she transfers other people's bugs to her. She's not to go where unwashed people and animals have been—to protect her. She's being legitimately and graciously . . . allowed a relaxed calm lying-in time, at a time when sanitation didn't exist. We know how important this is, because in the 1600-1800s that's exactly the 'time' that mothers died from puerperal fever and other infections, because doctors didn't understand God's design, and the need to wash their own hands before dealing with a labouring woman. Neither did the doctors in the 16-1800s understand the need for separation of pregnant and post delivery mothers from corpses and the worst types of filth.

"So the last thing a woman needed in those days was to be forced to go INTO the temple where there are animals, birds, people, dirt, bugs etc. And frankly, men are pretty heartless sometimes, and I suspect without God telling the men to back off, and making this a law, women would get a raw deal. So God lays down the law to men, so that a woman isn't forced to have sex or go places which put the raw unhealed lining of her uterus at risk. This law enabled a mother to rightfully stay at home quietly, without guilt, and NOT be poked and prodded, while the lining of her uterus healed and the cervix closed and any tears to the perineum healed. Women knew the law in those days. They were often enterprising, and just as intelligent and protective as women today.

"To me, this law is an indication of just how much God valued, loved and respected women, and wanted to protect them from what he knew men were capable of. How it could be interpreted any other way, beats me.

> " 'When the days of her purification for a son or daughter are over, **she is to bring to the priest <u>at the entrance</u> to the tent of meeting** a year-old lamb for a burnt offering and a young pigeon or a dove for a sin offering. He shall offer them before the Lord to make atonement for her, and then she will be ceremonially clean from her flow of blood.'

"Note that: 'the entrance to the tent'. She wasn't even to go into the outer courtyard because God knew that was too filthy for a woman who had stopped bleeding but might still not be 100% healed.

> " 'These are the regulations for the woman who gives birth to a boy or a girl. But if she cannot afford a lamb, she is to bring two doves or two young pigeons, one for a burnt offering and the other for a sin offering. In this way the priest will make atonement for her, and she will be clean.'

"So God is asking the mother to go and buy the sacrifice herself, and to go to the entrance at the time where her bleeding has stopped and she is now at far less risk of infection. I guess if God had wanted to be really condescending he could have said that the man do it and leave the woman at home."

I had also said to Miriam, "I get the sense from the Bible that women were simply second-class citizens." To which she replied:

"You have difficulty with a virgin birth, and you think women were simply second-class citizens. Let's look at Jesus' mother Mary. Mary was a very bright cookie, and an independent thinker. She was a poor young girl, who did her very best to understand God.

"God chose her, because he needed a smart woman to be the mother of his son. The assignment for her was huge, and would stretch her understanding and faith to the limit.

"God knew that in order for Mary to understand the importance of her pregnancy, and how she needed to bring him up, He had to do two things: explain the deal to her, and get her permission. God sent his head honcho angel, Gabriel, to explain his plan to her, and ask Mary if she was prepared to carry the son of God. Mary then asked a raft of sensible thoughtful questions. In answering one of them, Gabriel told Mary that her elderly cousin Elizabeth, known as the barren one, was six months pregnant. Obviously that message had a lot more importance in it, than a throw away one liner.

"After answering Mary's questions, Gabriel had to **wait for her agreement where she said, 'let it be done to me according to what has been said'.**

"Mary could have said no. She had a choice. Gabriel explained, and Mary accepted and agreed.

"Is this the action of a God who thinks women are second-class citizens who need their husbands' permission to think?

"At that time, the Jewish law dictated that a woman pregnant out of wedlock could have been stoned immediately when found to be pregnant. Mary was no dolt. She knew that. But she was smart enough to reckon that if God is polite enough to ask her, and tell her that the child would be born and become the saviour of Israel, then God had that law covered. Which meant she would live. To say yes under the law, took belief on her part in God, and not to look at what the law said.

"Then what is the next thing she does? She packed up and hurried to stay with her cousin Elizabeth for three months! And, Mary did NOT tell Joseph about Gabriel, or what he had said.

"Actually if you want to call anyone a 'second-class citizen' I wonder if Joseph sucked a lime later and said, 'Why didn't Gabriel come and ask me first?' or 'Don't I have a sperm in this?'

"Why did Mary hurry to Elizabeth first, rather than talking to Joseph? Elizabeth's husband had had an audience with Gabriel about seven months before, which didn't go quite so well. Zacharias decided to argue with Gabriel, got in God's dog-box and was made mute until the baby would be born. Nevertheless Mary knew that Elizabeth and Zacharias would understand what her innermost worries were.

"Zacharias and Elizabeth were chosen to be parents to John the Baptist, because their hearts were in the right place with God, and Zacharias understood the significance of scripture. God knew that they would bring up John the Baptist well.

"When Elizabeth opened the door and saw Mary, the Holy Spirit straight away spoke through Elizabeth (a woman, no less!!!) verifying the words that Gabriel had said to her.

"What a relief that would have been. I wonder if Mary had worried all the way there, 'What will these two say and think when they hear my story?" Mary needed to hear that from Elizabeth. I would love to have been a fly on the wall listening to the conversations in that house for the next three months, because I bet most of it would have centred around God's plan through the ages, and what was to come next for both Elizabeth and Mary.

"But more importantly for Mary, even if Zacharias couldn't speak, as a temple priest he would be able to show her the scriptures she needed to fully understand what Gabriel had said, and the significance of scripture relating to Jesus' future. "Mary's presence reinforced the words Gabriel said to Zacharias and Elizabeth, and strengthened their faith. Being with Zacharias and listening to Elizabeth, strengthened Mary's faith and trust, so that she could face what was to come when she returned, and her blossoming belly would naturally raise questions.

"So here are two examples of where God does something without reference to a man. Gabriel speaks to Mary, before speaking to Joseph, and Elizabeth immediately speaks God's word to Mary when she arrives, not Zacharias. So here are two very strong women, chosen directly by God, supporting one another. There is nothing second class about that.

"Then think of Jesus, and his huge respect for women through his life and ministry. Never once did he treat a woman as a second-class citizen. While cultural dolts might have, second-class citizenry was never part of God's plan. It's no fluke that after Jesus rose from the dead he appeared to women before appearing to any of the men. He spoke first to those who loved him with a heart belief and were . . . all women.

"Even earlier in the Old Testament, Abraham really loved and respected his wife Sarah. So did a lot of the OT men. Women *bought, sold, traded and had things they did for God in their own right, without men being around.*

"I believe that even in the Old Testament, women who were not airheads had as much respect and acumen as men did. Certainly, until Miriam spoke against Moses, she had great respect amongst Israel. After her racist outburst against Moses for marrying a black African woman, God temporarily struck her with leprosy as punishment, and her ministry was finished. Right there, that tells you what God thinks of colour discrimination!

"And there were other amazing OT women prophets, judges and lots of ordinary women like Ruth and Esther who we may never know about, who God deeply loved and honoured. Priscilla is one of many mentioned by name in the New Testament.

"Remember that the first four books of the New Testament are actually under the Old Testament law, so in God's eyes, the New Testament begins, after Jesus rose again. If you read the Bible carefully, you will always find the answer to your question somewhere, because the Bible is a commentary on what happened in all countries, including Israel, when they turned away from God:

"We all have the ability to listen to voices, make our choices, and take our consequences. So you need to ask the Holy Spirit to explain it to you, instead of reading it with just your mind."

The emails between Miriam and me took place over several months, and during that time, I was rethinking a lot of attitudes and assumptions I had had, and facing the fact that Wicca and then shamanism had not helped with my feelings of emptiness or depression. They had opened my eyes to other ways of thinking, but to what end?

In retrospect, me blaming God for not intervening and stopping man's inhumanities, of any kind, was like holding barbers responsible for the existence of long-haired hippies, or blaming the appearance of ambulances for accidents. What had I actually known about God? Nothing really. I had been jaded and making assumptions, and didn't know what I didn't know.

Suddenly Mr. C. LeJoy came back to my mind along with my revelation while studying Fourier analysis decades before.
At that time, with no understanding at all of Jesus or God's heart, I knew that all of this beauty, all of this organization and cohesiveness that we are, and the ethereal broth that we are marinated in, did not evolve out of a random outward-flinging bang. That would be more outrageous than going to Mars and finding a functioning Apple computer next to a steaming gourmet meal and concluding that it evolved there. I just understood that God did these things, and it was intentional.

When thinking on it, I also surmised that the mind of God, who created this magnificent place and everything in it, must be too awesome for God to explain, or for any human to understand. I also understood that instead of looking for God, I had looked for a god that suited my idea of what a god should be.

Similar thoughts about a creator being had come back during the first year of medical school, when dissecting cadavers. As we pored over amazingly designed, intricately made, and unique bodies, labeling parts, pondering the complexity of the eyes, the glandular systems, and the way cells make proteins and duplicate, my knowing solidified more. Man could not have evolved from an ameba which arose from a primordial soup, which came alive in the dust from a big bang.

Even recently, as I've become even better acquainted with the intricacy of God's immunologic blueprint, total awe continues. Kinesin is one example of a living protein that acts like a walking shuttle down micro-tubule filaments.

Microtubules form a packed cytoskeleton network, which give cells their structure and shape. I studied microtubules in the laboratory in 1989 but we didn't yet understand how the transport of proteins actually, physically, occurred even though we tracked them biochemically. It turns out that it occurs using kinesin. The life and motion of kinesins[37] support intracellular shuttling and cell division. These amazing proteins even know WHERE to walk, and how not to bump into each other! Most kinesins walk towards the positively charged end of a microtubule.

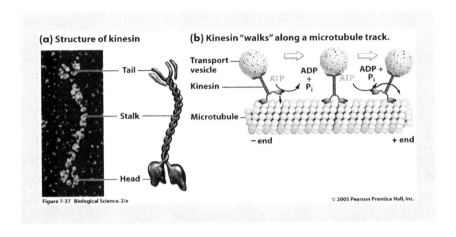

(a) Structure of kinesin
Tail
Stalk
Head

(b) Kinesin "walks" along a microtubule track.
Transport vesicle
Kinesin
Microtubule
ATP   ADP + P$_i$ ATP   ADP + P$_i$
− end   + end

Figure 7-37 Biological Science, 2/e   © 2005 Pearson Prentice Hall, Inc.

Then there are dyneins, which are similar motor proteins that move towards the microtubule's negative end. It's remarkable, and there is no way that primordial soup evolved into proteins that know the electrical charge of their shuttle destination and how not to bump

[37] Freeman, S., and Hamilton, H., 2005 *Biological Science.* Upper Saddle River, N.J: Pearson Prentice Hall.

into anything along the way. To me, science has proven over and over that there is a thinking, living creator God.

While there was no doubt to me, that God made everything as the most supremely intelligent and powerful force in the universe, I did not know Him. Like lots of new age people today, I wanted some of that god power for myself, through my own effort. I wanted a god who rubber-stamped my idea of who God should be. Meditation, yoga, shamanism, and everything else happening around me, was all about finding god within, and making our futures come to pass through what we did, by reframing our own thoughts. I would learn later that the new age 'science of mind', was a whole different ball of wax to Christ's version of "renewing the mind"[38].

It dawned on me that Miriam was correct. Her Jesus, and the Jesus of Mr. LeJoy, was a Jesus I had never known.

[38] Romans 12:2

Spiritual Duplicity

During my 10 years of shamanic observance, I had seen supernatural flickerings in Medicine Man's midst, and also began to experience smatterings of my own clairvoyance. Even though Jesus Christ had healed Mr. LeJoy, I did not understand that his living God was a giant compared to the gods and spirits of shamanism.

Shamanism seemed like a very practical spiritual orientation for many people who worked with Medicine Man, because he never required or suggested anyone rescind their own religions. We were told that Buddha, who enlightened people to the truth of their attachments, and the archetypes and gods of Hindu spirituality, who brought universal truths to human consciousness, and Jesus who brought grace to the planet, were all valuable contributors to humanity's spiritual evolution. According to Medicine Man one did not exclude the other.

To Medicine Man, there was no such thing as Satan. The dualistic thinking of 'good and bad' were just different aspects of what 'is'. According to this thinking, by realizing our oneness with 'Source' or 'Spirit', we can supposedly become inwardly free from the

242

apparent troubles and ills of this 'dream life'. We supposedly have the ability to see loss and gain, sickness and health, and life and death, merely as fascinating chapters of a dream that we can think of as our lives. I didn't have the knowledge then to realize that Satan existed, and could also display counterfeit miracles, signs, and wonders to a degree.

Even so, out of the other side of his mouth Medicine Man would talk about "darkness" and "low-frequency entities" and help us protect ourselves against "negativity" and tell us what to look out for and avoid when in a state of shamanic journey, because there were dangerous entities that could come in to you and torment you. When questioned about these discrepancies, Medicine Man usually made up an explanation on the spot, and when he changed how he did things after telling us it was the right way, he would just say "My truth changed."

Much of what the group discussed and did at my house was what some would call the teachings of the Mystery Schools and, in new-age thinking, it was accepted as quite hip.

Along with meditation and yoga came Kabbalah, ancient Hinduism, shamanic meditation, and 'secret' shamanic techniques via the shamanic oral tradition. Nothing important in the upper echelons of shamanic tradition is ever written down, because common ordinary man would not do it justice or protect these supposedly sacred teachings—so sacred that only a select few, after untold lifetimes of teaching, were permitted entrance. A quick look via Google will show you that shamans today are proclaiming themselves in every culture and every profession. According to them, they are changing the world and 'holding the space' for those of us who are stunted and held back in 'ordinary reality', until we progress through karmic lessons and can take their places. According to Medicine Man, the secrecy required is such that my karma could be seriously damaged for even talking about this today.

Medicine Man informed us all that Jesus was an enlightened being who came to bring the "Christ consciousness" to the planet, and that Jesus was also a sort of shaman, mediating the sacred from God to man. According to today's modern shamans, several biblical characters like David, Jacob, John, and Peter also experienced shamanic journeys. Medicine Man said that some Christian scriptures had value, and we should all have a copy of a red letter Christian Holy Bible and read it, especially the Book of Revelation. The only problem with that is he so belittled Judeo-Christian thinking at the same time, that any practicing Jew or Christian was asked to consider that his or her religious mindsets was limited, dualistic, and unevolved. Medicine Man had also stated, "I've never seen Christianity as a path to enlightenment," which was intended to have us believe that he had seen people find the path to enlightenment, but stupid Christians were not among them.

According to Medicine Man, human enlightenment was a spiritual evolution process that could take a person hundreds to thousands (or more) lives on earth to learn the lessons and progress to the upper echelons of an advanced soul; shedding ego, and ultimately becoming more and more light and energy than solid matter, and defying the laws of 'ordinary reality'. But apparently this could only happen if you apprenticed and paid a lot of money to a more advanced soul to stand-in as your mediator and keeper of the secrets, until you became evolved enough to become a mediator yourself.

We were encouraged to make a quiet room at home, with an altar on which we should place icons, pictures, candles, incense, sage, and images of power animals used in shamanic 'medicine'— anything that reminded us of who we are in 'essence'. This room was to be our 'sacred space'.

As time went on, I also started noticing Medicine Man had a pattern of lying and not keeping his word. The theories he taught us, were not panning out within his own life. His 'truth' constantly changed.

Lots of problems had become evident by the eighth year of listening to him. I put one foot outside the door as my own veils began to drop and I saw yet another naked emperor in the image of a shaman. Even though his psychotherapy training and skills were as astute as any other psychotherapist I had listened to, I started to see that the rest of what he taught was yet another pig in a poke.

One day he could be saying, "Fear is the lowest frequency," and the next day I would realize his inconsistency. He was hermit-like: scared to eat most types of foods for various and sundry reasons, afraid to swim, and confined within a legion of his own limitations. Plainly, whatever god was in him didn't touch his diverse assortment of problems or fears. We would be told that we, with 'The Light', could transcend all negativity and darkness, yet he could not transcend his own personal problems or food intolerances, to the point where he was nearly impossible to cook for. This anomaly was explained away by inferences that his advanced 'high-frequency' energy would be reduced or dampened if he did not feed his body properly. It was not a fear . . .

As I looked around, it was plain that none of my classmates were evolving at any appreciable rate at all. In fact the older students, some of whom had been working with Medicine Man for 20 years, seemed rather stunted compared to his younger apprentices. I asked him about that once, and he offered that he had refined his teaching methods over the years, and the younger class was the beneficiary of that. Looking at everyone who had made it as long, or longer, than I had, it was blindingly obvious that not one of them had had their core ego problems shifted. All they had was more awareness of them. That is just psychotherapy; not blessing, not power, miracles, or evolution. I could also see that the same applied to me. My deadness was as dead as ever. At the rate we were all going, we'd certainly need a few thousand more lifetimes to get anywhere!

Medicine Man never had any trouble buttering-up whomever was sitting in front of him, at the expense of who was not. Then he could turn around and say the total opposite to the one outside when he was face to face with them. The discrepancies and hypocrisies mounted to a level matching the Vatican. It was becoming clear that the power Medicine Man claimed he wielded, was primarily a lucrative mirage.

I was the only student in our group who took him on; challenging his discrepancies and the things that felt wrong to me. The rest of the group often fidgeted in discomfort while we debated. Someone once said to me, "I could never argue with him like that. I am too afraid he won't love me after that." I watched as the group of 15 people reduced down to five. Medicine Man became desperate and pretended to teach Christianity, in order to retain the three of us who had caught on to the difference. He said that "Nothing compares to the love of Jesus," and had us do some new meditative exercises in healing past wounds. Desperate actions couldn't deceive those who were starting to see—two more followed me out when I left, leaving only two.

For whatever reason, I think people are less amenable to seeing spiritual duplicity than they are to seeing scientific duplicity. It is politically correct to adopt a gracious attitude towards religious freedom, because people tend to feel that anyone who believes in a god, and looks like they have something good going, should be trusted and respected. It's all part of respect for cultural differences and freedom to practice your own version of what you think makes you a good person in the eyes of your god. Most people tend to trust a person who, somewhere in their eclecticism, has convinced them that they are held accountable to a god for whatever they teach.

The thing is, I don't think that people like Medicine Man or cult leaders actually believe that they have to answer to a god, because they've deceived themselves to the point where they think they are a god, answerable only to themselves and guided by their 'Divine

Essence' which is . . . 'god'. That was plainly true in how Medicine Man acted and what he asked of us. Even though he would sit and 'bring in' lessons and truths from the 'Great Spirit', it became obvious that he was the man behind the curtain, and we were, at least in the beginning, the naïve trusting counterparts of Kansas' Dorothy.

Rock Meets
Hard Place

In spite of Miriam's suggestion that her Jesus would come to my rescue, the discussions between us had set bundles of nerve endings on fire.

I continued to fight fire with fire, and landed email after email on Miriam with questions about many things in the Bible that made my small intestines pretzel. Every time, clear, succinct answers came back to me, with perfectly reasonable explanations. I was really determined to find the chink in the armor in her defense of her God. More emails, more questions—and, much to my chagrin—more perfectly reasonable answers. She never lost her temper, never told me I was stupid, and was always willing to answer anything I asked.

Another thing I hit her with, was the violence of the Old Testament such as Joshua 6:21, *"And they utterly destroyed all that was in the city, both man and woman, young and old, ox and sheep and donkey, with the edge of the sword."*

I said that God must have condoned such behavior because He commanded Saul do the exact same thing in the book of 1 Samuel 15:3, which says, *"Now go and attack Amalek, and utterly destroy all that they have, and do not spare them. But kill both man and woman, infant and nursing child, ox and sheep, camel and donkey."* How is this a God who also told Moses to pass on the commandment "Thou shalt not kill" to the Israelites! This is a God we are supposed to trust and love? So many crimes and murders since then have been committed in the name of Jesus and commissioned by supposed holy men that it makes my head spin. I just couldn't get on board with that: Jesus, yes . . . but, God of the Old Testament? No! How can one reconcile those diametrically opposed personalities?

An email came back saying:

"God doesn't have a split personality. Do you have ANY idea how society lived back then? There are two aspects to this. First, remember that the nation of Israel had lived as slaves in Egypt and for a long time, all male babies were murdered at Pharaoh's order. Moses escaped that fate. Pharaoh had a huge army for good reason. Normally daily life consisted of one country over-running another country. Moses was a highly trained military general who had been in charge of the total submission of Ethiopia, and much of the wealth Egypt amassed before Moses was forced to flee and live in the land of Midian for forty years, was the loot he brought back from Ethiopia. That's just historical background. But consider this: Why did most cities have very thick impregnable walls? Do you think it was just so that people could hang flower boxes and sunbathe on the top?

"The first city Joshua had to take was Jericho. Have you studied the archeological findings from that? Joshua never attempted to take down those walls because it would have been impossible. God simply reduced those walls to rubble and they climbed over the top. But to really appreciate the situation Joshua was going into, consider what the helpful and meritable harlot Rahab told the spies before they took the city. She recounted that the inhabitants of Jericho had lived in total fear of the Israelites because they had heard about the ten great plagues, and of how Egyptian wealth and society was disemboweled after the Israelites left. They had also heard what God did for forty years as they travelled through the wilderness. They knew that the God of Israel meant business.

"Every other city that Joshua was instructed to take, and leave no man and animal standing, was totally justifiable. Study what there is of secular history of the times. Sodom and Gomorrah in Abraham's time was bad enough, but by the time Israel moved into the Promised Land, humans had descended well below that. Human sacrifice was well established. Not only did many families sacrifice a baby to the gods Chemosh and Baal, it was tradition for a baby to be killed and built into the walls of houses to 'protect against evil spirits'. It was considered normal to have sex with animals. Adults were sacrificed as well. If you want one abject lesson of how bad things were a few hundred years later, go and study Assyria, and a later king, Sennacharib. Then you will know just how far humans can stoop. God saw all that coming, and did not want his people involved in any of that. He said very clearly to Israel, 'Go in and kill everyone and all the animals' because immorality was such that even animals were perverted. However, also note that the Bible clearly says that Israel did not do what God said to do, and they would pay for that later.

"God also warned the Israelites never to marry into certain other nations, and not to have those nations living among them because if they did, their attitudes and their gods would become thorns in Israel's sides. Again, Israel did not listen, and even under Joshua, certain groups were allowed to stay and the very people that Israel had mercy on rather than do what God had said, were to be their undoing later on. Goliath is just one example. He descended from a group Joshua told one tribe to destroy early on, and they didn't do it."

"But Miriam," I responded, "Some of the OT stories are totally ridiculous and so unbelievable that no sane person would believe it. Just take Jonah and the whale. I mean, come on. You don't believe that do you?!!!"

Strangely enough she did. She responded:

"Have you thought about what it would take for a known prophet like Jonah to hear God's voice, fearfully disobey God's request, and run away?"

Knowing I would have said no anyway, she continued, *"He ran in the opposite direction, because Nineveh was the capital city of the Assyrian empire. Do you have any idea, just how Assyria behaved? Nineveh was a beautiful rich city. It was beautiful, courtesy of the relentless looting of distant countries by the Assyrian army. Study their war tactics. You're a doctor but your stomach will not survive just how the Assyrians went about as a killing and destroying machine. The only thing that limited their disgusting fighting practices was that all fighting was done by hand. Had they had nuclear weapons, we probably wouldn't have an earth today.*

"Jonah wasn't a tin pot ignorant prophet. People in those days lived on travelling news, and the gossip grapevine. He knew exactly what the King of Nineveh was capable of, and he knew that a very likely outcome for him would be to be hoisted on a stake with the point inserted under his rib cage in the market square, and left to die being laughed at by the inhabitants. So he ran.

"And if you want to, you can think that three days in a whale is totally improbable but it's not. You can find written records of people who have survived inside a whale. But regardless, God can do anything. He had a lesson to teach Jonah, and it took three days in a putrid, stenching, nasty, gastric-juiced environment to do it, which shows how bad Jonah's fear of the Assyrians was. No person in their right mind went near Assyrians.

"This is my personal opinion, but I believe that BEING in a whale actually gave Jonah credibility, and protected his life. The Ninevites worshiped the half-fish-half-man god, Dagon, whom they believed came out of the sea and founded their nation, sending occasional messengers from time to time.

"Probably clenching his teeth, and shaking like a leaf Jonah went to Nineveh. He wouldn't have had to slowly elbow his way through packed crowds. They would have smelled him coming. Jonah didn't exactly pack soap, hair shampoo, deodorant, washing powder and fabric softeners. You can smell the stink when a whale blows, so can you imagine what people thought when he walked into Nineveh? It doesn't say what they said, or what Jonah said, but I'd imagine it went something like this: 'Cor, blimey what a STINK!!! How did YOU get in such a filthy mess?' The Assyrians wouldn't have even wanted to lay hands on a stinking mess who might have been sent by Dagon.

"In my imagination, what Jonah said might have been something like this. 'God told me to come and tell the King and you scumbags to repent. Normally you would kill me without thinking about it, so even though I'm a prophet why would I want to come to this moral hellhole? I ran, got on a ship going the other way, but because it was plain the storm was caused by my disobedience, I got tossed off the boat, sucked up by a whale, sulked and argued with God for three days until I said, "Okayyyy . . . I will do it!" Whereupon the whale spat me out, and I'm here. And God has said that I, this stinking heap, should tell you that if you don't repent, then he's going to kill the lot of you in a few days, so I'm going to go and sit on that hill up there, and wait and watch.'

"Jonah stomped off in a pissy mood and did just that.

"What do you think the King of Assyria did in that time? He was no kitten. I bet he sent out emissaries to check at the docks Jonah said he had boarded at, ask the captains and sailors what happened, and whether he got thrown overboard. He didn't need to check the whale story because apart from the fact that Jonah stank, his clothes would have been a streaky bleached mess, and that would have been visual evidence enough. I guess that once they realised what Jonah said was true, they took God seriously and decided to repent. So yes, I believe the story. Sometimes the only thing that gets into the heads of violent heartless people is something so disgustingly unlikely, that it shows God means what he says."

Well, that was a new wrinkle of what I used to see as a story that had previously made little sense.

In total desperation, I kept coming back to all the gods, avatars, and prophets I was familiar with courtesy of Medicine Man. Why not Buddha? Why not Krishna and Kali? Why not Mohammed? What was wrong with those benevolent gods and really nice people's thinking who ascribed to their existence and parables?

And she said:

"Tell me one other deity, shaman or whoever, that says they are God incarnate? Who so loved humanity, that he (or she) created a human form of themselves, who could experience humanity and all the sensations, temptations and emotions, and shows us what God is really like in the same circumstances we have to live in? What deity, do you know of, who performs miracles yesterday, today, and forever? Tell me one other God who accepts us for who we

are, and doesn't demand a list of things that we must do to earn his acceptance, love and favour. Everything you've practiced until now has been about 'doing'—about works for earning enlightenment and knowing some 'truth'. God is not like that."

I wasn't yet ready to relent because I remembered back to another of my medical dislikes, and sent another email asking:

"Don't you think circumcision was a bizarre request by God to his 'chosen people'?"

Miriam replied:

"God didn't ask Abraham to circumcise himself until Abraham's faith was secure. Why did he ask? Who knows? But it wasn't because he wanted other people or nations to see that sign. If God wanted a visible sign, then he would have picked something else.

"Perhaps in those days, a penis was something men placed great value on, and as part of a personal commitment to God, God was asking, 'Would you be prepared to mark your instrument of value, as a token of the worth of your relationship with me?'

"After all, it's easy to sacrifice something that doesn't hurt, isn't it? To cause pain to something you value highly, is no small matter. So was God saying, 'What matters more? Your thing of value or your God?' Personal circumcision was not something that Abraham verbally broadcast through the grapevine. Circumcision was supposed to come out of a heart response to God, but has no part in the New Testament covenant.

"Abraham said yes, and as far as we know, he also covenanted to lead his family in that way. God also told Abraham that his people would later live in captivity in Egypt.

"In my opinion, in order to really understand circumcision, you have to understand history and why any law was handed down by God in the first place. So, fast-forward to Moses:

"For whatever reason, the people of Israel did not perform circumcision at all in the 40 years in the wilderness. Plainly God didn't consider that right, or desirable at that point, because He never mentioned it again, until just before Joshua went into the Promised Land. Then all the men and children were circumcised on the same day, as a mark of their covenant, and once they were healed they went into the Promised Land. Obviously, the penis is used for populating and God told Abraham that his offspring would be numerous, and he promised him Canaan at the time when Abraham was circumcised. Then as the descendants with Jacob were about to fulfill that promise again and re-enter the land that God promised Abraham, they were once again asked to perform the ritual of circumcision."

The whole business of the Old Testament law was still really confusing to me, so I asked, "Okay, so why did God give the law in detail, after already giving the Ten Commandments? Why did God not give laws to Abraham to start with?"

Miriam wrote back stating:

"Abraham, Isaac, Jacob and also Joseph didn't need laws. All of them had a personal relationship with God, and didn't require a written law in order to do the right thing from faith in their heart. Their children were not cut from the same cloth though.

"During Israel's time in Egypt, no one had a really strong personal relationship with God even though many still loved God. Even Moses was a newbie at it all. He had an innate knowing which stemmed from around the age of 40 but not a specific understanding, like Jacob and Abraham had had. When God called him at the burning bush, he asked, 'Who will I tell the people of Israel that you are?' (Exodus 3:13). If there was someone in Israel with a better belief, wouldn't you think that God would have chosen that person?

"God initially told Moses that he wanted to make them a holy nation and a nation of priests. So first, God gave the people the Ten Commandments, and I believe that's all that God was initially going to give them. He also specified that at no point were the people to take gold or silver to make gods for themselves (Exodus 20:23). But before God spoke the Ten Commandments to the people Himself, he asked Moses to bring the people up to Mt. Sinai so that they could ALL hear him explain the Ten Commandments to them. But the people then got scared and said, 'No, no Moses, you go talk to God and tell us what he says.' Moses immediately relayed a message back to them that no gods (idols) were to be made out of gold or silver. God specified a few more living principles, so that the people would have a roadmap in social decency and good health.

"Right after that, Moses, Aaron, Nadab, Abihu and the 70 elders of Israel, went up to Mt Sinai and had lunch with God. I can't imagine it was a silent lunch or that the 74 had no concept of what was happening. Immediately after that, the 73 went back down while Moses stayed to receive the Ten Commandments written on tablets.

"While Moses was still on the mountain, the people went to Aaron and asked him to make them gods to lead them since

Moses hadn't yet come back. Idolatry was a recognised offense to God, long before the famous Ten Commandments were given by Moses."

"'And Joshua said to all the people, "Thus says the Lord God of Israel: 'Your fathers, including Terah, the father of Abraham and the father of Nahor, dwelt on the other side of the River in old times; and they served other gods.'[39]

"It was because of that idolatry that Abram was asked by God to leave, separate himself and go to a new land, so it was a known sin in the days before Abraham, and that was 430 years before the Law was given at Sinai. Wouldn't you think those 73 who had lunch with God, would counsel the people not to do this? Apparently not. Usually when a person spoke in defense of God, the Bible details it. Aaron of all people, asked for all the gold earrings to make the moulded golden calf. Plainly he too had a hearing and comprehension problem.

"Israel had agreed to abide by the Ten Commandments, and then immediately broke the first one. It is clear that Israel's version of 'I agree' was expedient. It didn't matter to them, the many miracles they had seen in the four months since leaving Egypt. Having lived in slavery for a long time, it seems they were a nation without principles or a moral compass who refused to have a personal relationship with God and wouldn't allow God to write his law in their minds and hearts, as God did with Moses.

"So God laid down even more written laws for several reasons, one of which was to try to stop them sliding into the total evil which permeated the countries around them.

---

[39] Joshua 24: 2-3

"Many of those laws were very sound laws. Others look ridiculous, but we don't have a full understanding of life then. The nations around them had some very nasty and barbaric practices, which extended a lot further than we could imagine today, and they were going to get worse as time went on.

"The law set a standard of obedience that was much higher than a human could attain. What God really wanted was for the people to see that the law was impossible to keep, and to come to him, as Abraham, Moses and Joshua had done in faith, but most would not. Obviously a few like King David, and the prophets did. What Israel did was outwardly obey the obvious rules, thinking that going through the motions would earn them righteousness points, so that God was pleased with them. But God was not pleased, because the law eventually became an outward ritual, while the people were as corrupt as ever on the inside, and then started worshiping other nations' gods inside God's own temple.

"Repeatedly throughout the Old Testament God says things like, 'Do you REALLY think I want all these sacrifices and offerings? What I want is your hearts, and for you to walk humbly with me, and with mercy towards others and love one another.'

"God never required the complex Law of Moses to be adhered to by Kings Nebuchadnezzar, Darius and Cyrus—and there were a lot of other people in many surrounding nations who knew who God was, and believed. They will be in heaven too, yet they never partook of the Law of Moses, nor were they circumcised. The Old Testament law was solely for Israel, to set them apart."

Over a period of three months, these and more explanations, started to make sense. As I read more carefully through the Bible that Medicine Man had said we should read, I started to see for myself a God that I had never seen before, and a history that I would not have imagined from my school days.

I started to see the lawless lands of the past and understand that the human race was also corrupted by a Luciferian lineage: *"There were Nephilim (men of stature, notorious men) on the earth in those days—and also afterward—when the sons of God lived with the daughters of men, and they gave birth to their children. These were the mighty men who were of old, men of renown (great reputation, fame),"*[40] now made sense.

However, one detail got me well and truly stuck. It wasn't the crucifixion of Jesus itself. Historical documents told the blunt truth about the Romans' penchant for horrific death. It was a bit I was reading about the moment Jesus died. Yes, there was an earthquake and an eclipse, but Matthew 27:51 talked about the temple curtain, which was double thickness and about 60 feet high and 30 feet wide, being torn from the top to the bottom. It sounded such an irrelevant detail, and I didn't get why it was so important, so I asked Miriam about it.

The explanation was mind blowing:

"Suzanne, it was THE biggest event and in some ways, it was even bigger than Jesus' death and resurrection. To the Israeli people it meant everything because the curtain separated the people from God. This was the Holy of Holies, a place that one of the priests was allowed to go in once a year. No one else was allowed access. The curtain was made very heavy, so that no draft of wind could move it into the place called the Holy of Holies in the temple, which represented the core or heart of God, in a space which was narrow but high. That event is

---

[40] Genesis 6:4 Amplified version

even written up in Roman history and the writer Josephus, described the curtain was made very heavy and thick with thick gold strands all through it. Josephus wrote that the curtain was so tough that you could put a team of horses on both sides, and they wouldn't be able to rip it. No man could rip it top to bottom. If they **could** have tried, it would have to be ripped from bottom to top, and they couldn't have ripped more than a few feet before they hit the walls and couldn't pull any more. Only God could have ripped that curtain.

"God was showing the world that people didn't have to go to the temple and talk to God through the priests, or secondhand rituals any more. He ripped the curtain to tell the world that now people could come to him directly without any human intermediary.

"The temple priests were aghast. That news not only spread through Jerusalem like wildfire, but everyone knew that it wasn't done by man. The gossip would have been, 'The priests would never have done it, so why did God do it?' The ripple waves from that were even felt in Rome. Otherwise, Josephus wouldn't have thought so deeply about it, and have written such a clear description.

"The ripping of the curtain was also a personal statement by God, defining the purpose and the power of his son Jesus, and telling everyone that we can come to God through Jesus, who was sent as a living express image of who God is, to demonstrate to the people, the heart of God. God was saying that if we want that relationship, we can do it ourselves, on our own, wherever we are. Even in the middle of nowhere."

Days stretched into weeks, and Miriam never flagged. We discussed shamanism and whatever other circuitous objections I had to things in the Bible, in depth.

All the while my mother was inching closer to death, my desperation was deepening, and I had to make a decision whether or not to return, and if I did, how to cope.

I had no more questions for Miriam.

The reality was that nothing I'd done in the past—psychotherapy, meditation, shamanism, Wicca, yoga, or you name it, had done much of anything that was deep and long lasting. At best, it filled a void in time, and sometimes was entertaining enough so that the depression had something else to think about. Yet everything that I had done, made me more amenable to seeing Jesus in a new light for the simple reason that shamanism is eclectic. To the occult, Jesus is often portrayed as a prophet and 'good'. In a way, Medicine Man showed me an up close and personal experience of comparative religions at a time when I had fully adopted a seriously anti-Christian slant for 10 years.

Deep inside I knew that I had to be with my mother. I didn't know why but at the deepest level it felt true. Because the burden of helplessness had only grown bigger, I didn't think I could handle this assignment.

But I also knew I needed help that no human could provide. By this stage I knew clearly that Medicine Man's 'Great Spirit' was impotent, otherwise he would not have suggested I owed Mom nothing and that I could stay away with no karmic repercussions. I had experienced shamanic 'light' intimately, from personal experience, and it held no joy, no peace, and no lasting answers.

In a strange way, shamanic 'light' provided the ideal counterpoint from which to judge the worth of what was about to happen.

In desperation, I emailed Miriam yet again, and asked her how I could get to know her Jesus. Maybe I wanted 10 easy steps or something, but she wasn't going to give me that. She replied:

"Read Psalm 139. Jesus knows you better than you know yourself. He hears every word you say, and every thought you think is known in heaven. Jesus also knows your mother, whether she realises that or not. I can't tell you how to do it. But doing it, is really simple. Matthew 7:7 says 'Ask and it will be given to you; seek and you will find; knock and the door will be opened to you.'

"It's not like a formula, a saying or a mantra. You have to want to do it. You have to choose to believe that God is, and that Jesus is his son, that God unconditionally loves you with open arms, and that everything you have known to this point has missed the mark. Believe that he will meet you where you are at. My Jesus isn't the Jesus you thought of. I know that if you ask my Jesus into your life, He will carry you through. But I'm not going to tell you how to ask, because that has to come from inside you. If you ask, and really mean it, Jesus will never say no, and he will send the Holy Spirit to help you. John 16:13 says, 'But when he, the Spirit of truth, comes, he will guide you into all the truth. He will not speak on his own; he will speak only what he hears, and he will tell you what is yet to come.'

"Better than that though, you will know it, deep inside. There is no mistaking when it happens.'"

The crux of it was true. I had spent years trying to make myself into something spiritually deeper, and magnanimous, yet failed miserably. I had spent decades looking to myself, and another decade looking to 'the ancestors', and various human and spiritual intermediaries.

Miriam refused to be an intermediary because this was to be my choice, my stepping out, and asking the Holy Spirit to lead me to truths that even she could not.

And the men who journeyed with him stood speechless, hearing a voice but seeing no one. Then Saul arose from the ground, and when his eyes were opened he saw no one. But they led him by the hand and brought him into Damascus. And he was three days without sight, and neither ate nor drank.

~ Acts 9:7-9

Crossing
the Chasm

If Jesus could help me, then what was there to lose? I had no plan, nothing. A beacon inside me just switched on, and the distress flare screamed out. I knocked and said, "Jesus please help me."

There was instant calm. Just like a turbulent plane landing suddenly and becoming smooth with no squealing of tires.

I decided to act on blind faith, got in my car, and went to my mother. I walked into her house, not knowing what to expect, and while the expected abuse came out from her mouth like a babbling stream, it washed right over me. Something had changed. A calm had descended, and whatever Mom said, moved on past, instead of lighting a fire. I could stand back, think about her comments, and respond with love.

I called my brother and my sister, and to my amazement, our relationships felt different. Every day, I would get away on my own for a while if one of Mom's friends was there, and get to know the God of the Bible and his son Jesus. Suddenly, I 'got' where my sister was at spiritually for all those years that I thought she was a foolish brainwashed Bible-thumper. I started to glimpse what 1 John 2:27

means when it says that *"You have received the Holy Spirit, and he lives within you, so you don't need anyone to teach you what is true. For the Spirit teaches you everything you need to know, and what he teaches is true—It is not a lie."*

As the days rolled by, compassion, empathy, and words came out of my heart, which had been impossible before the distress beacon had been set off. I had once scoffed and laughed at the term born-again Christians, because I thought they were worse than stupid. I was one of those ignoramuses who would say, "I don't need to be born again because I got it right the first time." But what I once thought born again meant, and what was actually happening in me, were worlds apart. How totally ignorant, and how totally dark, that side of me had been. I could see it now, because I took that step and got the biggest revelation first hand.

I kept re-reading the emails Miriam had sent me about the Old Testament. Suddenly I understood what it meant, when the Bible says:

> But the natural man receives not the things of the Spirit of God: for they are foolishness unto him, neither can he know them, because they are spiritually discerned. [41]

I understood why nothing had made sense before. Miriam had walked with me, through the last six months, demanding nothing. Charging nothing. As I read back over her old emails, things she had written came to light in a new way. Before, I had struggled to understand some of what was written when she first wrote it, but now it lit up and made sense.

Then I asked the Holy Spirit who Jesus is, and I was given the understanding that you can pour water from the ocean into a cup, and that water is a small part of a larger body of water with all the

---

[41] 1 Corinthians 2:14

same characteristics. Jesus is that drop of the vast ocean of God, and that what Jesus said and did was identical to the real heart of God.

It was easy to see why Jesus had never planned to keep his disciples at his side, forever charging money to do so. He never withheld deep hidden meanings of things until his disciples evolved to a certain level by which time they could be trusted to hold the secrets. Besides which, Jesus had no secrets. Nothing was hidden or withheld. He never suggested any intermediary be used between Him and his believers. After Jesus went back to God, he sent them the Holy Spirit—a direct 'phone-to-phone' connection, to help them in their day-to-day lives.

My new spiritual relationship was totally self-sustaining with no allegiance required to human intermediaries like those a church, a shaman, or a psychologist expects.

41 Resolution

Was being with my mother easy? No. Was it bearable? Yes, because I didn't carry the burden. I handed it to the Holy Spirit and waited for the response.

Mom went into hospice in December because she was really scared after she stopped all treatment and transfusions. The staff at hospice were amazing. I thought that if the rest of medicine had staff as compassionate and caring as they were in this hospice, we'd be so much better off. They were a great comfort all around for Mom and us.

Mom's sister came up from Florida, which was a treat for me. She's a really interesting and fun lady with many artistic talents, who, at 70 years, looks a bit like an amazon Dolly Parton, and has never cared what people think of her. She and her husband used to do a professional show where he sang with his smooth, polished voice as Elvis and she looked like Dolly. I've always enjoyed her spunk and finesse.

Drugged into semi-oblivion, Mom finally started to relax; she knew that doctors and nurses were right there if she had a sudden bleed or crisis. We also stayed around the clock with her, but after a few days it became obvious she was not going to die right off. After about a week of unnecessary inconvenience with one of us continuously being in the institution with Mom, I looked at my brother and said, "Why are we all here? Why not see if we can bring her home and tend to her with some professional assistance." The hospice staff and Mom were fine with that, so we went home and all enjoyed the comforts of our own beds, kitchen, and familiar environment. A nurse came every day to evaluate the home situation, take drug inventory, check vital signs, and deal with any medical issues going on.

Mom sat in her rocking chair in the living room dozing on and off for days. We would put her to bed next to John, her partner, and then help her up in the morning, feeding her whatever she would eat and drink in between, and medicating her pain and anxiety. After a couple of weeks, she must have become so anemic that her energy just took a dive and it was really difficult to get her to walk anywhere. My brother, with his giant bear strength, was a blessing, because if she didn't want to move, he just picked her up, and danced her into where she needed to go, taking the weight in his arms.

Then came the point where she just went to bed, stopped eating, and started to die. I spent a day in bed with her, holding her, singing to her, and stroking her head like I had never done before. I told her how much I cherished and loved her, and that I was sorry I couldn't have done it better before.

As she was dying, I prayed and put on her favorite music, Susan Boyle's album, and read the book of Genesis from the Rotherham's Emphasized Bible translation, that Miriam recommended. Blown away at how beautiful the words were, I sat contentedly with Mom all that day. Then night came. John, who was about 85 years old, just put on his PJs, got into bed, and went to sleep as if it was just a regular night.

Mom started agonal breathing, for about an hour. My brother and I kept her comfortable, and then her heart stopped. We then had to wake John up. He knew immediately why we woke him, and just held her and cried. Then we called the doctor who personally came to the house, pronounced her dead, counted up all the narcotics, and called the mortuary.

The funeral mass started a couple days later, with a pianist singing Amazing Grace, which left me in a puddle. My sister's kids held onto me, trying to give comfort, but the sadness just melted out all over the pew. I was glad to not do a eulogy; my relationship with Mom was too complicated and my feelings were still all over the place.

I was gobsmacked when the priest told my sister's family and me, from his place on the altar, that we should go up for communion with our hands crossed over our chests, to indicate that we would not receive communion because we were non-Catholics. I was really miffed and went to the altar and took communion, knowing that Jesus would not agree with the outlandish concept of Catholic transubstantiation nor that we, his faithful and loving brothers and sisters, were not suited to do what he asked during His last supper to "Do this in memory of me."

Aside from the communion folly, the Indian priest did an amazing job with the eulogy. Sensing the discord within the family, he really seemed to get the big picture—probably because she had talked to him and her church friends over the months. He said, "Everyone is a sinner, and everyone is good. We all have both good and bad in us. Our sister Pauline was a believer and will be forgiven for all her sins, and we pray for her."

Sometimes I think it is harder to say goodbye to the people we have had the hardest time with. There were so many questions, and memories, which only intensified later when we went through Mom's belongings and pictures. I saw photos of her in her teens and early 20s that I'd never known existed. Those pictures showed me another side to her life, which I wish I could have talked about with her while she was living.

Even though I was still a very young Christian, I had a lot of concern about where Mom's soul would reside in eternity. The vestigial Catholic in me wanted to plead for her soul and tell God that she was really a good person beneath the hard, hostile shell that abused those who were closest to her. I wanted to intercede for her. But I knew that there would be none of that in the eyes of a just God, who knows everything from the beginning to the end, and will do what is right . . . so what was the point?

Mom was cremated. She had made sure it was okay with the Catholics first. Apparently it is, because one infallible pope decided in 1963, to overturn the decision of previous infallible popes. The interment of her ashes in the cemetery was equally sad. The funeral director moderated the ceremony. It was too cold to put her ashes next to Dad's in the military graveyard, so all that was done was a little ceremony with us standing around a pathetic cardboard box of ashes. I know it sounds crazy, because the person is dead, but I wanted more than that for her. The cardboard ash box, and a rented casket for the funeral, was her request.

If there was a silver lining to the weeks, it was that a very generous friend gave me and my sister's family use of her parents' large furnished house in Moorestown. It was about to be placed on the market and the timing was just perfect for us. My sister and her family drove back and forth between Virginia and New Jersey whenever they could and we had the time together at the house to debrief, relax, laugh, and just enjoy each other's company.

I was so grateful to Miriam for the countless hours she spent redirecting my lost soul, to the point that I was able to stick it out, with grace, through the Holy Spirit's comfort and guidance. Thanks to her, I will not have to live the rest of my life regretting that I abandoned Mom in her final weeks of need. She died knowing I loved her, and did not abandon her.

Even better things were to come. While growing up, my older brother and I had an incredibly hateful and contentious relationship. From the time I was around eight years old, it seemed like all of the insane hostility Mom dumped on my brother when he was young, he dumped down on me threefold. I hated him with great passion and while I can't speak for him, I suspect the hate was requited. I used to think that if I died, it would be by him killing me in a violent rage. One of the best and most peaceful years I could remember was when he went into the US Army for a year, at the age of 18. The house was relatively quiet and there was no giant bully lording over me emotionally and physically.

As the years passed, he calmed down and we were able to tolerate each other in the short times we spent at Mom's, maybe every two years or so.

When he and I helped Dad during his death, I felt a little closer to him. But during those weeks with Mom, I'd seen my brother in a new light. I started to care much more deeply about him. Mom died in the early hours of the morning and by the time I could leave her house, it was around 3 AM. My brother opened the door for me to leave and said "Don't let anyone know this, but it was really nice spending the week with you."

The fact that my brother and I are now good friends is a miracle. In the years since Mom passed, we visit together twice a year, even though we live on opposite sides of the country.

I've always cherished my sister too, but now there is a different bond, and a knowing of something greater.

But know this, that in the last days perilous times will come: For men will be lovers of themselves, lovers of money, boasters, proud, blasphemers, disobedient to parents, unthankful, unholy, unloving, unforgiving, slanderers, without self-control, brutal, despisers of good, traitors, headstrong, haughty, lovers of pleasure rather than lovers of God, having a form of godliness but denying its power. And from such people turn away! For of this sort are those who creep into households and make captives of gullible women loaded down with sins, led away by various lusts, always learning and never able to come to the knowledge of the truth.

~ 2 Timothy 3:1-8

The Showdown

Seven hundred miles north, as I turned the car into my Maine driveway, I knew what had to be done next, but not how to do it. I again reached out to Jesus and asked how, but all I got was a leading to simply say it how it was.

The next meeting with Medicine Man was at my house, and I had chosen to allow that to happen on the day I arrived home. It was a full weekend meeting and I showed up late in the morning on the second day. I was trusting that, with the Holy Spirit inside, I would be shown a clarity that had eluded me up to that point.

What I was unaware of, was just how naïve and daft I had been. My belief was that Medicine Man was a gentleman, and would be delighted at my discovery, and elated that I had found my own truth and was leaving to pursue it. After all, who was it who had once told us that if he could take a walk with any person who ever lived, Jesus would be on the top of his list? Who was it who had told us to get a Bible with red lettering and study the words of Jesus, because he had said some very important things and the Book of Revelation was spot on? Medicine Man. Funny that.

Perhaps that had confounded me, and led me to believe that Medicine Man believed what he had told us. He had told us once that he used to teach from a Christian viewpoint but, as his groups hated it so much, he stopped. In between his second and third marriage, he dated a Christian woman for a while and during that time, there was more Christian inclusion and even a statue of Mary and Jesus appeared in his office. Rumor had it that he was even baptized during that time. Because of all of this, I never dreamed he would have any negative response to my leaving to pursue a journey with the Holy Spirit.

During the group meeting, I watched with new eyes. The whole scene in the room appeared as the ridiculous process it was: Medicine Man leading a group of grown adults, all agreeing that he was the wise man; the intermediary between us and the Great Spirit. I found myself giggling internally and at some point, I could not control my uproarious laughter. Then I told Medicine Man that I had things to tell him but I was not prepared to do it in the group and that we would talk in private. He seemed satisfied with that.

Strangely, he led the group in an exercise where he first talked about the love of Jesus as the most powerful love possible, and did a guided meditation on that. Then we were instructed to relive one of the worst parts of our lives, but with Jesus' love in our hearts. I had no trouble telling the group what happened with me in the weeks before. An angry long-term member, who resented my leaving the group, later informed me that my discourse turned a few heads that day.

When I saw Medicine Man alone during the week, I explained that I had an opening to Jesus and had been flooded with power and love that rocked my world. I told him that spending the last few weeks with my mother, was the best thing I had ever done. I told him that I now knew, for certain, that Jesus is the only path to God. He drew forward and slowly uttered two words that shook the room. "Says ... Who?"

I simply offered "The Bible says . . ." to which he sat back and shrugged. Stupid little Christian that I was, in his eyes.

Then I told him that I realized a personal relationship and union with Jesus, isn't enlightenment, but a personal revelation leading to a new life and to my spirit literally being transformed into a new creature—like being . . . born again.

In the most telling Freudian slip of all, he breathed out, "And who have you ever known, who has had a personal relationship with God?!" Right there in his anger, he had just told his own truth: that he didn't have a relationship with God and wouldn't know one if he saw it. I muttered in truth, "I . . . once . . . thought . . . you . . . did."

I hadn't planned on saying more but after that, in a surge of courage, I said that I was going to leave the group, which would no longer meet in my house.

Medicine Man grew stiffer and angrier, asking pointed questions, and trying to get me to talk about Miriam. I refused to have that relationship attacked by him. Yes, it was true that Miriam had an impact on me, but only because she made more sense than Medicine Man ever did with his sexy fancy Mystery School jargon, that led everyone nowhere. She helped explain this Bible with red words in a way Medicine Man had never even tried to do.

I recall another time when Medicine Man referred to the Bible. It was very early in my 10 years with him. He was talking about the importance of our words. He said the first line in Genesis is "In the beginning there was the Word," and tried to make a case that the whole universe was built upon just a word out of God's mouth. For anyone who doesn't know, that is how the **Gospel of John** begins, but the 'word' that Medicine Man was talking about was the words out **of our** mouths. He was trying to drive home an important point, that everything coming out of our mouths matters and can have long-lasting consequences, both negative and positive, which is true. However, in misquoting and misinterpreting the Bible, it is clear that he was clueless to the obvious fact that John was referring to Jesus as the Word.

Such loose associations were the norm in Medicine Man's so-called spiritual authority, even though he touted precision and 'being highly conscious' as interrelated to one's karma, which to him was of uppermost importance. To Medicine Man, we got to where we were going to go, by being 'human doings', over thousands of life times.

It's a beguiling position, because we are brought up in a world that judges our worth by behavior and results. If you do good, you are good. If you do bad, you are bad. One of the things that had always stood between me and any concept of God was why God would allow such wickedness, such terror on earth, and making our lives miserable. I looked at my mother and wondered what the price of her making our lives such an emotional battlefield might be.

I also thought about the difference that I was now experiencing, coping in life with Jesus. I felt no judgment, no condemnation, just total forgiveness and love, which made me feel completely free inside. I compared that to coping with a life of seemingly endless works recommended by Medicine Man. Where, for that matter, did Medicine Man stand in the eyes of God, by leading us all on a wild goose chase? But then, I had chosen that of my own free will. Why did I first choose Medicine Man and not Jesus? Because I couldn't see Jesus making a difference in the lives of people around me. But then, neither could I see Medicine Man making a difference either.

When I refused the obligatory 'exit interview' with the group, and he felt that I was rubbishing my apprenticeship of the last 10 years, he said to the remaining members, in frustration, "Even Jesus was crucified." When I heard this, I laughed uproariously: that he could consider himself to be equal to Jesus, and equate my refusal of an exit interview, to me crucifying him. I wondered just how Medicine Man conceptualized the meaning or significance of Jesus' resurrection.

The Holy Spirit showed me clearly that the crucifixion of Jesus[42] was the atoning sacrifice for not just my sins, but also for the sins of every person that ever lives in the world. The sin that stood between me and God wasn't that of following Medicine Man, or anything personal I had done, but the sin of NOT believing, trusting, and asking Jesus to help us. For the first time, I understood Mr. LeJoy clearly. All things are possible[43] through Christ in us.

It was then that I fully understood Jesus' grace and mercy, not just to me, but to my mother. In spite of her personal sin, which Jesus paid the price for, if she truly believed in Jesus, my mother would find herself in the presence of God. God took everyone's personal sin out of the way through Jesus, to make salvation an equal-opportunity occasion, and as easy as possible for everyone, from the least to the greatest, to have a relationship with Him because He doesn't think anyone has more status[44] than anyone else.

It is the Holy Spirit's job to comfort, teach, and convict every person on earth. But to convict about what? I saw it clearly in Jesus' words when he explained that the only thing that the Holy Spirit would convict[45] us of was not believing that Satan had been judged and defeated, and not believing that every person's personal sin was

---

[42] 1 John 2:2

[43] Matthew 19:26

[44] Romans 2:12

[45] John 16: 8 - 11

paid for by Jesus, and the righteousness granted to Jesus and those who believe in him.

That also applies to Medicine Man. Whether he realizes it or not, nothing he has done, stands between him and God, because he was also part of the redemption. The only thing that stands between him, or anyone, and God, is the same thing that stood between me and God.

But even better was yet to come. Even though Jesus had led me through the time with my mother with compassion and joy, I still felt the weight of helplessness, failure, and future uncertainty. One day, while standing in my house, I became aware that I had another choice to make. I suddenly saw the depression for what it was, and where it came from. I took that depression and everything that went with it and, in blind faith, handed it to Jesus. I trusted him to remove a problem that had plagued me for decades: a haunting hollowness that at times had stalked me despite pharmaceutical's best drugs, constant diversions, fountains of sorcery, psychology, and all of my own effort.

It lifted like a load removed, and has never returned, despite the fact that my life now has none of the security that money, or the medical brotherhood, has to offer.

The God of Abraham gave me a miracle that stands strong in my mind and heart forever, and grows stronger every day.

April 2012 marked the end of shamanism for me, and the rising into a new and more abundant Life.

43 Wiping The Slate

As I looked around my house, I knew straight away that everything that had any connection with other gods and my previous life had to go. As my eyes looked around wondering what could go and what could stay, an internal voice said, "This must go, that must go." The Holy Spirit made it very clear exactly what had to go, and it was pretty much everything.

Out it went. And every room that was cleaned out was prayed over.

The journals with all the shamanic teachings and my writings were burned in a fire pit.

I had collected four boxes of statues, idols, icons, crystals, books, tarot cards, and the like. There must have been several thousand dollars' worth of items by the time I'd rounded everything up. Those things never bothered me in the house before, but when they were all sitting together in one place, under my new eyes, under the new conditions, it felt like a dangerous mass of roaring anger. I was actually reluctant to put them in my car and drive, out of concern for having an accident, but I prayed for protection and went to the dump. After the fellow that worked at the dump saw what I was tossing into the metal bin, he stopped me and took them out. He said that someone might want that stuff. I tried to argue with him, but it was clear he was bent on taking them and doing something with it all. In retrospect I should have taken them back and buried them in a hole, but I didn't.

It was a total relief to have them out of my car and out of my life; in part because they were tainted goods, and in part because it was an important element of a cleansing process that had to happen.

When I got home, everything felt different. But it was also different in another way. God started dealing with me on an even deeper level.

After I had started with Medicine Man, a couple who had been in the group were having marital problems. My moral compass at that time was my own and so, as time went on, I saw nothing wrong in getting into a relationship with a divorcee with children, even before they were divorced.

Our relationship lasted eight years in total. The relationship was rocky from the start, as it usually is where an angry ex-spouse and shared custody is involved. There was never a time when drama wasn't being played out. I had wanted out many times, but hung in there primarily out of responsibility for the children, who I thought needed stability, but also out of hope that things could improve. But they never did.

The Holy Spirit convicted me heavily over the relationship, showing me that if I'd really had compassion for the children involved, I would have stayed clear away and insisted the parents work out their differences.

My involvement solved one problem because I provided financial security and company. And for me, it provided what I thought was love.

As I looked around, I knew then that the house wasn't mine and that I had to leave Maine, the house, and the relationship. God showed me that the degree of my ignorant complicity was such that, for the sake of the children, I needed to sign the house and all the equity over to my partner, leave all the furniture and appliances, and not take anything that would disrupt their lives.

I did.

Months later, the Holy Spirit showed me why the relationship was wrong on every level: morally, physically, and spiritually. Then I understood why it was always so difficult.

Homeless, jobless, and with a small amount of money in the bank, I left Maine to head back to Virginia with what fitted into my car and a small trailer.

44

Into The Wild Blue Yonder

Rewind a few months, to June 2011.

I had spent 15 years 'treating' people for kidney failure, hypertension, auto-immune, inflammatory, and metabolic disorders—treating, not healing them. Even though I had no idea how I was going to survive financially, walking out of the hospital in June 2011 was, in one sense, a joyful liberation because I never had to do that kind of work again on someone else's terms, unless I wanted to.

I had taken two weeks before going to my mother, just to do nothing but read, hang out with the dogs, and clean the house. It was a time of peace, exhaustion, and confusion. One of the things that allowed me some comfort, in resigning my job, was the concerted effort I had put into clearing the half-million dollars in high-interest student loans over the time I had practiced in Maine.

There were no more golden handcuffs keeping me locked into a job, with lips zipped shut, while watching policy overrule good medical care.

Even though I had not figured out a future, there were a lot of unanswered medical questions, and now there was time to put in some serious study instead of just snatching the odd hour here and there. After my rest, I had gone full throttle into polio research, even while with my mother and in my camper at night.

Around the same time, two other people, besides Miriam, gifted me with their libraries of old polio data, which were amazing resources. One of them was Dr. Herbert Ratner's family member, who gave me the entire library of all the documents he saved over decades, including his time as Oak Park Illinois public health department director, and his subsequent published criticisms of the polio vaccine after the Cutter incident, and SV40. It was an amazing endowment. There were references that I would never have found in any library because they were destroyed a long time ago. The information in there sometimes rocked me off my heels and sometimes made me laugh at the irony, but mostly showed me I was right to question the polio paradigm the public had seemingly swallowed—hook, line, and sinker.

Regarding flu, measles, and pertussis vaccines, all sorts of other fascinating information tumbled out of PubMed into my lap. I oscillated between gob-smacked wonder at what I'd never been taught, and downright dismay that piles of important information are withheld from medical education. Yes, we drank from a fire hose at medical school and during internships, but this other information was important. Exactly what were we doing to the immune systems of our patients? The more I read, the more upset I became. If I could easily find solid science that impacted my patients, then those writing medical education syllabi should also have known that what they were saying was carefully crafted and sometimes lying by omission.

After my departure from the hospital practice, I could have opted for financial security and hung my own shingle out to start a busy private practice, but I felt I had a different mission. Two actually. The first was to write a book. I thought that it might be on polio. My parallel mission was to read and get to know the Bible better, and listen to the prompting of the Holy Spirit as to what to do next. I also knew that the last 30 years were for a purpose and, right now, the subtle scorn of my medical colleagues was still reverberating in my ears.

Everywhere I went, I heard, "But if we don't vaccinate we could go back to the big, bad old days!" I continued researching and started to write a book, trusting that by doing what felt right, doors would open.

Roman Bystrianyk, engineer, computer scientist, and father of children who were adversely affected by vaccines, contacted me after hearing me speak about smallpox and polio on the radio in New York City. Roman had begun to analyze the history of vaccines, sanitation, and death declines over the past 100-plus years in various countries, and he had made graphs showing a reality most people are unaware of.

While I was prepared to speak about polio publicly, writing a book was problematic. There were far more urgent things to discuss, including the message of this book: the way the medical education system censors and massages information in order to train very bright people into captive automatons.

But bright people don't get deceived, right? What an affront to my intelligence that I'd been stupid enough to be deceived. The problem is that, being deceived, means you don't know you are deceived. It was the polio information gifted to me, and deep delving into PubMed, that showed me the extent to which the wool had been pulled over my eyes. Once I saw it, it was not so hard to come to terms with the fact that intelligence is actually the veil that blinds, because never once did I doubt what I was taught. As doctors, we are proud of our achievements, coronation, and the letters after our name, which are the stamp of authority, and what makes us different from the people we treat. That is, in fact, what most pro-vaccine zealots are defending—the integrity of their brightness. I'm often asked, "If this is true, why are there not more experts saying these things?"

The answer: Doctors stick within the rut of regulated information, because they believe . . . bright people don't get hoodwinked.

In my nephrology fellowship, Dr. Charlie Swartz had clearly seen the coming of automaton ignorance in the field of nephrology, which is why he hammered so much valuable information into our brains every Wednesday morning. He is most definitely one of the most important figures in my medical travels.

I was initially reluctant to agree to write with a total stranger, but Roman came to Maine for a visit and showed me his graphs and what he had written. I could definitely see the value of what he had started, and that he was a solid researcher with an abundance of integrity. I've never once regretted working with him.

At first, *Dissolving Illusions* was going to be written by Roman, with just a polio chapter by me.

But after the first year, as my research broadened, I couldn't stop reading, adding, and working out all the other chapters. By August 2013, *Dissolving Illusions*[46] was completed and we decided that, even though it was an equal effort, my name should sit as the first author.

Amazon/CreateSpace is the vendor and reviews have been stellar. There has only been one critique of the book even worth responding to: A self-labeled 'crunchy mom' who blogs on medium.com and has four followers. The critique reeked of a pharmaceutical ambush. We initially ignored it, but because there were so many questions about it, published a detailed response on September 2015.[47]

---

[46] Humphries, S., and Bystrianyk, R., 2013 *Dissolving Illusions: Disease, Vaccines and the Forgotten History.* CreateSpace/Amazon.

[47] Dr. Suzanne Humphries and Roman Bystrianyk: Response to "Isabella B's" "Why Dr.Suzanne Humphries, an anti-vaccine activist, is lying to you about measles." http://tinyurl.com/gn6mu6u

Had I not taken that human leap of faith in 2011, not knowing how my bills would be paid, there would be no *Dissolving Illusions*. Had Roman not heard me speak about polio, pushed me to write the book that he had the vision for, and seen it completed long before I could, it would not have happened. I have a handful of people that I owe so much to, for their various levels of generosity, faith, and support in what was one of the darkest, most difficult times of my life.

O faithless and perverse generation, how long shall I be with you?
How long shall I suffer you?

~ Jesus, from Matt 17:17

The Valley Of
The Shadow Of Death

Before *Dissolving Illusions* was printed, a looming shadow reared its head.

Years before, I had had a carcinoma removed from my chest wall. And while it was visually gone, except for a keloid scar, not everything felt gone. I knew deep inside that everything in the right lung was not what it should be, but for years I lived in serial denial. If I got any infection, it would go 'right there' but I would push away the thought that all was not well. Sometimes recovery from a simple cold could take months.

I developed a horrible cough in January of 2013. Again, while remaining in denial, lots of excuses came to mind. While I had organized my Maine home before leaving it, lots of packing and paring down of belongings had to be done. Thoughts like, "This cough is what you get when throwing out moldy items, taking belongings to thrift shops, and setting everything in order," came to mind.

The months passed, and the chest pains and cough waxed and waned. Wanting to research information that would add value to *Dissolving Illusions*, I booked a long-distance flight, halfway around the world. A few weeks before my scheduled departure, there was a new cough on top of the old cough. As the time came near, the spasmodic hacking got so bad, that I wondered if it was one of the nasty new strains of pertussis that were blindsiding vaccinated people around me. I had been DTaP vaccinated numerous times, and was intensely exposed to two ripe, diagnosed cases over a period of weeks about five years previously, without getting any cough that time.

With the worsening symptoms, I did everything I knew to do and managed to get things under control enough to stay semi-silent in the 18-hour airplane haul. Unbeknownst to me, my destination wasn't exactly clean, salubrious lodging. Even if the company was pleasant enough, I found myself in filthy surroundings, far worse than at any time in Central America.

My room and the whole house was filled with statues of demonic origin, which I felt the minute I walked in. I turned some in my room to face the wall, covered some over with scarves and tucked others into the closet. However, as I opened the closet, I realized it was laden with mouse shite, as was the shelving next to my bed, and the drawers in the room. The deep-pile shaggy blanket on the bed was impregnated too. I'd never seen what mice could do when left unchecked for years and it was beyond disgusting. So much for the one dozen cats living in this house, which must have been more recent additions. From ceiling to floor the place was caked with a kind of filth I'd never seen in my life before. Fly-impregnated spider webs, so thick they could just about sell as sculptures, obscured the light in every huge bay window. Mouse droppings were everywhere, including kitchen appliances, in profusion.

The stench of mouse urine and detritus never let up, even as I slept. It was in the bedcovers, holes in the mattresses . . . everywhere. There was no escape. Even when I washed my clothes, they came out smelling. I later realized that was because the washing machine was where the makeshift cat box—towels placed on the floor where the 12 cats relieved themselves—was cleaned each day.

Days passed and the cough got worse, and worse, to the point where the only safe place to cough was sitting on the toilet. I became incontinent of urine and could not leave the house even to take a short walk. It got to the point where I thought I might pop an artery in my head. The headache was intense and made coughing something I dreaded, but at the same time could not avoid. There were times I was gagging, coughing, and urinating all at once, with no control at all. The cough controlled me and I was beginning to fear for my life. Sleeping sitting up all night was the only option for getting any rest whatsoever.

During this time, my walk with the Lord was getting plenty of practice as I read my Bible, gaining insight after insight, while negotiating the demonic oppression around me. I was reading through the gospels, soaking up how everyone who came to Jesus touched him with a healing purpose, or asked to be healed, and was. Every story hit my head like a Morse code signal, yet because I didn't really know how, I hadn't prayed effectively.

Every day, I had a sensation of thorny tentacles growing in my chest; and moving outwards and heading upwards to choke the breath out of me until one night when it all came to a crunch point where things were so bad, I could feel everything closing around me. I had the sense that this was indeed a shadow of the valley of death.

In total desperation, my distress beacon went full pitch for the second time, and I said to Jesus, "I know you can heal me, but I don't know if you will." Deep inside, it was as if a voice said to me, "Suzanne, you know NOTHING about faith!"

Instantly, the cough was gone. I inhaled, feeling for the sharp invading sensation that formerly occupied every inward breath for nearly a year, and it was all but gone.

The tentacles had receded. There was nothing but peace, joy, and a knowing that I was healed. I cried with relief, and understood Mr. LeJoy's emotions in a new way. I just knew I'd be able to ride a bike the next day, without losing control of my bladder. The following day, after pumping up the tires of an antique cruiser, I headed out for a ride, and continued to exercise every day, eventually working up to running, which was something I'd not done since years before.

That voice was right: I knew nothing about faith, but I decided to make it my business to get that knowledge and test it in the years to come.

Eye Has
Not Seen

After returning to the USA, I needed to return to Maine to complete unfinished business relating to the house, which had to be done in winter.

Back in 2001, daily snow and swathes of white fluff had been a romantic new entity, with cross-country skiing out my back door and fires in my huge glass and iron woodstove. But after a few years, the delight of skiing no longer outweighed the sheer slog of stacking cords of wood, constantly stoking flames, and tweaking thermostats just to keep warm. Worse, winter had become for me, a bleak, bleak drag, of dark short days with drab colors.

Frankly, I was dreading going back north. The prospect almost took on a heaviness similar to the past, but in that moment, a scripture leapt out and hit me:

> *Eye has not seen, nor ear heard, nor have entered into the heart of man the things which God has prepared for those who love Him.* [48]

As I took leave of my sister, to start the trek back to Maine, I wondered what this could mean. It's also true that to people who are depressed, the world is 'gray'. For me, it certainly had been, and while the depression had lifted in an instant, unbeknownst to

---

[48] 1 Corinthians 2:9

myself, I had become so accustomed to seeing washed-out colors, that I didn't know anything else existed.

As I traveled, the colors around me started to change. Arriving in Maine, I was seeing new colors, hues, and tinges. The world now emitted a glow and a pulsing that had previously been concealed. A radiance of yellow-orange light permeated everything. I knew I was seeing God's life everywhere, and that before I had not. And in that moment, I perceived what the world would look like if God withdrew—and it was not pleasant. It was a downright horrifying, cold sharpness.

That winter turned out to be a total delight, as everywhere I turned and looked, the cold sharpness had become sparkling, glowing images seen through new eyes.

Was this what it meant, when Jesus said in John 9:39 that He came to give the sightless back their sight? Was it as much about physical sight as spiritual sight? Either way, this change in physical vision was an unexpected and delightful result of the spiritual rebirth.

The time passed quickly; all loose ends were sorted and I returned to my sister, still in awe at the color and glow all around me.

My sister started introducing me to her friends. One family immediately asked whether I was going to be licensed in Virginia. Displeased with my answer, they paid for the process to be completed and asked me to be their family physician. From there my practice grew into what I wanted: a traveling, home-visiting doctor who also pays attention to the minutiae of home life, the kitchen cabinets, and social factors.

The next person to ask for my help was a woman caught between a rock and a hard place. The hard place was lichen sclerosis, and the rock was a large ovarian growth, which, in the surgeon's experience, never regressed, and in order to be totally safe should be surgically removed. The daily norm also included large amounts of accumulating pelvic fluid that doubled her over in pain. Every which way she looked, it was all bad. I went with her and her husband to the surgeon and reviewed all the tests and indeed, this was a rock and a hard place. His exact words were, "It won't shrink. They never do. The best we can hope for is that it will not grow larger and that it is not malignant, but given the characteristics, it doesn't look good."

He told her to go home and think about it. Like so many other Christians, and indeed myself at one time, the fact that Jesus healed was something that remained between the covers of a book in her house. Hers was a faith wherein Jesus was her King but when it came to healing herself, 'seeing' that Jesus does still heal, was indeed a leap.

It's interesting though, that universally, being between a rock and a hard place cracks the shell of hardness of both thought and heart. There, you ask whether what the medical system sees with its 'eyes' and the miracle they believe to be impossible, could actually be possible. You wonder if those words in that book might actually be living, and contain more power than you assumed, and your yearning that they do, expands into faith.

I told her what happened to me a few months before, and in her desperation she wanted that too.

One night as we were texting on our phones, I joined with her in prayer and she agreed with a heartfelt cry to be healed and together we told the pelvic lump and lichen sclerosis where to go, in the name of Jesus. Soon after that, both were resolved.

Four weeks later, a family member dragged her to the radiologist. She kept saying, "Why are we doing this? I am healed!"

Sometimes, going to the doctor for confirmation has to be done—at least to please those who love you and still their worry. A new scan later and the surgeon had nothing to say, although perhaps he thought to himself, "I can't see anything. It must have regressed after all!" He couldn't blame a bad diagnosis; the proof from weeks prior lay in what he saw between the scans in his left and right hands and in the medical chart. There was no mass in the ovary to be seen or felt and no pelvic fluid could be found, no matter how hard the radiology technician looked, or what angle she took.

A year later, returning for a routine exam, a new doctor read the old records, did a bi-manual exam and declared she felt the ovary and lump. My friend was in despair because she knew she was healed so the exam result made no sense. I was also distressed and said, "Let us just see what the next scan shows." Once again, no ovarian lesion was visible on radiology studies. The job was done by Jesus and it was not going to be undone. Sometimes, the miracles of Jesus can be seen. Sometimes the miracle can be such that something that was once seen, is no longer seen.

Curse Of The Fig Tree Revisited

I pondered the meaning of my jaw and head fractures for many years. Was there something to be learned from the incident? I remember telling Medicine Man that I felt like it was a giant cosmic slap in the face but I could see no meaning to it. Was 'the Universe' trying to get me to do something different? Was 'the Universe' trying to tell me something? In my pagan years, even after journeying to the spirit world, and using divination to try to figure it out, no insights were forthcoming.

And I didn't think about the fig tree at all, even after giving it away for the second time. I concluded that both were just random misfortune. That is . . . until very recently. Today, I can see full well how they are related.

Jesus was making a point and not committing a random act of judgmental violence as I once thought. He didn't command the fig tree to bear fruit or heal it, even though He could have. He had the power to make fruit appear just as fast as he restored Malchus' severed ear after Simon Peter lopped it off. He killed the tree as an act of finality to send a very specific message to the religious system via the rampant social grapevine, which had heard everything he said and did while driving the moneychangers out of the temple.

I was just as worthy of destruction as the fig tree Jesus cursed. Even though I was in my own wilderness, God was trying to send me a message, which I took no heed of.

There were two messages for me from Figgie. One was personal and the other was about the medical system.

Today, I know exactly the answer to the riddles.

Stinking
Thinking

For over a decade, in the midst of my medical career, I had wondered why I felt so dead. At times I would share that question with trusted friends and family. Nobody really understood how someone with two degrees, success, and money, could be anything but elated. The only way I could have been elated was if I could have embraced being dead. At the height of success, I was an automaton with power, expected to shut off my natural curiosity and propensity towards curing people, in order to satisfy the approval and acclaim of the brotherhood.

'Curing' is only allowed to be attempted with methods contained in the manual and under protocols approved by the medical system. See a simple earache: prescribe antibiotics. See high blood pressure: prescribe hydrochlorothiazide—a diuretic—even though all doctors are taught the consequences of that. Cholesterol levels outside robotic norms? Simple: prescribe statins. Furthermore, what the system defines as a cure, may simply be the removal of one condition, with the result of spawning another.

Looking back now, when I consider my first degree majoring in physics, it stretched my brain. I was constantly forced to solve puzzles, to understand, and to join dots. In contrast, medical school wasn't nearly so difficult or intellectually challenging. It was more a question of relentlessly drinking from a never-ending fire hose, and having the capacity to embed copious facts into my memory without question. There is no time to question. There is far too much in the syllabus for everything to be understood at a deep level. Yet an implicit assumption, which we took as gospel, was that there was always a fundamental biological plausibility to everything, and therefore a logical rationale to underpin the information we were being fed. No student would take out huge student loans if the information wasn't considered worth knowing, and we all assumed that at some point we would understand everything. However, the reality is that by the end of medical school and as residents, we were at best, parrots. Becoming a parrot is the act of accurately remembering and reciting an encyclopedia of stuff, which often you don't understand. What's actually worse is that the students don't know what their teachers don't understand.

Doctors who prescribe by the rulebook and run approved hospital services are considered successful and brilliant. The rulebook protocols ensure that in different ways and under different schedules, everyone will be jabbed, pilled, scoped, and poked, 'just in case'. It's supposedly 'gold standard healthcare' cradle to grave, but it's mainly money for thoughtless jam. There are doctors out there, who think it's all wonderful that their lives just tick over, like well-trained dogs. They never question the fact that their patients come back over and over, and get sicker and sicker, while their medication lists get longer and longer. They don't really have to think at all, while the money just rolls in.

Yet, those of us who feel like a cog in a financial wheel and have a lot of questions are dismissed as outliers with, "low cognitive complexity in thinking patterns"—even though we have spent years in libraries and medical literature to find better answers, and have stretched our thinking patterns far beyond what is expected of any medical doctor.

This leads to a new problem because those who broaden their knowledge base beyond convention, whether doctors or laypeople, are targeted as quacks, nutters, and perhaps conspiracy theorists, by default. Doctors love their high standing in society and hate to be called quacks. Most will do whatever it takes to not stick their necks out—even if that means delivering fewer choices and more dangerous treatments than necessary to their patients.

The media today capitalizes on the financial vulnerability and fragile self-images of doctors, branding any who do not tow the party lines as, "twisted, simple-minded, lacking in evidence, misguided, resting on anecdote, touting myths of danger where none exists, ignorant"[49], a danger to society, and more.

At the same time, those who embrace conventional medicine and vaccination in every form, are portrayed as barely lower in ranking and infallibility, than the pope. These medical clergy profess safety and effectiveness of all their practices through "extensive testing", "constant monitoring by numerous independent investigators over millions of doses", and "copious clinical evidence which comprehensively debunks any opposition", by those who peddle dangerous, "emotive narratives" that may unfortunately allow "falsehoods" to "cloud the good judgment" of believers in all things medical.

If the media pick up a story that questions or critiques vaccination in any way, then instantly the reporters are characterized as *"irresponsible people who have suspended their critical thinking faculties and used anecdotes to scare the public with their 'vapid' opinions, against all sound logic and scientific evidence"*. Any reporter who dares to deviate from the limited palette of safety allotted them, and gives voice to any parent of a vaccine-damaged child, is labeled as *"poorly researched and inciting panic by using sensationalism"*. The rhetoric has gone so far as to suggest

---

[49] Grimes, David, January 11, 2016. "We know it's effective. So why is there opposition to the HPV vaccine?" *The Guardian.* https://www.theguardian.com/science/blog/2016/jan/11/why-is-there-opposition-hpv-vaccine-cervical-cancer. Accessed February 19, 2016.

"journalism jail" for such renegades and citing vaccine-critical reporting as compulsorily "faulty".[50]

The 1984 *Federal Register*[51], which states *"any possible doubts, whether or not well founded, about the safety of the vaccine cannot be allowed to exist in view of the need to assure that the vaccine will continue to be used to the maximum extent"*, has a continual effect on what doctors are taught in medical school, and what is considered freedom of speech in the media.

Doctors are supposed to give informed consent to patients, but there are a couple of problems.

First off, doctors don't get a well-rounded education and thus have no idea what they don't know. Their ignorance consequently blinds their clinical judgment so that when they see something, the trained diagnosis that usually registers within their head is the politically correct one. This really bothered me because the result was that too many diseases remained 'idiopathic' and the resources I was given to do battle with disease were inadequate. However, there were lots of approved laboratory and radiologic testing, to help me pick which drug to prescribe from the many options within the approved *Physicians' Desk Reference* encyclopedia of drugs.

If I was short of an idea, a really nice drug company rep, with really delicious food and a smooth patter, could be sure to deliver a glowing 'unbiased' font praising the latest, greatest, safest, and often . . . *the* most expensive pharmaceutical to match the problem.

---

[50] Kroll, D., "Dr. Paul Offit: 'Journalism Jail' for Faulty Medical Reporting," *Forbes Magazine*, March 29, 2014.

[51] Federal Register. Vol. 49, No. 107. Friday, June 1, 1984. Rules and Regulations. Page 23004. Final Rule. DEPARTMENT OF HEALTH AND HUMAN SERVICES Food and Drug Administration. 21 CFR Part 630 [Docket No. 84N-0178]

For instance, I can remember back in 2004, our nephrology group being literally wined and dined by a drug company rep, who was touting the benefit of a really expensive drug called fenoldopam, marketed and patented by his company.

Kidney failure is a big problem in medicine and especially from cardiac catheterizations because some image-enhancing chemicals (ionic iodinated contrast agents) are very hard on kidneys. Cardiac catheterizations are often done on patients who have underlying medical conditions, like diabetes, that affect the kidneys. Because they are done when people are sick, the risk of complications can be quite high. This drug was promoted to prevent kidney shutdown from iodinated contrast during heart catheterizations, by starting the fenoldopam infusion one hour before the procedure and continuing for 12 hours afterwards.

Our nephrology group was relieved to hear that some drug company had made a breakthrough and patented a drug that could be given before the radiology test, with the aim to prevent kidney damage. We were willing to sit and listen to the talk by the drug company's hired medical doctor and get a very nice expensive dinner, because this drug just looked so promising.

Afterwards, we went back to work and enthusiastically prescribed fenoldopam, which cost around 1,500 USD average (more for larger people or if there was any delay in the catheterization procedure).

But the buck stopped there. I was not capable of giving a patient really informed consent on fenoldopam, because all I knew was the report from the drug company. I might have hoped it would help, but in reality it was more expensive and more dangerous than other drugs we were already using, like the anti-oxidant N-acetyl cysteine, which is still used to prevent kidney damage, and is actually good for you.

A few months later the drug was withdrawn because further studies showed there was too high a risk of low blood pressure, and it didn't work. We realized that that we had been sucked into purchasing a pig in a poke.

But never to be put off by failure, a recent medical article that admits the failure of IV fenoldopam infusion, suggests another trial is warranted with the drug directly infused into the kidney arteries!

Similarly, before 2009, I was also unaware that I was incapable of giving patients information so that they could give an informed consent for a vaccine. Pretty much all I knew was when to jab them, and a little bit about how to test if the vaccine stimulated the immune system. Nephrologists have to test for the immune system response, because their patients are so immunosuppressed that three hepatitis B jabs might do nothing, in which case six, or even nine, injections might be ordered. And even then, the result might still be no antibodies. And because we were so dead to questioning the rationale of sticking these injections in chronically ill patients, any deterioration in health after any of those hepatitis B shots was because the people were already sick and vulnerable, not because the vaccine had knocked them sideways. Vaccine reactions were just 'coincidence disorders'.

> *"Doctors are given limited information and in turn, those same doctors and the various branches of medicine are advised to limit the amount of information given to parents in order to achieve a desired health behavior, instead of high-level knowledge.*[52]

> *"Our experience and that of patient education specialists indicate that current materials contain an excessive amount of information that most patients do not find useful.* **The**

---

[52] Davis, T., 1996 "Parent Comprehension of Polio Vaccine Information Pamphlets," *Pediatrics*, Jun;97(6 Pt 1):804-10. PMID: 8657518

*number of concepts per pamphlet should be limited.
Pamphlet authors should **determine the key points** that the
patient or parent needs to know **to achieve the behavioral
objectives.** Nonessential concepts can be deleted. The **key is
to write for the desired health behavior rather than for
high level knowledge.**"*

The main problem I see is that these sentiments also determine the
theology of those who write the medical school syllabus. From the
position of what I know now, I'm aghast at the encyclopedia of
essential concepts that were never taught to me in medical school,
and which I now find make the biggest difference for the patients in
my practice.

Those in the highest ivory tower positions have stated that anyone
who poses any doubts about vaccines is guilty of "**conspiratorial
thinking, denialism, low cognitive complexity in thinking
patterns, reasoning flaws, and a habit of substituting
emotional anecdotes for data**"[53]. The first time I saw such
accusations was in 2011 but, since then, there have been numerous
vaccine enthusiasts who have used the exact same language to
continue the attack against all doctors, parents, and media who
dare to question the accuracy of policy or information about
vaccines. It doesn't matter whether or not those parents' views are
well-founded, or whether those parents were compensated with
millions of dollars by the vaccine court for an injury to their child,
or themselves. It doesn't matter if growing numbers of doctors,
questioning the limited tools sanctioned by various advisory
committees, have legitimate concerns either. The concept that no
doubt can be allowed to exist, is my definition of "low cognitive
complexity in thinking patterns".

---

[53] Poland, G. A., and Jacobson, R. M., 2011 "The Age-Old Struggle against the
Antivaccinationists," *New England Journal Medicine*, 364:97-9, January 13,
2011. PMID: 21226573

Being of "low cognitive complexity in thinking patterns" is, in my opinion, a form of deadness, and is something that all doctors are expected to do, in order to stay within the narrow lines of accepted practice. It's little wonder many doctors feel like technicians; pushing buttons and pulling toggles in a pre-ordered sequence, like a marionette, much of the time.

It is preferred that doctors keep any conspiratorial thoughts to ourselves, and remain in our caskets among the graveyard of highly trained medical zombies who, every year, create **MORE** sick and wounded patients through preventable medical errors and 'correctly' prescribed drugs, so-called 'curative' procedures, and medically induced secondary infections, than were once created by all the infectious diseases of childhood, put together.

Stranger In A Familiar Land

By January of 2013, I had moved to Virginia for its warm climate and some family who were established down there. I was the consultant family physician to friends of my sister. My duties were primarily related to the children and occasionally the wife, but not her husband Lazarus. However, in August 2014, Lazarus emailed me some test results ordered by his insurance company doctor and said, "When you get a chance, will you have a look at this and tell me what you think?"

Lazarus was 44 years of age and had no known medical problems. He had a very small potbelly, but was not obese or unfit by any standard. I knew the house was always kept around 64 degrees Fahrenheit, whether winter or summer, and that Lazarus was a sweaty guy, but he said he had been like that for years. He told me that a recent episode of food poisoning had left him really flat out, and lacking in energy but aside from that, he was strong and healthy. I also knew his wife wanted him to eat better, reduce the fast food, and think more of going gluten-free and sugar-free paleo, like she was feeding the rest of the family.

The labs were strange: signs of real diabetes, and not just a little hyperglycemic episode, with a HA1C of 7.4% (normal max 5.6%). Also his blood pressure was high on the insurance doctor's exam at around 140/100. His kidney function was normal but there was a small amount of protein in the urine. The EKG showed evidence of mild thickening of the left ventricular wall. I asked him a few questions about stress, given that he ran his own business. He said no stress, and had no idea what I could be talking about because he was happy. Hmm, I thought, well this is just bizarre.

I suggested he get the abnormal tests repeated to see if there were any changes and to verify the results were real. Some were repeated within a month but the HA1C and urine protein were not, so the repeat labs were not very helpful.

It looked like what is commonly called metabolic syndrome, but I was still uneasy about the diabetes numbers and why he would have that. I again suggested that the missing tests should be repeated in a month or so, and that he should consider getting a glucometer to check his own sugars.

He told me he thought he had white-coat hypertension to which I responded dubiously, since he had target organ effects in his heart and kidneys. Lazarus told me he had committed to starting an exercise regimen and eating gluten-free, and would see how that went. Then I went overseas for the winter. When I returned in June, I asked if he had the missing labs repeated and was told he had not. He said he was feeling better since losing a few pounds and being gluten-free. I subsequently never saw any repeat labs and figured they were dealing with it through the doctor who did the insurance physical.

But in August of 2015, at 9:30 PM, Lazarus' wife called in a bit of a panic to tell me that he was having a really rough day and that he had asked for me to go over and have a look at him. The guy lying in bed, breathing very rapidly and abnormally, was not the Lazarus I knew. His color was ashen-gray. His blood pressure was 190/100, and pulse was beating around 200 per minute and so rapid it was actually difficult to palpate. Aside from a hard non-tender abdomen with scant high-pitched bowel sounds, the rest of his exam was unremarkable. He told me that his symptoms began after drinking a Starbucks mocha latte coffee and he thought he was poisoned. He wanted to just stay put and sip on some Perrier, thinking this episode of 'food poisoning' would resolve just like the last one. He said that he felt like he just needed to relax and then he would be okay. We prayed together and he seemed to be doing a little better for a short time.

But I was still very concerned and not happy to leave. I sat at his bedside and watched him go in and out of sleep for about 20 minutes, noticing that he was intermittently apneic and groaning when he fell to sleep. Differential diagnoses like ischemic bowel, perforated viscus, sepsis, and all sorts of food-poisoning ideas were a reality. After all, I had seen firsthand what happened in a church with a pot of arsenic-laced coffee. His vital signs were becoming more concerning and because whatever was going on was not clear to me, I woke him up and suggested he go to the emergency room for an evaluation, just to be sure I was not missing something.

Lazarus slept the whole way, partly reclined in my passenger seat, and when we got there, he didn't want to wake up. He said, "Oh it just feels so good to sleep." I told him he could sleep again once we got inside. He dragged himself out of the car and slowly sauntered into the ER reception, Perrier in hand, and at the reception window Lazarus slouched into a chair. When asked why he was there, he offered "shortness of breath". The ER team immediately swept him into the cardiac evaluation room and began an admirably rapid investigation.

His vitals at midnight were the same as at home, but the oxygen level in his blood was too low. There was also a huge accumulation of acid in the blood, with severe hyperglycemia over 500 mg/dL.

The doctor came in to examine him and ask questions, but first was diverted by a happy, jolly talk about the fact that they both had kids in the same school. After the interview, I introduced myself as a physician and family friend, because she didn't ask the questions I thought were pertinent. She wanted to know if I worked at that hospital and I said no, that I was in private practice and a fully licensed, American Board of Internal Medicine certified specialist nephrologist in the states of Virginia and Maine. Even so, my opinion was simply brushed aside like soot.

The attending doctor must have thought Lazarus only had a bad case of food poisoning because, as she was walking out of the room, she nonchalantly said, "Okay, but you don't have any other medical problems like high blood pressure or anything, right?" I stopped her and said, "Actually yes, he was diagnosed with high blood pressure last year, and strangely his hemoglobin A1C was also 7.4 in February last year." She curtly retorted, "Oh but that doesn't have anything to do with what is going on today." I was stunned at her brush off and arrogant certitude. For a brief moment, I felt irritated that she was not considering the clinically pertinent history I had just given her. I went to my cell phone and forwarded the year-old labs, vitals, and EKG to her because she kept saying that the kidney failure could be old. I kept saying it was not long-standing because I had the proof—his kidneys were working normally the previous year with the exception of a small amount of protein leakage. This kidney failure was new.

She was in a hurry, and besides the schmoozing with Lazarus, her focus seemed to revert to dealing with the orders and computer work that is obligatory for doctors today. A nurse came in and set up an IV in the hand, and another in the forearm. Adenosine, amiodarone, and saline were put through one IV to try to break the high heart rate, and 5% dextrose, insulin, sodium bicarbonate, and furosemide were administered through the other one.

Or so I thought. What I did not know, at the time, was that they ALSO administered the beta-adrenergic blocker, labetalol, in an attempt to slow the heart down and lower the blood pressure. I had watched lots of drugs going into Lazarus, but didn't know labetalol was one of them.

Although Lazarus was in distress at home, he did not have heart and lung shut down. Only after the labetalol, did the records chart Lazarus' accelerating downhill decline as his lungs and heart could no longer keep up with the additional drug-induced stress.

A highly competent phlebotomist from the pulmonary lab came in and, like a stealthy mosquito, gracefully drew a small amount of fresh blood from Lazarus' radial artery in the right wrist. He didn't even flinch. This is usually a painful procedure, made worse if a novice goes in fishing rather than having a good target aim. This phlebotomist was awesome, one of the best I've seen.

The lab results started trickling in and the doctors were having a hard time determining what the problem was. There were such severe metabolic derangements; it was hard to believe he walked himself into the hospital. The blood pH was barely compatible with life, which explained why the breathing was so fast. The attending doctor was clearly confounded and, when I asked what she thought, she half-jokingly said in frustration, "Why don't you have a look at these labs and see if you can figure it out." With a profound metabolic acidosis, and severe hyperglycemia, the acid and base derangement was becoming clearer. But Lazarus also had a huge lactic acid buildup, which was a bit confusing. The reason for that would become evident a short time later.

For now, there was a suspicion of ischemic bowel but no unifying diagnosis was forthcoming to any of us. It was certain that he needed insulin and sodium bicarbonate because the pH was so profoundly low. There were at least three obvious reasons for his acidosis: hyperglycemia, breathing fatigue, and kidney failure. But it still was not adding up. Acid was coming rapidly from somewhere else. Instead of stabilizing, Lazarus was getting worse.

Three ampules of bicarbonate were pushed into the vein and the insulin drip was continued. Still, there was barely any change in the pH at 7.1. Lazarus was tiring out quickly from breathing so fast for so many hours, and because he was tiring, more acid was going into his blood.

Because the belly exam was abnormal with distension and lack of normal bowel sounds, Lazarus was sent for a CT scan of the chest, abdomen, and pelvis. Sometimes, a CT can be thought of as a 'grope-a-gram' when used without distinct signs and symptoms, because it is just groping for any more clues. This CT was helpful though, because it showed a large mass, the size of a grapefruit, sitting where the left adrenal gland should be.

On hearing the CT scan results, the unifying diagnosis was instantly clear to me—a pheochromocytoma—the phantom that every nephrologist looks for, but almost never finds.

A pheochromocytoma puts out the equivalent of a category-five hurricane into the endocrine system, and it's deadly because it can intermittently secrete uncontrolled levels of catecholamines. Lazarus' problem was not food poisoning and neither was the episode the previous year. Possibly the chocolate and coffee from Starbucks, and a very strenuous day on his boat in the hot sun, had been enough to trigger the pheochromocytoma to bleed and release a cascade of adrenaline, the likes of Niagara Falls: this time pushing Lazarus to the limit.

It's not a tumor you want to leave undiagnosed and growing for a year. All the signs had been there but because the tests the previous year weren't repeated properly, the insurance doctors had missed it, and I missed it. In my intermittent chats with Lazarus, he was nonchalant because of having lost weight and feeling a little better.

Regret at not pushing harder for Lazarus to repeat the tests the insurance company ordered, and for not having forced a third repeat of the tests, flooded coldly through my brain and I face-palmed. This exemplifies why doctors should not allow a patient, who says they are feeling better, to brush off the idea of a proper physical examination and a complete history of present illness. Even if a doctor is only being consulted on the side, they should hound reluctant patients into getting a proper follow up.

And there it was, on the CT scan. I was told that the radiologist had seen a large mass on the adrenal gland, 6.9 x 6.1 x 8.5 cm, with a hemorrhagic core. I kept saying to the doctor, "Well, don't you think that it's a pheo?"

She ignored me, saying they needed to call in cardiology to make sure his shortness of breath was not cardiac in origin because his cardiac enzymes were elevated and his heart muscle was not contracting normally. I said, "But he is 44 years old and with pheo, the blood pressure alone is enough to stress the heart like that, plus his kidneys are beginning to shut down and that can raise the heart enzymes, which are not even that high." I also pointed out that he had just had a chemical stress test with the high blood pressure and heart rate of 200.

At 3 AM, the cardiologist showed up and did an echocardiogram. Then he jumped right to the plan of doing a cardiac catheterization, without taking much first-hand history at all. I tried to talk him out of it, saying, "Look, the CT scan and tests give a unifying diagnosis of pheo, so why expose him to the risk of the intravenous contrast when his kidneys are shutting down?" Looking right past me, he went to Lazarus and said, "We need to make sure you are not having a blocked heart artery and heart attack so I need to take you to the lab and do a cath." In disbelief, I watched that conversation like a bad dream. Nothing I said mattered to the cardiologist either. The CT scan results appeared to be secondary in everyone's thinking.

No one listened to me or connected the dots as I had. Instead, their well-trained cognitive complexity in thinking patterns deduced that this 44-year-old man was just having a garden-variety occlusion of the heart arteries, commonly known as a heart attack. I was told they would wait until later in the morning and make sure his kidneys were stable before doing the cath.

At around 4 AM, a different phlebotomist arrived. It was plainly obvious that the next blood gas was not likely to go well. The technician sauntered in; looking a little lost and more annoyed at having to be at work at all, and began pushing objects around the room, then setting up. She went into the wrist and no blood returned: a total miss. Then she came out and went in again, this time deeper. Lazarus winced and looked at me like, "Is this for real?" I hated feeling helpless but there was nothing I could do. She then began moving the needle all around inside the wrist, finally got into the artery, and left with the prize. But Lazarus was left with a throbbing right radial nerve as his reward.

After about two hours of telling him how good he looked compared to his worsening blood results, everything had deteriorated to the point where doctors began badgering him to get put onto a ventilator. This was not acceptable to Lazarus who looked at me in disbelief and panic, and asked what I thought. It was a tough call but I could tell he really didn't want to be paralyzed and vented so I advocated that they listen to him, hold off, and keep up with the bicarbonate.

Then the ER staff became hell-bent on putting in a nasogastric tube, just in case there was a lot of fluid in the stomach. Lazarus wasn't keen, so they made a false promise to him: stating that if they put a nasogastric tube into the stomach and didn't get out any fluid, they would take out the nasogastric tube, and that this maneuver could keep him off the ventilator. It was an outright lie but they knew they could use the threat of ventilation as leverage to get the nasogastric tube in.

At that point Lazarus would have done anything to stay off the ventilator, so he agreed. I was appalled at the technique used to stuff a stiff plastic tube into his nose and down his throat. They didn't use lidocaine gel and had no regard for his gagging and spasms, as they accidentally went into the trachea instead of the esophagus. The second attempt brought the tube out his mouth. At that point I'd had enough of buffoon-watching. I stepped in and said they needed to get a cup of water with a straw and insert the tube slowly and properly. I said, "I've done this a hundred times and I would never do it without a cup of water and the patient sipping on the straw to open the throat. Then you slip the tube past the open glottis as they swallow." After following my instructions, the tube went in fine with minimal pain and gagging. Lazarus was clearly overwhelmed by what must have felt like outright torture.

At 5:30 AM, after more verbal torment ("Don't you care? Don't you want to live? If you want to live you will let us paralyze you and put you on a breathing machine," and to his wife, "How do you get him to listen?") and badgering by the pulmonologist, Lazarus reluctantly agreed to be placed on a ventilator and into a medical coma. The stress, high sugars, inappropriate drugs, the beta-blocker, nasogastric tube, and two painful arterial blood gas sticks had pushed Lazarus to a point of exhaustion. He was no longer coping, and cardiopulmonary collapse was imminent if nothing else was done.

A beta blocker can be a potentially devastating death-threat for someone with a pheo. Labetalol had been started before the diagnosis was known, but worse, it continued to be administered **after** the pheo was found. It is well known that the beta-adrenergic blocker should **never** be started first with a pheo, because a blockade of vasodilatory peripheral beta-adrenergic receptors with unopposed alpha-adrenergic receptor stimulation can lead to a further elevation in blood pressure and worsening of heart and lung function. Beta blockers can be used later, but in a specifically controlled manner.

This was all classic hammer-and-nail medicine. Lazarus was lucky that all that happened was that he was placed on the ventilator.

By 6:30 AM, everything seemed settled down enough. I had spoken to all of the doctors and been over the lab work, so decided to go back to my friends' house where I was pet-sitting for the week to deal with dogs who had been alone over 10 hours. I also needed to sleep and planned to return in a few hours. I told the doctors that once the blood pressure and heart were stable, his kidneys would improve and because his acids would be controlled by giving insulin, IV bicarbonate, and being mechanically ventilated, he didn't need dialysis.

But once again, nothing I said mattered. As soon as I walked out the door at 7 AM, they immediately performed the unnecessary and dangerous heart catheterization, in the middle of an endocrinologic storm and impending kidney shutdown, having said they wouldn't do that. Lazarus' wife then texted me, stating that he was now being put on dialysis. I couldn't believe it.

Later in the morning, Lazarus was transferred by helicopter to a large tertiary medical center for more specialized care.

Those doctors corroborated the diagnosis of pheo, and that the dialysis was unwarranted. In addition to it being unnecessary, dialysis is something a person with a pheo can do without because it causes huge amounts of reactive oxidative stress and hemodynamic instability, which is actually harmful to kidneys, and which could have made things much worse. Fortunately, Lazarus stabilized anyway.

After a few days on a ventilator and given the proper drugs, Lazarus' vital signs and kidneys normalized. More tests were done to verify the pheo, and after coming off the ventilator, Lazarus was sent home to regain some strength before the major surgery that would remove the mass. When I saw him at home, he did indeed look like a man raised from near death, complete with holes in his groins and neck, from large venous and arterial catheters, that he said still really hurt.

He handed me a copy of his files. I settled down to read them and it was then that I saw that labetalol had been used, and probably precipitated Lazarus' subsequent sudden clinical deterioration, and was continued even after the pheo was suspected.

The cardiologist was blinded by his irrational need to rule out coronary artery disease. Both the dialysis treatment and the heart catheter were unwarranted, but that is how automaton medicine works. The overbooked specialist is called. They see the one body part they are expert in, do the procedure they know how to do, and then get out as quickly as possible, so they can return to the office or dialysis unit and take care of all that is waiting for them there.

Lazarus and his wife were happy that things turned out okay. I was still smarting at the unnecessary, invasive, and potentially dangerous procedures, as a result of being ignored by the hospital physicians. Lazarus and his wife understood my frustration and forgave me for not pushing hard for further testing or thinking of a pheo a year before. I have yet to forgive myself, however. We were all lucky. The surgery went very well and despite a huge scar about 12 inches long over the left flank, Lazarus is back to normal after a month of postoperative wound drainage and infection. The diabetes and high blood pressure have gone, his heart function is perfect, and he is considered tumor-free thanks to two amazingly precise and meticulous women surgeons.

So now, one might ask why I put this story into this book. It's not just because I was blown off by doctors at the potential cost of my friend's life. For many years, I was a teaching professor whose job was to help young nephrologists see the bigger picture, so that patient safety was paramount. Through my professorial eyes, I watched a friend of mine suffer because doctors in a small community hospital had lost the ability to correctly put together a unifying diagnosis, and were ignoring the obvious. They were unable to accept a diagnosis arrived at by someone else, who was trained appropriately and put all the pieces together correctly.

Instead, they looked at the body through their specialty parts and hoped someone else would take ultimate responsibility for whatever the underlying cause was.

The minute I walked out the door, a dialysis plan was started, even though to my face everyone agreed that it didn't need to be done. The nephrologist, who didn't even show up until the dialysis was started, was educated 20 years after me. He probably never had the advantage of someone like the great Dr. Charlie Swartz, who out of concern that nephrologists were becoming automatons, made sure we were extensively and broadly educated.

Something is seriously missing in that nephrologist's global medical education, which makes him a risk to the patient and the profession.

Dialysis was done to Lazarus in order to supposedly save time and get things over with.

If Lazarus had been my hospital patient, I would have set the plan to keep the correct drips going, and then approached accordingly with caution. The heart catheter and dialysis would not have been done. An alpha blocker, which would have made a difference in his heart, would have been started and the ventilator would probably not have been needed.

Lazarus' family and I were relying on doctors to come to a safe diagnosis, and to be patient advocates as well. Because I was there, Lazarus' wife understood that things were not going as they should have, which was very distressing for her.

The reason why medical treatment can have the potential to go so badly, is that doctors know that uninformed family are essentially a captive audience with little say or ability to assess a doctor's fitness to practice. This is perhaps one reason why the numbers of annual hospital deaths from preventable medical error in the USA are so high. If all family members knew the difference between correct or incorrect diagnosis and treatment, perhaps doctors might take more time and think more carefully. But that will never happen. So families sit and watch, holding their breath and wondering what is going to happen next. Fortunately, for some patients, they live—in spite of the mistakes made. And for doctors, fatal errors are often buried with the patients, without the family even realizing it.

Why do doctors make potentially fatal errors? Because most of the time, just like when I was a resident, automaton medicine is practiced on the spur of the moment. Your 'training' just kicks in. When doctors don't think about what they do, and the physiological rationale behind it, the potential for harm is always there.

One area of ignorance, which I recognized even as a hospital nephrologist, is the giving of prescription drugs without regard to the human microbiome. We like to think that antibiotics will just fix a problem, but when they also destroy good flora in the gut, lung, vagina, and skin, other microbes can fill those spaces and cause serious disease. The logical approach to the problem is to protect the human microbiome while, at the same time, pushing out the suspected rogue pathogen. But so often, the antibiotics destroy good colonies, and often don't even eliminate the original pathogen.

Destruction of the microbiome can have huge consequences for adults. The ramifications can be even more dire, however, at the start of life: when the microbiome has a very specific role in educating the immune system.

50 The Microbiome Miracle

The undeniable scientific reality is that the microbiome consists of complex communities of biota (bacteria, viruses, and fungi) that are an essential element of the immune system, and life itself. No ecosystem could survive without it. Every year more 'essential' facets of the microbiome are being fleshed out. A person's immune development, and their physical and mental health, depends on bacteria, viruses, and fungi all living in balance with each other.

There have been huge gains in the ability to measure different parts of the microbiome and the insight into mitochondrial health and disease—just for starters. PubMed contains a growing body of knowledge for a huge array of potentially wonderful treatment possibilities. The medical system could choose to use that knowledge to develop real health in newborns, and all patients, which would go a long way to fulfilling my original dream.

While some of this research is brilliant in its fundamental concepts, the problem I see is that the conclusions and concepts are often perverted by corporate manacles. Most researchers are forced to compromise both the focus and the goals of their research in a bid for money. Funding applications, for limited dollars, are a competition between researchers and tainted by the ever-present demands from those who hold the purse strings and ask, "What's in it for me?" Drug companies expect an eventual return, which forces the researcher to take something valuable and turn it into a golden-egg-laying goose for the stockholders.

317

Pregnancy, and the first two years of life, lay down a crucial foundation for adult health and longevity. The immune system of an octogenarian is, in many respects, determined by how well that person was nourished in utero and the microbiome development during pregnancy and the first two years of life.

Babies receive their first round of microbiome while gestating. Then, as the baby descends the birth canal, it picks up a second and very important dose of the mother's vaginal microbiome, which continues the process of colonizing that baby through the mouth, nasopharynx, and down to the intestines. Breast-milk bacteria provide dose number three, which carries on the chain of proper seeding and microbiome growth. Colonization is different in vaginally vs. c-section-born babies.

Ideally, the baby receives the second round of microbiome from the mother's vagina, and not from hospital workers' hands or the mother's skin after a c-section. C-section babies are susceptible to a range of metabolic and immune disorders, which in part have to do with abnormal microbial colonization that occurs on day one.

On the basis of work done in animals, which proved the principle of microbial seeding, scientists have experimented with immediately seeding newborn c-section babies with the mother's vaginal flora. They report that the microbiome can be partially restored at birth in those c-section babies. When I read the article by USA mainland and Puerto Rican researchers, I was glad to see that what is common sense to many had arrived on the laboratory bench to be blessed by the hand of science.[54]

But soon after the paper was published, a group of scientists from the UK and Australia cautioned against the practice of seeding the

---

[54] Dominguez-Bello M. G., et al., 2016 "Partial restoration of the microbiota of cesarean-born infants via vaginal microbial transfer," *Nature Medicine*, Mar;22(3):250-3. PMID: 26828196

newborn with bacteria it would have received in a normal birth! I was astonished. In one of the most shortsighted obstetric statements ever, Cunnington et al., stated that *"There is not yet sufficient evidence to recommend the procedure, and more importantly, because there are potential risks associated with the transmission of known pathogens."*[55]

Why do I consider the statement daft? Because we know that natural birth is crucial for the microbiome seeding of the mucous membranes and is instrumental to setting in motion the correct adaptive programming of the neonatal immune system. A c-section changes and undermines microbiome programming, and has its own inherent 'potential risks', which appear to be acceptable to doctors like Cunnington. To make a blanket statement and withhold seeding from all women, just because a tiny percentage test positive for either herpes or Group B strep, is astonishing.

Why then, is it considered 'safe' for doctors to routinely prescribe antibiotics, and other drugs, which alter the microbiome and can seriously impact the way the immune system works?

Why is supplying the baby with the vaginal microbial seeding it would have received, had it been born vaginally, bad for babies? To imply that it is NOT okay, aligns with the same type of limited cognitive complexity that agrees with NOT giving babies the placental and cord blood that belongs to them!

Very little is actually understood about vaginal symbionts, or the impact of the microbiome, as a whole. What experts call pathogens, are only 'potential' pathogens. Group B strep (which obstetricians live in fear over) affects less than 1% of babies whose mothers happen to be carrying it, and the carriage of strep B is often transient. You can be tested for it and not have it, yet a week later,

---

[55] Cunnington A. J., et al., 2016 "Vaginal seeding of infants born by caesarean section," *British Medical Journal*, Feb 23;352. PMID: 26906151

have it, and assume you don't have it. And, because most babies aren't affected by strep B, who would be any the wiser?

Some maternal infections can lead to preterm birth. While intrauterine infection and inflammation is important in understanding the etiology of preterm birth, relatively few studies have examined the uterine microbiome of healthy, full-term pregnancies owing to the false sterile-womb paradigm that persists despite mountains of growing evidence to the contrary. Bacterial existence in healthy human infants has been verified at the level of umbilical cord, amniotic fluid, fetal membranes, meconium, and placenta[56]. Bacteriophobia persists among doctors, despite evidence that all babies are exposed to intrauterine microbes before birth, and during birth. Microbes are a normal essential part of immunity and proper brain function[57]. It's time conventional medicine caught up with the facts.

Throats of normal healthy babies are colonized with haemophilus influenzae type b, group A beta-hemolytic streptococci, strep pneumoniae, and staph aureus.[58] In countries where antibiotics are used as a matter of convenience (for the doctor) for any infection, the rates of antimicrobial resistance are rising. Those 'potentially pathogenic' bacteria just so happen to help keep each other and everything else in balance, and most 'normal' throat swabs contain all of them at one time or another, in addition to the dreaded Neisseriae.

---

[56] Funkhouser, L. J., and Bordenstein, S. R., 2013 "Mom knows best: the universality of maternal microbial transmission," *PLoS Biology*, 11(8). PMID: 23976878

[57] See also my video on infant immunity at http://tinyurl.com/l2trzqj

[58] Berkovitch, M., et al., 2002 "Colonization rate of bacteria in the throat of healthy infants," *International Journal of Pediatric Otorhinolaryngology*, Mar 15;63(1). PMID: 11879925

In the gut, E. coli is potentially pathogenic, but it and other potentially pathogenic species are vital for synthesis of certain nutrients. Toss an antibiotic cluster bomb into the body and you can totally mess with the gut synthesis of vitamins B and K. That's just the tip of the knowledge iceberg. To arbitrarily decide what is a pathogen, when so little is known about the 'microbiome community effect' is ignorant and short sighted.

Many procedures in labor and delivery work against the best interests of the child, like cord clamping, yet experts do it anyway. Precautionary approach doesn't apply there! Similarly, it is still considered normal, in 2016, to toss antibiotics into pregnant women as if they are safe—yet mimicking normal fetal colonization at birth is considered dangerous.

Why are experts blind to physiological normality and the 'right' way to birth babies, while compulsively needing to control everything? Why does the medical system, which knows so little about any microbiome in context of both the balance and working of the whole body, think that the only views that are important are their own? Does this 'pathogenic' mindset—that seeding isn't a good idea—imply that all babies should be born by c-section and seeded with a standardized, patented microbiome, approved by 'experts', on the basis that maybe mothers may be carrying potential pathogens? And in spite of these experts' own insufficient knowledge and understanding of what is actually normal inside a microbiome?

Seeding a baby, born by caesarian to a mother without pathogens, is a natural form of probiotic supplementation. The use of probiotics is crucial for all age groups.

Anyone who has done the biological and historical research knows that natural probiotics are very valuable. I understand, and have experienced, the benefits that traditional foods such as kefir and sauerkraut confer to the body. Both hold affordable keys to many of today's most common health issues.

The medical system knows this and has been studying probiotics for a long time: isolating one or a few probiotics out of a balanced eco-system, in order to satisfy the patent demands of the company sponsoring the work. This has resulted in contradictory results, of course, because probiotics never 'work' in isolation. Such strategies enable researchers to secure life-long funding, while producing drugs and supplements, with limited applications, rather than looking at the bigger picture and endorsing a way of life that has historically been proven to work, and which could result in immediate improved health today.

Conventional medicine has effectively enabled microbiome destruction through the indiscriminate use of drugs (not just antibiotics!) so that, these days, hospital patients are at very high risk of nasty pathogens such as Clostridium difficile, MRSA, VRE, and new drug-resistant pathogen overgrowth, which result in serious potential health issues, and can be almost impossible to resolve. Yet the answer is sitting right on the seats of doctors' chairs.

Have you ever heard of fecal transplantation? About 15 years ago, there were isolated rumblings in the medical literature over how to treat the worst drug-induced bacterial-overgrowth intestinal problems. As a last ditch effort, someone thought of taking the stool from a healthy person who had not had antibiotics, and transferring it into the sick person's intestines. It was sometimes jokingly, but realistically, termed as the 'one-use blender' treatment for serious gut dysbiosis.

Around 2010, meaningful study and discussion about the microbiome really began to flourish, and the potential use of fecal transplantation became obvious. The simple procedure has provided real cures and hope for many patients who previously were left to die as a result of doctor-induced antibiotic napalming.

"FMT's [fecal microbial transplantation] high cure rates of multiply recurrent CDI [C. difficile infection], 83% to nearing or at 100%, and reported safety supports the viability of FMT as an acceptable treatment method. In a recent systematic review, based on seven studies that represent the best available clinical research evidence on FMT for CDI, analysis concluded that most patients (83%) experience resolution of diarrhea immediately following the first FMT procedure."[59]

It seems clear from medical literature that fecal transplantation is a step in the right direction, but even here the arrogance of ignorance blazes out for those with eyes to see.

The people researching fecal transplants have difficulty with the fact that while it works in a very high percentage of patients for a variety of medical issues, they have no strict control over the biota species, the quantity, or sterility (facepalm). Researchers only perceive the need to take fecal transplants out of the visceral 'eeeuwwww' category, and to transform the currently 'crude' process, into a methodical, regulated captive market—using a standardized, patented, controlled product. Of course, this will come at a high cost. And the irony is that the necessity for fecal transplants has arisen, for the most part, because of standardized, patented, controlled 'gold standard' protocols and accepted medical treatments, in the first place.

Another irony is that, although these people still have only a skeletal understanding of the microbiome, they think that their limited knowledge entitles them to formulate new purified fecal

---

[59] Rohlke, F., et al., 2012 "Fecal microbiota transplantation in relapsing Clostridium difficile infection," *Therapeutic Advances in Gastroenterology*, Nov;5(6):403-20. PMID: 23152734.

gold standards, which they believe will work better than the current 'raw real deal'. Obviously, there is a need to make sure that the fecal donor is healthy. That's a no-brainer. Particularly when there are now very few people in the world who haven't had their gut flora damaged to some degree by antibiotics, foods, and drugs.

Considering how the system treats alternative practitioners, it's also ironic that if fecal transplantation was performed initially by natural practitioners, using the current anecdotal plausibility criteria, then mainstream medicine would have taken them to court and imprisoned the lot of them under the guise of being a danger to human health, because they had "limited cognitive complexity in thinking patterns".

Patenting certain pharmaceutical brands of bacteria will never be the same as transplanting an already functioning complex microbiota from one person to another. Many new viruses and non-cultivable bacteria are being found all the time. Without a complete understanding of the whole system, we can't reproduce it. Taking a part of a functioning system from one healthy person and putting it into a recipient, is probably the best practice given the limitations of current knowledge.

If only conventional medicine understood this enough to cease giving random antibiotic cluster bombs to pregnant women, babies, and children: bombs that wipe out these beneficial bacteria, viruses, and fungi as if everything will quickly grow back just the same. Medical literature shows that once you wipe out a human microbiome with the first dose of antibiotics, it is almost impossible to get it back to what it was before.[60]

---

[60] Jernberg, C., et al., 2010 "Long-term impacts of antibiotic exposure on the human intestinal microbiota," *Microbiology*, Nov;156(Pt 11):3216-23. PMID:20705661

Try tossing a bottle of bleach into your garden and see how fast the microbes in the soil return to pre-bleach levels. Then consider the effect of doing this every six months, or more, to a human body, which is at a disadvantage to the garden. Why? A garden has a better chance of replenishing than a body does, because it's impossible to really sterilize soil unless it's put on a synthetic sterile surface and isolated in a glass house. Inside a living body, however, we know that antibiotics can totally destroy good flora in a limited area and, because there isn't always a joined area with the same healthy microbiome, replenishment often doesn't happen. Giving antibiotics to one member of the family can result in resistant bacteria that spread and infect other family members. Most doctors know not to put harsh cleaning products into their gardens but don't think twice about tossing the 'just in case' antibiotics or repeated courses of non-curative antibiotics, into a human. Most of them never even wonder about an alternative, or perhaps cultivating a healthy ecosystem to push out the perceived enemy, instead of killing off everything in sight.

Turning fecal transplantation into a standardized one-size-fits-all marketable product ignores everything these researchers already know, which is that every individual has their own biochemical uniqueness.

Standardization, once again, locks the medical profession into a one-size-fits-all 'gold standard' empire, which is solely focused on pharmaceutical returns and lorded over by a select few.

It's the same sort of mentality that resulted in the general attitude that immediate cord clamping is normal and that the blood left in the cord is useful for research, or banked, at a cost, in case a baby needs it later. The concept that cord blood has vital physiological and repair functions within a baby's body, doesn't enter the minds of a lot of obstetric staff.

I am willing to testify and offer proof that immediate cord clamping at birth causes attention deficit disorders, learning disabilities, behavioral disorders, mental retardation, respiratory distress syndrome, and intraventricular hemorrhage, and cerebral palsy.

~G. M. Morley, MB, ChB, FACOG, August 29, 2001

Childbirth: Issues Of Blood

While living in Virginia in 2014, I started studying neonatal physiology relating to birth and the development of the immune system, in order to better understand some of the problems that babies have. One of the first things I studied was physiological fetal circulation changes at birth: when a baby changes from an effectively two-compartment heart to a functional four-chambered heart. What really goes on inside a baby in the first 15 minutes of extra-uterine life is something many doctors either don't know much about, or don't really care about after learning it in embryology. This process is essential, so that the baby begins to breathe and its lungs become responsible for bringing in its own oxygen, instead of the mother's blood providing oxygen. During obstetrics training, we were simply taught to immediately clamp and cut the cord — a process that had always seemed wrong to me.

Up until 2014, most of what I knew in terms of natural birth came from my experiences in Nicaragua and Guatemala.

Immediate clamping of the umbilical cord violates every fundamental principle of normal cord closure physiology. In 1899, the original clamp was created to keep the sheets from getting a few drops of blood on them. Such a trivial problem raises the question of, 'What about all the mothers who ripped the perineum, or bled before the placenta was delivered?' Everyone has read old-time novels where just about every second woman seemed to bleed to death after birth. Really? Presumably, those delivering babies must have had methods of delivering the placenta without routinely cascading the bed with blood, except for the minority who hemorrhaged.

The first clamp patent explicitly stated not to apply it until the cord had stopped pulsing.

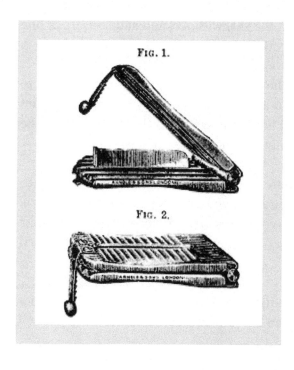

FIG. 1.

FIG. 2.

*"In the old method of dividing the umbilical cord the accoucheur after tying the first thread pressed the blood in the vessels some distance along the cord which was then held by an assistant until the second thread was tied, the object being to avoid the **escape of blood on to the bed-clothes**. This part of the accoucheur's work may, however, be accomplished more conveniently by making use of a clamp which I have designed and which is represented open in Fig. 1 and closed in Fig. 2, for it by the same movement cuts the cord and compresses both the cut ends, thereby supplying the place of scissors and ligatures. The clamp having been opened, the cord **when it has ceased to pulsate** is placed between the blades, resting on the plain side; the knifed edge is then pressed firmly down and retained in position by the catch. The*

clamp is removed a few seconds after application, and if the accoucheur is afraid of haemorrhage (although French authorities say there is no need for ligatures) he can tie the cord on either side of the clamp before releasing the catch. The instrument is neat and easy to use. Messrs. Arnold and Sons, London, are the makers."[61]

~Edward Magennis, MD

When my senior obstetrics resident in medical school told me that, if we didn't immediately clamp the cord then the blood would run out of the baby and back into the placenta, it made no sense. But it never occurred to me to wonder who runs around all the other mammals, on land and in the sea, with a clamp and scissors in one hand and a vitamin K injection in the other.

What I was taught was the 'see one, do one, teach one' of when to clamp, how not to make a bloody mess everywhere, how to let daddy feel involved, and how to move on to the next issue on the checklist as fast as humanly possible.

Unfortunately, immediate cord clamping is still considered to be normal in most hospitals. If you are very lucky, the obstetric staff will wait 30 or maybe 60 seconds before the ants in their pants cause them to snap on the cord clamps and cut the cord between them.

In 1957, Gunther[62] measured that immediate clamping deprived a baby of anywhere between 100-200 ml of blood.

The average total amount of blood in the placenta and cord is 166 ml[63], of which 115 belongs to the baby. So when the cord is clamped

---

[61] Magennis, E., 1899 "A Midwifery surgical clamp," *Lancet*, May 20; 153(3951):1373.

[62] Gunther, M., 1957 "The transfer of blood between baby and placenta in the minutes after birth," *Lancet*, Jun 22;272(6982):1277-80. PMID: 13440024

immediate, the baby misses out on roughly one-third of its final blood volume and 60%[64] of its final red blood cell volume.

So in a 4,000-gram baby, immediate cord clamping results in a total blood volume of 280 ml inside the baby. A three-minute delay results in a volume of 360 ml. Longer delays than that can add in another 50-plus ml, which pulses in at a slightly slower pace than the volume transferred in the first three minutes.

When parents or birth attendants do nothing at all with the cord and wait until it's flat, white, and hard, the hemoglobin levels of these babies are much higher than clamped babies.

During the stressful event of being born, a baby's oxygen level can dip to 60%, so, if the clamp is not applied, this infusion of oxygenated blood from the placenta, keeps oxygen saturations in the baby raised over the timeframe of three to 10 minutes.

This placental and cord blood transfusion is also important for effective heart-blood flow transition, and the efficient changeover from the fetal to the child circulation. The blood that the baby is deprived of through immediate cord clamping might also prevent various health problems from happening, both short and long term.

The range of what is considered normal hemoglobin levels in babies born in a hospital, is determined by averaging out the hemoglobin after either immediate cord clamping or maybe 30–60, or however many, seconds later. In the UK[65], normal values are

---

[63] Buckels L. J., et al., 1965 "Cardiopulmonary effects of placental transfusion," *The Journal of Pediatrics*, August Volume 67(2):239-247.

[64] Rabi, Y., et al., 2006 "Oxygen saturation trends immediately after birth", *The Journal of Pediatrics,* May;148(5):590-4. PMID:16737866

[65]http://wps.prenhall.com/wps/media/objects/354/362846/London%20App.%20B.pdf

14.7–18.6 grams/dL for newborn boys and 12.7–18.3 for girls. In New Zealand[66], the Auckland District Health Board considers 16.8 the median, and one USA website[67] quotes 14–20 with 17 being the optimal level.

However, hemoglobin levels of 23–25 grams/dL (230-250 grams/L) in non-clamped babies are not unusual. When cords are clamped immediately, babies have significantly lower levels of hemoglobin, red blood cells, and albumin, in comparison with unclamped babies.

The reason the hemoglobin levels are higher in babies without clamped cords is not just because they got the 'extra' blood from the placenta.

A cascade of events maximizes the baby's blood thickness. If you do not clamp the cord, the infused placental volume that the baby receives diminishes over the space of four hours by virtue of fluid movement out of the vascular space flushing through tissues. Any excess is then excreted into the urine.

After the diuresis, the blood viscosity rises (thickens) because the plasma colloid, albumin, and blood cells remain in the blood vessels. This increased plasma colloid osmotic pressure is a survival strategy that helps keep the lungs dry. A wet diaper soon after birth is evidence that the baby has had a decent placental transfusion[68], with the subsequent normal fluid movement, and the right hemodynamics to close off the valves that are no longer needed in the fetal circulation.

---

[66]http://www.adhb.govt.nz/newborn/Guidelines/Blood/HaematologicalValues.htm

[67] http://www.cprworks.com/Labvalues.html

[68] Oh, W., et. al., 1966 "Renal function and blood volume in newborn infant related to placental transfusion," *Acta Pediatrica Scandinavica*, Mar;55(2):197-210.

The current so-called normals of newborn hemoglobin levels, and the use of vitamin K, were established at a time when most babies had their cords clamped, immediately depriving them of a significant volume of blood.

There is also a blanket assumption among obstetricians and neonatologists that all babies need vitamin K. Am I saying that low vitamin K issues are non-existent in infants? No, because a tiny minority of babies can suffer as a result of mothers who ignore or have no idea about vitamin K-rich foods, just as deficiencies of vitamins D, A, C, B, folate, and iron in utero and after birth, can also have consequences for the baby. If a mother isn't eating enough vitamin K during pregnancy, the chances are that other vitamins and minerals are also absent. Vitamins K, C and D are also crucial for a baby's bone development and growth, so every mother should have a clear understanding of her baby's metabolic needs, both in utero and when they are being fed. Physician education on these subjects is sparse, so mothers usually have to be self-educated.

A few mothers who have frank vitamin K deficiencies, or who take medication like warfarin or seizure medication during pregnancy, can have babies who have bleeding issues at birth and need vitamin K.

Vitamin K-refusing parents need to remember that their babies may have had enough at birth, but if busy mothers are only eating easy carbs, processed and junk food on the run, and ignoring vitamin K-containing foods, then their babies can have late-onset hemorrhagic disease as a result, starting weeks or months after birth.

Infant formula has vitamin K in it, which is why late-onset hemorrhagic disease shouldn't be an issue in formula-fed babies. Even so, formula is not the same as human milk, which is an immunologic and developmental programming organ, in itself.

For the majority of well-educated mothers, vitamin K bleeding problems in their babies should not even be an issue.

However, as the medical authorities who make the recommendations will be quick to tell us, vitamin K-deficient bleeding has increased in babies in the era that women have become more enlightened about ditching formula in lieu of their own dairy bars. It's actually true that forward-thinking, breast-feeding mothers' infants are statistically at higher (albeit miniscule) risk of such vitamin K deficiencies than formula-feeding mothers. That's all mothers will be told though, because that's pretty much all doctors know.

The issues, though, may not be solely related to nutrition. Did you know that the food additive, antioxidant butylated hydroxytoluene (BHT), produces a deficiency of K-dependent factors? It is found in hydrogenated vegetable oils, margarine, carbonated drinks, ice cream, dry breakfast cereals, cheese spread, fried snack food, and commercially baked goods. Mothers need to review the everyday convenience foods that are easy to gravitate to—not only because they may be low in vitamin K, but because they may contain ingredients that can lower the vitamin K-dependent clotting factors too.

Other liver-damaging compounds such as PCBs (polychlorinated biphenyls) PCDDs (polychlorinated dibenzo-p-dioxins, and PCDFs (polychlorinated dibenzofurans) can cause severe vitamin K deficiency[69], and prolong clotting time. They also pass into breast milk, and can do likewise in babies.

Maybe vitamin K depletion is not just an issue because mothers breast-feed more today than they did in the 1960s and 1970s. Glyphosate is getting some well-deserved negative press lately, and it fits right into this discussion. It is well-published that glyphosate

---

[69] Koppe, J. G., 1995 "Nutrition and breastfeeding" *Eur J. Obstet Gynecol Reprod Biol* Jul; 61(1):73-8. PMID: 8549852

(Roundup) binds to the compound 5-enolpyruvoylshikimate-3-phosphate synthase (EPSPS) in the shikimate pathway. EPSPS is a key enzyme involved in aromatic amino acid biosynthesis. The EPSPS reaction is the penultimate step in a crucial pathway for the biosynthesis of aromatic amino acids and many secondary metabolites, including tetrahydrofolate, ubiquinone, and vitamin K[70]. Furthermore, many other biologically active molecules, including serotonin, melatonin, melanin, epinephrine, dopamine, thyroid hormone, folate, coenzyme Q-10, vitamin K, and vitamin E, depend on the shikimate pathway metabolites as precursors. Gut bacteria and plants use the shikimate pathway exclusively to produce these amino acids. In part, because of shikimate pathway disruption, our gut bacteria are harmed by glyphosate, as evidenced by the fact that it has been patented as an antimicrobial agent[71]. Clearly, glyphosate poses dangers, which grandparents of the past never needed to consider.

Doctors therefore, need to tell their pregnant and lactating patients that not only should they be consuming plenty of leafy greens and broccoli, but these should be organically grown. If a mother cannot do this, then the mother can take a daily oral vitamin K supplement.

[70] Alibhai, M. F., 2001 "Closing down on glyphosate inhibition—with a new structure for drug discovery," *Proceedings of the National Academy of Science of the United States of America*, Mar 13;98(6):2944-6. PMID:11248008

[71] Samsel, A., and Seneff, S., 2015 "Glyphosate, pathways to modern diseases III: Manganese, neurological diseases, and associated pathologies," *Surgical Neurology International*, Mar 24;6:45. PMID: 25883837

Eden And Arthur

Comparatively low hospital pediatric 'normals', and attendant misconceptions, have the potential to create nightmares for some parents whose babies' cords are not clamped at all. Doctors don't realize they are dealing with a different physiology in babies who have higher hemoglobin levels than the upper end of the so-called 'normals'. This can result in problems; informed parents are subjected to harassment when they don't want to automatically comply with hospital 'gold standards'.

Recently I was an audience to two incidents that highlight some misconceptions surrounding cord clamping and blood clotting.

These two educated and well-informed mothers had ideals that differed from conventional medical practices on some key points. As a result, neither baby had their cord clamped until it was white and hard. Neither mother wanted the vitamin K injection to the baby, either. Both mothers mainly came to ask for clarification on microbiome and clotting issues.

The first mother contacted me because she had issues with the medical mindset. She was a home-birth mother and had recently birthed her fourth baby. The newborn baby girl, Eden, had a very significant hormonally mediated uterine bleeding[72], which started

---

[72] This phenomenon occurs in about 25% of newborn girls, but is only obvious in about 3.3% of them. The bleeding is considered physiologic and not pathologic. It comes from the mother's hormones being rapidly withdrawn after months of stimulation on the infant's uterus. PMID: 973490

hard on the heels of meconium and lasted three days. She was obviously in abdominal discomfort and not too keen on feeding. Even an adult with menstrual cramps can appreciate that. I saw the diapers, and know the baby was bleeding quite a lot.

The midwife went into instant panic and harassed the parents about the Guthrie test and vitamin K. When the Guthrie[73] test was done, the midwife had to prick Eden's left heel three times, and the right heel twice because, while she bled okay, the blood wouldn't soak through the test spots because it kept clotting too quickly. At the same time as the midwife was observing Eden screaming after five heel pricks and the blood clotting too fast, she was continually hounding the parents to have the vitamin K injection. They said no, so she left a vial of oral vitamin K with them as a reminder of what could happen.

The midwife harassed the parents about vitamin K every day. Because the parents continued to say no, she tried to involve the nearest Neonatal Intensive Care Unit, without parental permission, and the pediatrician determined that the baby should be admitted to the hospital. Again, the parents said no.

While this was going on, the midwife received notification that the Guthrie test had come back outside the normal range for a genetic disorder called fatty acid oxidation. However, they noted that there was too much clotted blood on the card and wanted to redo the test by the end of the first week. This was done and the test came back normal. So Eden was a physiologically healthy, normal baby who didn't need vitamin K, but because everything wasn't within the 'normal' perception of the eyes in the system, the family was put under serious emotional stress.

---

[73] Metabolic screening for potentially serious disorders such as phenylketonuria (PKU), cystic fibrosis, and congenital hypothyroidism.

What I saw though, was a mother almost pummeled into submission by a medical professional who had an inability to think for herself, or cope with anything outside of 'normal'. The midwife also didn't know that macroscopic uterine bleeding in a several days' old baby is a physiologic variant of normal, and happens to 3.3% of female newborns[74]. Why did a nephrologist know about hormone withdrawal bleeding in a female infant, but not a midwife? And, seemingly the hospital staff had the same perception disorder. Because the father had become a tiger, he continually stood watch between his wife and the medical profession and supported the mother's decisions.

Fortunately for the mother, the midwife went on vacation and her stand-in midwife was of a different temperament. She saw that the baby's uterine bleeding was slowing down and left the mother alone.

The next mother who contacted me had a slightly more complicated situation. Arthur was baby number three to a healthy 39-year-old New Zealand mother, who was very diligent in her home pregnancy care. She had refused any scans during pregnancy, but had three blood tests done to check that the usual things were on track.

Her first baby had been a spontaneous labor, and vaginal frank breech delivery. Her second, was a normal, head-down delivery in a birthing unit. Arthur was born at 12:02 PM, after a 10-hour labor, at the same birthing unit as her second baby. He was 39.6 weeks gestation, weighing 4,350 grams, and was born with the mother in a standing position, with hands-on support by the midwife. The baby

---

[74] Huber, A., 1976 "The frequency of physiologic vaginal bleeding of newborn infants," *Zentralbl Gynakol*, 98(16):1017-20.

came out shocked, and with an omphalocele[75]. With stimulation and free-flow oxygen, breathing was established within two minutes. In the next 40 minutes the baby was grunting, crying and had nasal flaring; the parents declined vitamin K, and breastfeeding was established successfully, with the mother on hand and knees over the baby to protect the covered omphalocele.

A hospital with a pediatric unit was contacted. The midwife was advised to wrap the baby's omphalocele and lower torso in plastic cling wrap, and clamp the cord at the placenta, and that the hospital would send an ambulance, to "retrieve" the baby—as stated in the records.

The placenta was delivered 52 minutes after the baby was born, after which the cord was clamped. By that time the cord was flat, white and hard, and was clamped at the placenta end, as requested by the hospital. The baby was again put to the breast for an extended feed.

The ambulance arrived two hours after the birth. Arthur's stomach was suctioned, and 10 ml of fluid was removed. In the newborn intensive care unit, he was put on broad spectrum antibiotics, and predictably, the parents were nagged about vitamin K. Blood work was taken, showing that the baby had a hemoglobin of 230 grams/L; well above the highest limit of normal. A coagulation screen was done, and the baby was slap bang in the middle of the stated range of normal, so there were no coagulation issues evident

---

[75] An omphalocele (exomphalos minor in this case) occurs in approximately 1 per 5,000 births, and is where some contents of the intestines protrude through a hole in the abdominal wall, but are contained within a balloon shaped two-layer amnionic-peritoneal membrane, which protects the intestinal contents from the amniotic fluid. The sac comes out of the hole where the umbilical cord should insert, and the umbilical cord inserts into the top of the membranes of the sac containing the intestines. In this baby's case, the sac only contained the large intestine, and not the small intestines or the liver.

on admission. Yet, the records clearly show that the next day, the only thing that seemed to matter to the clinical director of newborn services was the vitamin K. He wrote extensive notes on what was said to the parents, and their declination.

He was unsuccessful in his attempts and, after a further pediatrician confronted them about it, a bigwig pediatric consultant was sent in to likewise browbeat the parents, as evidenced by more, very detailed, hospital notes.

The parents challenged all specialists by pointing out his very high hemoglobin and red blood cell count, and the fact that during the heel prick test just done, the nurse had difficulty with blood that was clotting too quickly (that test also came back with a request to 'redo it please'). The parents argued that with blood clotting like this, he shouldn't hemorrhage, and it wouldn't matter if he lost a bit of blood during the operation since his hemoglobin was so high.

The parents asked for the APTT coagulation test to be done, which measures how quickly, in seconds, the blood clots. Vitamin K or not, either the blood clots at a normal rate or it does not. They were told by one of the specialists that such a test wouldn't be useful, yet he should have seen that the test the mother asked for was done the day before on admission and was perfectly normal. It was also stated that vitamin K used different pathways and they didn't have good normal values in a newborn, so a coagulation test wouldn't help direct management.

Of course this is nonsense: the APTT is a reasonable gauge as to vitamin K sufficiency, because clotting will not occur in a normal time period in the ABSENCE of vitamin K. Vitamin K is required for activation of factors VII, IX, X, and prothrombin. Any medical encyclopedia like *UpToDate*, gives accurate values on coagulation studies in newborns, so testing coagulation times is relevant.

One fact parents should be aware of, is that there is NO TEST that can gauge ACTUAL vitamin K deficiency in a baby. The only way to assess whether enough is present at birth, or not, is to check the coagulation profile, yet hospital staff stated this was supposedly not useful? Supposedly, the only way to treat a bleeding baby is to administer vitamin K and watch for the bleeding to stop.

Arthur passed all clotting parameters with flying colors and the surgeon was unconcerned about the parents declining vitamin K. In light of this, it's a total mystery why the pediatric specialists were relentless in their pressure. It must have been pretty harsh because a few days after, a nurse wrote in the notes, "Please do NOT mention vitamin K."

At 8:00 AM on his second day, the surgery was successfully completed. The procedure was uncomplicated with no transfusion required. The baby was back in NICU just after mid-day with no wound oozing.

The hemoglobin before surgery was 230 grams/L and after surgery was 217 grams/L, which is still well above the high end of normal. So the baby could afford to lose a few tablespoons of blood and plainly, declining vitamin K was not an issue. Antibiotics were stopped on day three.

The mother was very concerned about antibiotic-induced microbiome damage, as she understood that the ability of a baby to absorb nutrients and synthesize vitamin K is significantly affected by the microbiome. As a committed breastfeeder, she had been expressing and labeling her containers as colostrum and breast milk with sequential numbering. She was determined that her baby would get breast milk in the right order, so that her baby's gut could be properly prepared to accept food quickly and efficiently, and to give his microbiome the best possible start. Up until then the baby had had an IV infusion of 10% dextrose. The mother was extra vigilant about staff knowing her wishes, and

Arthur was discharged seven days after surgery because he was gaining weight and thriving.

The parents had stood their ground on two counts and the outcome cannot be argued with.

This case is of considerable interest to me for another reason.

In America, an omphalocele is usually confirmed during a scan after four months. Before four months, a sac outside the body is ignored because it's part of a physiological process. At around six weeks, the abdominal cavity can become too small to hold all the contents, resulting in protrusion of the intestines into the residual extra-embryonic coelom at the base of the umbilical cord. This is usually only temporary and is called a physiologic mid-gut herniation, and is usually seen in ultrasounds up to the 11th week. After that, the contents move back into the abdominal cavity and the umbilical cord seals normally. An omphalocele is simply the failure of the intestines to go back in. An omphalocele can be minor, as this one was, or major and include the small intestines and sometimes the liver.

'Gold standard' pregnancy management involves early detection, which marks the start of numerous scans, and usually a prolonged stress-inducing nightmare for the parents. They are immediately assigned to a high-risk obstetrician, a team of maternal-fetal medicine specialists, neonatologists, a pediatric surgical team, and a genetic counselor.

Then starts a grueling schedule of tests, tests, and more tests. Because an omphalocele is considered a mid-line genetic defect, the first tests run will be fetal genetic tests, amniocentesis testing (big needle into the pregnant uterus with a 1% mortality rate) for Beckwith-Wiedemann syndrome, and a fetal echocardiogram looking for associated heart defects.

Every three weeks the mother will be required to have a long ultrasound examination, which will look intimately at a lot of areas in the baby. Because fetal growth restriction and preterm delivery are not uncommon in pregnancies complicated by an omphalocele, ultrasounds become more frequent in the last trimester and after 36 weeks, weekly ultrasounds, nonstress testing and biophysical profile monitoring begin in earnest.

A caesarean delivery gives no survival advantage to a baby with a minor omphalocele, but the best a mother can expect with the medically managed model is an induction at 38 weeks. This is all planned in advance so that the retinue of 'experts' are on hand and ready to carry out their various 'plans'. However, a caesarean is often done, particularly if the omphalocele contents are considerable and the obstetrician feels that dystocia, rupture, infection or hemorrhage could occur during a vaginal delivery, and also if the sac has broken.

But the biggest problems for these babies often start after birth, and part of the reason for that is that the baby's microbiome is set back by the pre-and post-surgery antibiotics—usually cephalosporins, which impair intestinal vitamin K production. No attempt is made to address that problem, other than a vitamin K injection. The same gut microbiome destroyed by cephalosporins, also affects other synthesis pathways as well; also not part of any normal hospital management plan. Establishing feeding in these babies can be a potential nightmare, because the gut microbiome has not been prepared by the mother's flora, colostrum, and breast milk. Even if it was, continual antibiotics can render such methods ineffective.

In Arthur's case, he only had one more dose of antibiotics after surgery, and the mother was able to start the sequential process using colostrum the next day. But this is unusual. In America, the gold standard processes are so rigidly adhered to, and often babies with omphaloceles are in the hospital for weeks, if not months, and many are still being fed through a naso-gastric tube at discharge, even months later.

In America, in terms of what parents can expect, it's much the same as for gastroschisis, which is a more common and similar midline defect. The Seattle Children's Hospital has an explanatory video[76] on YouTube.

The UK has a similar one[77], which in some respects is worse.

My point is that we KNOW that omphalocele babies managed with the gold standard methods are often preterm and of low birth weight. Ironically, Arthur's hospital file has a list of 'problems', at the top of which was "large for gestational age".

Why might that be? Specialists might argue that low birth weight, associated with omphalocele, is part-and-parcel of the defect itself. I would argue that it is not necessarily so. Constant stress over several months can also result in intra-uterine growth retardation.

Arthur's mother refused all ultrasounds from the start of the pregnancy. She was not exposed to the encyclopedia of tests, and the stress of being scanned for this, that, and every other minute thing at each visit to the lead maternity caregiver. Arthur didn't live inside a uterus being constantly flooded with stress hormones by a mother who felt helpless and under helicopter management from every direction.

Arthur was assessed in the hospital for chromosomal abnormalities and nothing was found. He was also assessed with an echo-cardiogram and found to have a tiny ventricular septal defect of no

---

[76] Seattle university video on gastroschisis
https://www.youtube.com/watch?v=Npt_XbQXVMo

[77] UK video https://www.youtube.com/watch?v=gNPm-kccGtl

significance, which is expected to close by itself. Arthur did not suffer the sorts of intestinal problems that babies treated under 'gold standard care' would have, because his exposure to antibiotics was limited and his mother insisted on repairing that damage with carefully, sequentially collected breast milk and has committed to long-term breastfeeding.

What might be learned from Arthur's case? Will future medical educationalists bury their heads in policy, and use this case to reinforce into the minds of medical students that NO MOTHER should be allowed to reject pregnancy scans?

Will they learn that it's okay for a mother to choose her own pregnancy path?

Will they learn that their 'normals' for hemoglobin, and their attitudes to vitamin K, are not necessarily normal but simply reflect physiological medical mismanagement?

Will they learn that perhaps the skewing of neonatal microbiomes, and refusal to look at that aspect of omphalocele and gastroschisis management, contributes to the feeding problems we see on the Seattle video?

There is a lot of good that the system could learn from cases like Arthur's. The problem is that many practices or lead maternity caregivers won't provide care for a mother who refuses ultrasounds. It's a bit like practices that toss out families that won't vaccinate.

Also, there are very few omphalocele babies who have a mother with such a spine and focused determination within the hospital, so there aren't very many babies like Arthur with which to compare babies who are subjected to 'gold standard' hospital practice.

You can argue that Arthur's mother was just lucky: that it could have been worse and she could have had a dead baby if he had had an omphalocele major.

That could be true, but it is not what happened. For a parent who chooses not to have ultrasound testing and who is prepared to 'take that risk', I would argue that the outcome for Arthur was FAR BETTER than it would have been if his mother had been subjected to minutiae scrutiny and lived through 25 weeks of pregnancy in a constant state of emotional turmoil and testing. Is it possible that constant circulating cortisol in the mother being subjected to a gold standard omphalocele pregnancy, might itself result in intra-uterine retardation, a c-section, and antibiotic cluster-bombing?

Should Arthur's mother come to me for any advice with any future pregnancy, my only advice would be that if she were refused care, or constantly pressured in pregnancy for an ultrasound, to only allow one ultrasound, sometime after 34 weeks. Chances are it will be normal, and so allow the lead maternity caregiver to untangle their knickers.

Any possible doubts, whether or not well founded, about the safety of the vaccine cannot be allowed to exist.

~Federal Register, DHHS, FDA 1984

Stealth Bombs And Automorons

Doctors also have preconceived prejudices in another area: when they are confronted by parents saying their child experienced adverse effects after submitting their infants and children to vaccines. After listening to parents give first-hand testimony of their experiences, I have many questions about medical doctors, and in particular pediatricians.

It's interesting that, during a meningitis outbreak, parents will be told that if their guts tell them that their child is really sick, to take them to the hospital and be persistent, because at those times, parent's instincts are considered to be a clinically valuable indicator.

Yet, hypocritically, if the same parent considers that any vaccine caused a serious problem with their child, that parent now becomes viewed as a paranoid anti-vaccine threat to society.

Listening to adults tell me what they thought was wrong with their teenagers or children, who came to me with kidney issues or nebulous electrolyte disturbances, high blood pressure etc., always made my job way easier. To me, gathering every clue as to the path to illness from all possible sources in a person's life seemed like a good idea.

Doctors today are hell-bent on denying any vaccine as a cause for any adverse event because of their systematic brainwashing, and their lack of independent thought about what the medical literature says that vaccines can do within the body. I've seen temporally related seizures, headaches, high blood pressure, thrombocytopenia, projectile vomiting, depression, suicidality, oligoclonal bands in the spinal fluid test of a girl with new hippocampal enlargement, prolonged screaming, withdrawing from other people, loss of eye contact, and death, among the symptoms adamantly denied by other doctors as potentially associated with a vaccine.

The medical records show these children were well until the vaccines were administered, and then regressed or became ill within hours or days afterwards. Yet, the universal sound bite is, "It is definitely not the vaccine." Where do doctors learn this? How do they know? As doctors, we are told that any drug at any time can cause an allergic reaction and that all drugs have some potential side effects . . . but not vaccines?

Worse yet, when a person is injured by a vaccine, the doctor will go to great lengths testing for all sorts of sundry possible diseases, not related to a vaccine. I reviewed the file of a boy with multiphasic disseminated encephalomyelitis after a meningitis vaccine, in which the attending specialists ordered untold expensive testing overseas looking for every genetic, immunologic, and metabolic disorder under the sun, in order to try to explain away two identical reactions after two meningitis vaccines, resulting in many years of expensive treatment with an immunoglobulin called Intragam. The fact that problems started in the same time frame, after both vaccines, was blindingly obvious to the parents and onlookers, yet the specialists refused to admit it, even after all other tests came back negative. Instead, they tried to hedge their answers by suggesting that perhaps the right test didn't yet exist to explain the problem. They will create many different solutions and ideas of what could be going on, while tossing one drug after another at the problem. And if those don't work, they order another round of tests and drugs. However, in this case, the evidence was so impressive that the child was eventually compensated for vaccine damage. Yet, even at the very last moment, a plea was put in to dismiss the case, because it could be politically inopportune.

As I have witnessed, the inevitable result is that the solutions offered can just make the patient sicker, because the real underlying cause of reactions is ignored.

Another example, Kate, was age 13 when I first met her. She was a healthy high-functioning teen who received a series of three Gardasil vaccines at age 12. She felt unwell after each one. But the back pain, burning in the joints, pleurisy, and pneumonia from the 'weird virus' she was diagnosed with, were initially considered manifestations of hysteria and nothing to do with the vaccine. Or so said the medical doctors who were consulted each time. Because the hallucinations did not respond to sedatives, they were considered idiopathic and not related to the vaccine. After Kate was admitted to a child psychiatric ward, a doctor decided to do a brain MRI and a spinal tap. The MRI showed a swollen hippocampus and the spinal tap showed oligoclonal bands that were put together into a unifying diagnosis of limbic encephalitis. Kate was then given an emergency breast exam and scan of the ovaries because apparently limbic encephalitis is often associated with cancer, and those were the two types of cancer that needed to be immediately ruled out—in a 13-year-old girl.

In my opinion, a breast exam given to an acutely hallucinating, frightened teen, whose likelihood of having breast cancer is almost zero, was a really thoughtless move. But that is what was done, even though it could have been done later when she was less anxious.

When those exams were negative, the unifying diagnosis was switched to multiple sclerosis, which earned Kate intravenous immune globulin (IVIG) and steroids. They didn't work. So then a large dialysis catheter was put into her neck and plasmapheresis was begun in attempt to remove the offending antibodies, which her doctors 'knew' were not caused by the vaccines. Blood thinners, and pooled donor plasma were all part of this treatment . . . which also didn't work.

So what do you do when IVIG, steroids, and plasmapheresis do not resolve symptoms that are 'not caused' by the vaccine? You give chemotherapy of course, and you hit the immune system hard, to try to kill off the cells that are making this antibody—that is 'not caused' by the vaccine. And that didn't work . . .

After several alternative physicians, hands-on healers, and more allopaths were unable to help Kate with her extreme debilitation, she and her mother visited with me to tell her story.

I repeat it here, not to tell you that I've brought her to a wonderful recovery, but to show you that the arrogance of medical ignorance and automaton assumptions are far more insidious than even I had ever imagined. Each time Kate's mother asked the neurologist, "Could this possibly stem from the Gardasil vaccine?" the neurologist would firmly respond by saying "No, there is one thing we are sure of and it is NOT the vaccine."

But the misadventure did not end there. Kate broke out in an itchy rash. She received all of her childhood vaccines on schedule and the chicken pox vaccine twice. She also had chicken pox twice, at three and five years old, and she got it again in January 2015.

Initially, the emergency room insisted that she could not have chicken pox because she had been vaccinated and because she had had the disease too. The emergency staff were ready to discharge her with an antihistamine. How's that for ignorance of basic infectious disease knowledge?

Fortunately, her neurologist heard she was in the ER, and after looking panicked, admitted her to an isolation room for IV Ganciclovir administration to combat the viral proliferation in her pharmacologically immune-compromised patient.

Kate was finally sent home. She and her family continued trying to pick up the pieces, with Kate requiring many drugs including antidepressants, sedatives, and antacids.

So, the parents turned to 'quackery' administered by doctors who believed that the vaccine had everything to do with the new sickness. 'Quackery' is the only thing that has improved Kate's previously declining health and helplessness. She is now tapering off some of the drugs that didn't work, and starting to get back some of her life. It remains my belief that when Kate and her mother realize that the conventional medical specialist's drugs are doing more harm than good, Kate could improve even more.

Another mother related her recent experience with doctors, after she reluctantly agreed to allow her baby to be vaccinated.

"My youngest boy is 15 months now. In late March we decided to give him the rest of his vaccines. He had only received the 6 week ones, so at 3 months the nurse gave us the 5 month ones. **After getting the shots he has been ill.** *He has been* **vomiting almost every night since** *and also during the day sometimes. He's otherwise happy and playful. I've been in and out of the* **doctor's office with him, but to no help.** *First* **I was told I fed him too much (he used to be a great eater but after the vaccines, he did not eat much).** *I was told to only give him 100 ml milk.* **After that they said he had reflux and told me to raise his bed** *and not feed him before bed. When that didn't help they gave us infant* **Gaviscon, which just made everything worse.** *Next visit to the doctors they* **informed me he was probably lactose intolerant and we took him off dairy.** *That's a month ago now and he is still dairy free.* **Next time the doctor said**

it was the valve in his stomach not being strong enough, and because I feed him too much (!!!) it all comes up again. She had no answers when I asked why this suddenly would happen and just said it would probably pass and to just keep raising his bed head. We have mentioned to the doctors that we think it's the shots that caused this, but as I'm sure you can imagine it's just been dismissed and even denied."

It's the old story of finding a problem familiar to a doctor's trained and preconceived mindset, rather than a proper evaluation from a complete differential diagnosis list that includes all drugs administered, including vaccines.

These new illnesses are considered true, true, and unrelated. The vaccine court monetary compensation claims are said to be given out of generosity, and not because there is any real proof that vaccines cause damage. In the American case of Hannah Poling, the courts compensated the family for autism caused by vaccination. However, Paul Offit's view was that Hannah Poling's father, who is a neurologist, was detached from scientific reasoning. Dr. Offit wrote many columns about the case, which Dr. Poling responded to, but even the scientific evidence that swayed the court couldn't penetrate the shell created in Dr. Offit's mind by his prejudiced blinders.

Let's say you are a 'good' parent, do whatever the doctor says, and accept all vaccines on time. If your child gets sick immediately afterwards, vaccine enthusiasts may blame you for overfeeding, or even go so far as accusing you of shaking the baby to death.

Even worse, is the modern thinking of people who say, "Your child's problems were never caused by the vaccine," and that whatever happens after a vaccine is psychosomatic and caused by a parental mental disorder. It's not unusual for the child and the parents to be referred for psychiatric evaluation, or mothers of young children to be scrutinized for Munchausen syndrome by proxy:[78] All shades of the old days, when doctors were sure that autistic children were caused by refrigerator mothers.[79]

---

[78] https://www.nlm.nih.gov/medlineplus/ency/article/001555.htm

[79] https://embryo.asu.edu/pages/early-infantile-autism-and-refrigerator-mother-theory-1943-1970

Out Of The Mold

Looking back, my life has largely been that of a doctor and of researching, and it's no different today. Only now, I have more freedom as to how I live my life. I feel good knowing how many more of my patients recover from what would have otherwise meant lifelong drugs and worsening chronic conditions. The children I treat today are usually spared the insult of antibiotics and get to deal with infections and gain normal immunity with an intact immune system and full microbiome.

After I resigned as a hospital nephrologist, I still wanted to influence people's diseases for the better. I still wanted to serve the people who asked me for help. I looked back over the time comparing the Steiner children with mainstream children, and decided to try to find out what the difference was between the two groups. There is some published medical literature specifically looking at Steiner-educated children, but those types of children also exist outside Steiner schools, and the results are the same; healthy children with stronger-than-average immune systems. I needed to know all the details that went into making children as strong as possible. What opened my eyes was solid core research, which is only just starting to explain how an infant immune system is designed and how the first two years epigenetically program the development of the immune system at all levels.

There is much that is not yet understood. That fact alone should make any parent think.

Doctors recommend vaccines, yet what the emerging core research shows is that a baby's immune system is designed to stay quiet (anti-inflammatory) as much as is possible. The programming of the immune system is intricate, with breast milk as an important teacher and anti-inflammatory modulator of the program. Vaccines are designed to be inflammatory, to set up cytokine responses. Theoretically, inflammation has the potential to counteract the innate design of the neonatal immune system. Trained correctly, the infant immune system is a very strong foundation. Trained incorrectly, the child becomes a disaster waiting to happen.

This information helps explain WHY non-Steiner children are often so unhealthy in comparison.

After learning a lot more on infant and child immunity and non-drug treatments of common ailments, I went into private practice as a 'general practitioner' with internal medicine and nephrology knowledge, and vaccine expertise. I began to see more and more of the sickest of sick children—who were mostly casualties of conventional pediatrics, where treatment had done nothing positive for these children. Understanding what was really affecting these children involved a huge amount of study about pregnancy, birth, and pediatrics and all the interconnecting bits that go with that. Knowing that I, as an internist, contributed to the patient base of nephrologists, it came as no surprise to me that a similar situation exists between obstetrics and pediatrics, and that the knowledge base of both is limited.

You can never assume that doctors really know what they are doing. The totality of their education is the fire hose of information they tried to drink from, while sleep deprived and stressed out in medical school and residency. Add to that, the experience of being 'tested' during compulsory residency and fellowship; where doctors are climbing the ladder of experience, and teaching those below them. The higher one gets on that ladder, the more likely they might be to find time to read and see the bigger picture, provided they recognize that there is one. On overnight calls, doctors rely on pocket handbooks, Dr. Google, and the occasional compulsory literature review, and the next day, there may be a drug-sponsored meal with slanted lectures before morning rounds.

Looking back now, I can see how some people shouldn't have trusted me—or most doctors who are beholden to the system—to cure them. Doctors entrenched in the conventional system don't know what they don't know. I was once guilty of thinking that my judgment was accurate and my knowledge was the best.

People came to me for help because they thought that what a highly trained professorial nephrologist had to offer was the finest option. Everyone has been brainwashed into believing that mainstream medicine knows everything there is to know, and anything OUTSIDE mainstream medicine could be very risky, even when they can see that, time and again, mainstream medicine fails and maims. Some people eventually wake up and toss out their religious dedication to the system, but usually not until after the medical system's gold standard treatment leaves them with heavy consequences, and they run out of options. At which point, the system will sometimes consent to their aberrant choices, while smirking that nothing else could possibly work.

There are a few things that still make being a doctor an amazing thing. Early on, an older doctor told me that being a doctor is like "being in the front seat of the theater of life". That is as true today as it always has been. It is a privilege to be trusted with the delicate inner surfaces of people's lives and asked to guide them.

I will never tire of that. Doing our best to deliver the best options that science has to offer should be the priority of any good doctor. I believe if most doctors knew what I know and had the ability to practice medicine with an honest heart, they would walk away from the constraints of convention[80], or at least pry open the bars on the door and expand their repertoire. That is, presuming they could still keep their standing in society and their hearty income. But, as I have experienced first-hand, conventionally trained doctors don't have very high expectations. Dreams and hopes of being a healer are short lived once we see what the 'best practice gold standards' can deliver. Young doctors often degenerate into middle-aged high-paid technicians, who do the same thing day-in and day-out, becoming the walking dead.

And as I have also experienced firsthand, doctors who awaken to the reality that they were miseducated, and that healing really is possible outside the guardrails that separate 'real medicine' from 'quackery', are not treated well.

Am I saying that the whole system is rubbish? Certainly not! Lives are saved, organs are maintained, and some drugs are worth taking for some people. My biggest argument is that doctors and patients are not offered a full range of options, including many natural alternatives that have proven helpful in the medical literature. Doctors are taught that anything other than 'gold-standard' medical practice is quackery. That mentality is rubbish! So many people go to so-called quackery after the system fails them—and then they heal and become very wary of conventional medicine afterwards. When they return to their doctors to show them the proof, they are either scorned or ignored. The system's thinking can't cope with the fact that answers can lie outside of their limited paradigms.

Because of this, doctors can get aggressive towards parents who want other options, so when parents really do have to use the

---

[80] In a study of over 15,000 physicians, the average burn-out rating was 4.5 in a scale of 1-7. Among top reasons were too many bureaucratic tasks and increasing computerization of practice.
http://www.medscape.com/features/slideshow/lifestyle/2016/nephrology?src=wnl_physrep_160214_mscpedit&impID=990103&faf=1#page=14

system, they are too often rolled over within, and by, the system. Many parents are fearful for their children's health and concerned that if they don't do things according to doctors' recommendations, they will land up with no doctor at all, out in the wilderness, or will have their children taken from them because the doctor will call Child Protective Services. I have seen too many regretful parents who wish they had followed their own instincts and not the coercion of the doctor, or who wish they knew then what they know today. Many parents don't realize the problems created by blindly following doctor's orders, until they have one or more damaged children. When they chose to refuse the mainstream medical processing of subsequent children, who then have thriving health, they see the difference very clearly.

It surprises me to see how many doctors stop studying the minute they hang up the shingle. They think they have learned the bulk of what they need to know, beyond the minimum extra study required to gain their CME license credits or board recertification, which is just another form of drinking from the fire hose of new drug information and related facts, while trying not to spill a drop. Most doctors never go any deeper into understanding the bigger picture or total pathophysiology, immunology, nutrition, inflammation, or the many aspects of true health that are actually right there in their medical literature.

There is another sad fact that plays into what is broken about the system: Nobody, except you, profits from your good health. Doctors and hospitals mostly profit from diagnosing and treating disease, or never-ending tests done at 'well child' or 'well adult' visits looking for something wrong, topped off with a string of vaccines on the days when there is actually a well person in the waiting room.

While patients are usually discouraged from asking questions, the reality is that they can't ask too many questions or doubt the medical profession too often. You can always wait as long as you need to, before agreeing to any medical procedure that is not immediately lifesaving. Research the fact that, every year in the USA, the medical profession kills around 250,000 people[81], either by preventable medical error, hospital-acquired infections, or properly prescribed drug reactions. There would be even more misadventure if you added in plain old wrong diagnoses. It is no different abroad. The UK, Europe, Australia, and New Zealand have similar proportions of collaterally wounded patients.

So, what does it take to get a parent to wake up? Usually, being caught in the wake of desecration; caused by 'gold standard medicine', which totally fails them or their children.

---

[81] Starfield, B., 2000 "Is US Health Really the Best in the World?" *Journal of the American Medical Association*, Jul 26; 284(4):483-485. PMID: 10904513

More Eminence-Based Medicine

The next case exemplifies several common issues I hear about from parents in the USA, Australia, Finland, Sweden, Kuwait, UK, Canada, and Central and South America. Not only does the medical system fail children, but the parents cremate into a heap of raging frustration and insecurity, until they finally realize that if they don't take matters into their own hands, their children may never have a normal life.

Any medical professionals reading this book, and in particular any immunologists, should see what is so wrong with the current dogma, which is illustrated by the misadventures detailed in the next few pages. You should be right behind the science I have been presenting publicly since 2011, and hopefully you will remind your colleagues and your patients what you should all know from the medical literature.

---

[82] Poland, G. A., and Jacobsen, R. M., 2012 "The re-emergence of measles in developed countries: time to develop the next generation of measles vaccines?" *Vaccine*, Jan 5;30(2):103-4. PMID: 22196079

All pediatricians must be noticing patients presenting, again and again, who, after years of treatment with hammer and nail

symptom-suppressing pharmaceuticals, vaccines, and anti-microbials, only see their health getting worse by the day. When parents seek out help in the hope of healing their pharmaceutically injured children, why are they usually met with more of the same?

Jill is a mother who contacted me in 2013. This case is typical of many parents who call and write to me after being jostled around by a medical model that has limited incentive to think outside the box and which only knows how to respond with prescription drugs.

"I did not take any antibiotics during any of my pregnancies but I have suffered on and off from candida infections since I was a teenager. When I was nineteen or thereabouts, I had three lots of quite severe tonsillitis within six months of each other, which were all treated with antibiotics. This is when the candida infection really got quite bad and took hold.

"Then between the age of twenty and twenty-seven when I first fell pregnant I had a couple more courses of antibiotics for sinus infections and ear infections. As a child I was quite anemic (my hair would fall out by the handful) and I always had really low iron levels.

"My candida infection flared up quite badly during this pregnancy and I was prescribed a general anti-fungal cream and told to use it both externally and internally. I used it topically externally but just did not feel comfortable using it internally so I didn't. I did not clear this infection before my son was born. I was given an ultrasound scan at every appointment with my GP (I had opted for shared care so my GP was my lead maternity caregiver throughout my pregnancy). I also had the standard scans at about 8 weeks for dating, 12 weeks, 20 weeks and then I had a growth scan at about 36 weeks. During my labor I was given gas and a pethidine injection for pain relief. I was given an IV for de-hydration and in the end my son was delivered by

ventouse. He received the vitamin K injection and I was given the Anti-D injection (RhoGAM) at the maternity unit.

"He was an unsettled baby from the day he was born. When he was just a few days old he developed pustules on his tummy. I was given a purple liquid (probably gentian violet) to wipe over them and they disappeared a few days later. He had his first thrush infection when he was just a few weeks old and many, many more over the first few years of his life. They treated his oral thrush with nystatin and for his bottom and penis he had over three different anti-fungal creams over the first couple years of his life.

"He was also born with fluid on the kidneys. They pumped dye into him (intravenous pyelogram) when he was just a few months old to look to see if he had reflux and then gave him his first set of precautionary antibiotics.

"He had eczema (treated with hydrocortisone creams) and really bad bowel movements, ranging from frothy, mucous, diarrhea, undigested milk, occasional blood spots, which I was told not to worry about. They said he was just a colicky baby. However there was one extremely distressing incident shortly after his first vaccinations, where I was sitting on the couch and he was absolutely inconsolable turning blue, arched his back screaming at the top of his lungs and the veins on the side of his neck were popping out it. When I reported this to the GP, I was told he probably had acid reflux. He was then started on the prescription antacid, Losec and also given Gaviscon.

"After his vaccinations, things definitely got worse. He used to breastfeed well but that slowly got worse and worse until shortly after his three month vaccinations he started to refuse the breast completely. I remember him actually pushing me away and almost hitting me when I tried to feed him. This was again all put down to gastro-esophageal reflux. I was told by the GP that it wasn't vaccinations. Getting my GP to acknowledge there was any problem at all seemed impossible. Not once did he suggest I see a dietitian or nutritionist and when I asked about cutting certain foods out of my

diet to see if it would help I was told not to, as it would be bad for me and my baby. At around four months he suggested I try him on SOY formula. I was reluctant as I wanted to breastfeed. But for months now I had had a very unsettled baby who never slept more than 15 - 20 minutes at a time, and used to wake up screaming. I didn't know what else to do so I caved and put him onto soy formula. At first it seemed to help but then his eczema, reflux and bowel movements got worse. Then around five months he got diarrhea, which the GP just dismissed as not serious enough to be concerned about. I remember him getting small dark red spots of blood in his bowel movements from time to time, which the GP also told me was nothing to be worried about.

"About two weeks after the diarrhea started, he developed a really high temperature and we ended up in the hospital with him as he had become severely dehydrated. At first they wanted to discharge us and send us home as they didn't think he was all that bad but we couldn't get anything into him and he was also vomiting a lot more. The nurse and I were having an argument, when she tried to force Pedialyte down his throat with a syringe and he vomited on her and he went pale, floppy, and speckled in complexion.

"We then had medical personnel rushing in there to put an IV drip into him to get fluid into him. Five minutes prior they had been trying to send us home!

"The next morning his temp had settled and he had stopped vomiting because of something they had given him and they wanted to discharge him. I think I lost it at this point and they were telling me he had gastroenteritis. It didn't matter how many times I said that the diarrhea had been there for two weeks and prior to that he had strange bowel movements anyway and I didn't feel that he had gastroenteritis. In the end I just refused to leave until they could give me a better answer. So I stayed another night and saw the head pediatrician the next morning. He listened to everything I had to say, although by then I had given up asking about vaccinations and concentrated more on the reflux and allergy side of things. While we were talking, Luke passed a bowel movement and he agreed it wasn't normal even though this was how they had long been, and other doctors told me it was fine. So he then recommended to trial him on a formula called Neocate which is for kids with food allergies. A couple days after we got home from the hospital my son got a strange red spotty rash.

"I took him to the GP and he said it was roseola, but then the rash seemed to change so I took him back and he said he had German measles and that it was probably that all along and just sent me home saying he was over the worst of it and he would be fine. All blood tests were negative for both viruses. A few weeks into using the formula Luke's skin improved, his bowel movements stabilized and he appeared to be improving so we just proceeded as if he was a child with allergies and acid reflux. He was also on Losec and had been since he was just over 3 months old.

"Although he appeared to have improved in some areas, he still slept badly. He frequently woke up screaming for no apparent reason. He started talking early using clear words and definitely understood the meaning of the correct words, in context. People often thought he was older than he was, and used to comment on how advanced he was with his speech.

"Both my husband and I are sure that he had reactions to his vaccinations. I got nowhere with my GP or the pediatricians that we dealt with. My son also had allergies and just got sick all the time.

"He also suffered many tonsillitis infections for which he had several rounds of antibiotics. He was sick a lot before the MMR, but things got much worse afterwards.

"No matter how much I questioned giving him the vaccinations based on the fact that I didn't feel he was well or that I thought he might be struggling with his immune system, the GP just wouldn't listen to me and several times made me out to be a paranoid mother, especially as he was my first baby. He also said some very condescending things like, "Some babies cry a lot. Just deal with it." I still knew something wasn't right with him. Anyway long story short it was after his first MMR that I really got mad with my GP. I had delayed the MMR a few months due to not being happy about the state of his immune system, allergies, his general health. Shortly after the vaccination I saw what I knew was a reaction.

"A few days after vaccination as my son became unwell, running around the house pulling at his teeth and his head and saying 'Mommy head hurts,' along with a few other things but he just couldn't stop crying and telling me how sore his head was. I went back to the GP who dismissed my concerns about it being a vaccination reaction and he told me it was probably just a coincidence and that he was coming down with something or suffering from a bad headache or migraine.

"I didn't believe him so that was when I first started reading more. Over the next few weeks, he started stuttering, his balance was off, his behavior changed, and he became excessively hyperactive.

"Eventually I went to see my GP, very unhappy about my child's health in general and we had a big argument. He told me that he couldn't find anything clinically wrong with my child and I said, 'Just look at him. He is pale and has big black rings under his eyes and this is about as good as it gets. I want to know why his immune system is struggling so much.' In the end he agreed to blood tests but his attitude and arrogance really upset me. So that afternoon I booked an appointment with another GP that I had found out about that took a more holistic approach. After the blood tests my original GP phoned me a little sheepish and said to me that it appeared that my son was fighting something but they didn't know what or why and would I like to bring him back in (high CRP, anemia)? I said NO and took him to the other Dr. The other Dr listened to everything I had to say and put him onto Vitamin C, multivitamins, fish oil, probiotics and suggested

some changes to our diet which was already restricted because of his
allergies but basically we cut out as much sugar and processed foods
as possible.

"I had also started taking my son to a chiropractor as well. Slowly he
showed improvement but I was still very concerned about his balance,
gross motor skills and speech. When he was younger, he spoke well
and very clearly, but now his stuttering was getting worse and along
with it he was losing his confidence.

"Then one weekend we went away with very close family and friends
all people my son had grown up with and was very comfortable with
and his stuttering got so bad that he stopped talking, wouldn't
respond to anyone and just retreated into himself. He wouldn't look at
us. I felt like I was losing him. Everyone there was commenting on it
and quite worried. Up until then many of them had been telling me I
was overreacting. We took him to a specialist who basically just said
that because he was still so young there wasn't much we could do but
wait and see what happened!

"A couple days after we had seen the specialist I found my son sitting
up in bed having what looked to me like some kind of seizure. He was
shaking/convulsing and not responsive. It lasted less than a minute,
though I don't know how long it had been going on before I found
him. I couldn't get him to come round and fully wake up or make
sense and eventually I managed to get him to lie down and he went
back to sleep but kept twitching every few minutes. I took him back to
the original GP who told me it wasn't a seizure of any kind and that
he was probably just having a bad dream!!! I think he called it 'night
terrors'. It was like he had not even registered what I was saying. I felt
so helpless and so mad!

"We continued with the chiropractor and the vitamins and diet
changes. I read a book called Gut and Psychology. Although we didn't
go onto the diet fully, we adopted a lot of it, and slowly over the last
year and half he has improved significantly. The stuttering went

away, his balance appears normal for his age now and we have our happy, confident son back. It was a very scary time for us and we had very little help or support. I felt very alone in my views that his vaccinations had contributed to this.

*"My mother in law absolutely lost it at me when I didn't want to vaccinate my daughter. She swore at me in front of my son and called me a f****ng irresponsible parent and it didn't matter what I tried to say, or how much written scientific evidence of potential harm I showed her. She just wasn't interested in reading or hearing about it. Needless to say, my relationship with my husband's family has suffered massively because of our decision not to have my daughter (second child) vaccinated. Even my own mother was very unsure about what we were doing, but she at least read some of the stuff I sent her, and said that she was just happy she didn't have to make the decision in today's very different world. In the end, my mother decided to support us in our decision despite what she might think. My mother is now much more open minded about not vaccinating and far more accepting and supportive of our decision not to vaccinate our two daughters at all or continue with our son's vaccinations."*

If you think I am too hard on the medical system, can you please justify the behavior of doctors who deny or ignore the side effects of drugs and vaccines without even a second thought?

What would the average doctors say to this frantic mother who out of desperation wrote to me in April of 2016?:

"Dear Dr. Humphries

"I'm French, I live in France.

"Allow me contact to you for speak problem for my child aged 5 years.

"In September 2014, my child has received a vaccine, the MENINGITEC.

"15 days after injection, strange symptoms appeared when he never had any health problems before. He had three colds during the first 4 years of life.

"He began to have severe stomach pains every day, to have nosebleeds, has anemia, constipation or diarrhea, strong fever for 2 days without being sick, vomitting, ENT infections such as ear infections, tonsillitis, bronchitis and often struggled to heal despite antibiotics or cortisone.

"Then I learned that the vaccine was withdrawn from the market because it was suspected to contain heavy metal particles. The French authorities have not recognized the problem but today an analysis in Italy of a vaccine MENINGITEC confirms the presence of heavy metals such as zirconium, lead, steel ... in the vaccine.

"Thousands of children are affected, and nearly all children have the same health problems.

"I would like to have your opinion please, I am very afraid for my child.

"Thank you very much for your reply."

I receive a lot of emails like this, or about vaccine reactions of various kinds. Most doctors in the current climate just dismiss these problems as a coincidence, because, like me, they went to medical school, and learned little about the immune system or potential side effects of drugs and vaccines. On top of that, doctors read on Medscape, where vaccine patent holders like Paul Offit and Gregory Poland brainwash them into believing the dogma that vaccines don't lead to autism, autoimmunity, epilepsy, or death anywhere beyond the background noise. Those doctors then counter any parent who so much as asks about or insinuates that they saw their own child's health decline after a vaccine.

Regarding the French mother's account above, I have verified that the event occurred in 2014. At that time, the manufacturers insisted that there was only a small amount of iron oxide (rust) and oxidized stainless steel, which was said to have originated from faulty manufacturing equipment. Doctors were undoubtedly sent a memo to that effect, and naturally would mentally label any concerned parent as 'preoccupied with perceptions of vaccine danger'. In the media, the event was down played as insignificant because supposedly very few contaminated doses were said to have been administered[83].

However, after mass vaccination with Meningitec, hundreds of concerned parents hired legal counsel. An Italian investigator tested the vaccines. The results were reported as "alarming" when "considerable amounts" of stainless steel dust, lead, zinc, titanium, zirconium and even a "slightly radioactive" compound were measured[84].

Throughout history, vaccines have had contamination issues of one sort or another. The contamination can be something simple like shrink wrap particles in Gardasil[85], or something initially unidentified like 'adventitious' viruses, such has SV40. Smallpox vaccines were constantly contaminated with so many bacteria that

---

[83] Papple, D., 2014 "Meningitec, A meningococcal vaccine: worldwide recall issued," *Inquisitr*, Sept 29. http://www.inquisitr.com/1506968/meningitec-a-meningococcal-vaccine-worldwide-recall-issued/

[84] Stéphane, B., 2016 "Vaccin de Méningitec, un lot jugé dangereux pour la santé," *Initiative Citoyenne*, April 10. http://initiativecitoyenne.be/

[85] Loftus, P., 2011 "Shrink Wrap Found in Merck Vaccines," *The Wall Street.Journal*, July 28.
http://www.wsj.com/articles/SB10001424053111904888304576474562508701
184

the list would make a bacteriologist cringe. Even today, the European Medicines Agency has documents on their website that state that "degradation products" are in the MMR, but they are "neither identified nor quantified". Rotavirus vaccines have had previously undetected pig viruses in them.

Aluminum is used in vaccines because it has a strong positive electrostatic polarity that is attracted to the negative polarity of vaccine antigens like a magnet. Having the metal and antigen bound together, causes the immune system to create a red alert. Without the metal as a foreign body, the immune system wouldn't do very much with the antigen.

Zirconium and lead are even more positively charged than aluminum. In 1964, zirconium[86] was considered as an adjuvant candidate. Reports from the 1960s and '70s confirm that zirconium has considerable immune-modulating effects when paired with mineral oil. The problem was that it led to significant fibrosis, hemolytic anemia, and granuloma formation. Thus zirconium was sidelined and aluminum remained the darling of adjuvants, where it still stands today, despite the profound lack of safety studies and plethora of literature demonstrating its neurotoxic effects[87]. In 1979, another report[88] showed that zirconium, without mineral oil, had the ability to cause hemolysis, was toxic to macrophages, consumed complement, and induced foreign body granulomas. All of these things are extremely unhealthy effects.

---

[86] Braverman, I. M., 1964 "Zirconium: Its effect on the reticuloendothelial system and action as an immunologic adjuvant," *J Invest Dermatol*, Dec;43:509-18. PMID:14234857

[87] Youtube, *Trojan Horses and Clusterbombs: Trojan Horses and Clusterbombs: Dr Suzanne Humphries on aluminum in Finland.* A fully referenced lecture on aluminum toxicity.
https://www.youtube.com/watch?v=PWP6e2CYPo8

[88] Ramanathan, V. D., et al., 1979 "Complement activation by aluminium and zirconium compounds," *Immunology*, Aug;37(4):88108. PMID: 500133.

This could be why the manufacturers only admitted to stainless steel dust, rather than zirconium and other heavy metals.

Most doctors will only read the short bulletins sent to them by the system's informers giving the desired bullet points. Whatever those bulletins say is considered to be the truth. This is why some doctors still recommend acetaminophen after vaccines. Yet, it's hard to justify using acetaminophen after vaccines (or infection-related fevers) when the medical literature has so much to say about the negative effects of that drug. Acetaminophen has no biologically beneficial attributes.

When it comes to infection-related fevers why don't doctors at least implement probiotics, excellent nutrition, vitamins D and C and watch what happens? They might be surprised. Or perhaps the mandatory 15-minute time slot may not allow such attention to health creation?

In my practice today, I see many women who tell me of the terrible health of their first child, who was born, and conventionally medically managed. The mother was very compliant with doctors' recommendations and vaccines. They later have second and third children who were born at home with no interventions, and require no medical doctor at all. These children have never been on a drug or an antibiotic, and are strong and happy. This pattern is extremely common once parents wake up and see the issues for themselves playing out in real life.

The second and third children for these families have different health because the parents read lots of books, and through those pregnancies they did things completely differently, realizing that their first child (and sometimes the second one) was walking proof of the damage that can happen when parents unquestioningly listen to doctors' words and use their prescriptions.

The mother of Luke realized that she listened to the medical profession, took their word seriously, believed them, allowed them to push her into their mold, and became paralysed by learned helplessness.

She realized the voices she listened to determined the choices she made but only SHE had to live with the consequences. Only when she saw her child getting worse after every visit to the doctor did she make the decision to step out of the pharmaceutical/medical mold.

The real problem is that those medical 'voices' just sit behind their desks, leave you with the mess they have made, and refuse to understand or believe that much of the trail of destruction they keep prescribing for, is of their making.

First time parents often don't know what they need to know in order to make the right choices, because they don't get to hear the voices that can tell them how to make different choices. Unfortunately, doctors also don't know how to tell you that, because most doctors don't have a grasp on how little they know.

For you to make different choices as parents, you need to know what the biological foundations of good health really are. Your great-great-grandmothers and grandmothers knew what these foundations are, and most were very successful in working out what really mattered in their worlds. But now we live in the era of experts, and the inter-generational knowledge has been broken.

Even knowledge on how to treat simple diseases has been lost to the point where most mothers look first to a doctor for a solution, assuming that they are the only ones that have an answer. Often what doctors have to offer just makes things worse.

The whooping cough denied

What do you do when the medical system categorically denies the diagnosis and uses harmful drugs that make whooping cough worse? The story of a very sick two-month-old boy and his older two-year-old sibling follows. Both recovered and are well after home treatment with vitamin C in the form of sodium ascorbate.

*"As parents we are what our parents call "Google parents". We are ever ready to do research on our children and their health etc. Both our sons got whooping cough, one after the other. Our 2-year-old first and then we think approximately two weeks later our 2 month old picked it up off our 2 year old. We were onto it quite quickly as we spotted the tell tale signs. The more we researched online the gloomier we felt. By the time our two month old started coughing we were already in bits and felt that we were going to have to watch our precious baby be consumed by this illness til he is no longer with us. We found talk of high dose vitamin C online and started doing research. We found Dr Humphries and researched what she had published online regarding the use of vitamin C[89]. **We also found some material, which was very eager to depict Dr Humphries as a loon.** We weren't convinced and felt that everything she had said fitted in with our understanding of our babies and their general health. So we decided to go ahead and contact the Dr. At this point we felt like we knew what we were supposed to do, however neither of us had the confidence to actually do it. We both understood that at this point taking our son to the hospital and handing him over was actually the best thing for us to do FOR US and not for our son. The feeling of passing over responsibility was ever drawing. However a more powerful feeling dominated and didn't allow us to cower. This was the emotion of wanting the best for our babies irrespective of the pressure it placed on us as parents.*

---

[89] http://tinyurl.com/zy42ps7

"The image of our baby lying in a hospital with bright lights and being isolated and not feeling our warmth and love was one we were desperate to avoid. However we felt the pressure as I assume any parent would. What if we were completely wrong? What if this whole vitamin C thing is nonsense? What if our actions lead to causing harm to our baby? Tough questions we had to face and I suppose at the end of the day as a parent you have to make a decision that you think is best for your children and you have to go with it and be positive and optimistic about your decisions. As a side note here, going slightly off on a tangent, I'm convinced that our baby's emotional state in dealing with whooping cough is of paramount importance. When we were optimistic and in high spirits – it made a difference.

"So we contacted the Dr. and had an initial Skype conversation. I can categorically say, and this is not to take away for all the support and help the Dr. gave throughout, but this Skype conversation was the most important, and the whole direction and attitude we had changed after this conversation. It was all about the support and hearing that everything was going to be all right. Of course things can happen and the Dr was keen not to give us a absolute promise but we could both tell she was somewhat covering her own back and she was very confident that our 2 month old was going to make it through this. We needed that confidence as at this point we were lacking it and I believe our babies could feel our mood. Quite simply this Skype conversation gave us the confidence to do what was needed to give our babies safe passage through this situation.

"The Dr was keen to point out to us that this was not a race but more of a marathon. This was concerning to us as we already felt drained by the time we had contacted the Dr. Emotionally the worry and the online barrage of imagery showing dying or dead babies weighed heavy on our minds.

"Anyway to cut a very long story slightly shorter, the Dr gave us a level of support that I can only compare to how family behave. She was on the end of the phone whenever we needed her, and we needed

her frequently. One of the most admiring attributes of the Dr was that when she did not know something or when something was surprising to her – she would say exactly that. This may not be what some people want from their adviser, however for me it was extremely comforting, as I knew that when she confidently said something then she meant it. This characteristic reappears to good effect later in this story. So the Dr. guided us through the challenges and the difficulties of giving vitamin C to a 2 month old. In particular because we are in the Middle East and finding sodium ascorbate or lypo is near impossible.

"In the darkest and most challenging parts of the journey we went through our 2 month old was sleeping throughout most of the day and when his feeding reduced, the doctor advised us to go and get his vitals checked at the local hospital. This for us was the most dreaded part – as we were deeply concerned that our son would be kept at the hospital and the dreaded imagery of babies in hospital with whooping cough was vivid in our minds. Anyhow, as we had decided to go and get the vitals from the hospital we decided that we may as well have a test for pertussis done at the same time just to be 100% certain that we are actually dealing with whooping cough. The Dr at the hospital was ADAMANT that this was not whooping cough. I myself can be a very persistent person and I was not letting this matter go so I asked how the Dr could be so certain. She gave a bunch of reasons for which I countered with an explanation to each.

"Dr – I can tell from the cough it's not whooping cough.

"Me – You've only seen him cough once – it's much worse than this at night.

"Dr – We don't have whooping cough in this country.

"Me – We just flew from the UK two weeks ago.

"Dr – Babies under 3 months don't get whooping cough. I have only seen 1 case in 30 years.

"Me – That does not in any way mean our son doesn't have whooping cough, 'specially considering the pattern and sequence of events.

"Dr – Because your wife is so young she would have passed her immunity to the baby.

"My wife – I'm 32 (my wife does look younger than she is – and the Dr looked surprised at her age).

"Dr – Look I'm telling you 100% that this is not whooping cough and I don't have time to talk to you anymore.

"We ended up leaving her office with her shouting at us (a few moments from calling security on us), ADAMANT that we were silly to even suggest whooping cough, the only thing she gave us was a nebuliser prescription (steroid and bronchodilator) and a bill to have our 2-month-old's hips checked (completely unrelated to whooping cough, just a routine check done to all babies at this age).

"To be honest we left her office confused and for the first time my wife and I differed on how to proceed. We were faced with such a STRONG, ASSERTIVE Dr. with 30 years' experience with babies telling us that there is NO WAY that this is whooping cough and what we are dealing with is ALLERGIES and we need to give the nebuliser straight away. As it turns out this assertiveness and dismissiveness was actually mere arrogance. The one most important thing we did get from the visit to the hospital was that our baby's vitals were perfect. At this point we ended up giving our baby the nebuliser because we were confused, pressurised and somewhat convinced that we had been quack parents.

"The next 48 hours were the worst we had. God knows if this was unrelated to the nebuliser or not. When we got home from the hospital we contacted Dr Humphries and explained what had happened. Her response, which stood out to me was very confident, without the shred of arrogance. 'It is whooping cough. Doctors often

miss it because of how good they look because of the vitamin C you've been giving your baby.'"To be perfectly honest until this point I was not convinced that the vitamin C was making such a huge difference. This to me was the biggest indicator that it truly was.

"I believe that because we started giving our babies (in particular the younger of the two) vitamin C so early in the cycle of the disease we never actually saw the impact giving vitamin C makes on this disease. Dr Humphries' confidence in saying that it is whooping cough (which it obviously was, we went to another hospital and got the test which was POSITIVE) was very comforting and her confidence that the vitamin C was helping gave us the confidence to give our babies increased doses.

"THIS PAID OFF STRAIGHT AWAY and now for the first time both of us were confident that the high dose was making a distinct difference to the coughing intensity and duration. Both our babies got past the worst of it and are now well into their recovery. The challenges were not one or two, it felt like every day a new challenge would present itself. From my understanding the way each baby deals with whooping cough differs. With vigilance, lots of prayer and support from Dr. Humphries and family we got through this and our now looking forward to many years of immunity."

It's very important for parents to find a doctor who will listen and support them in what they want. It's also very hard, as a doctor, to feel isolated within a system and feel that you're the only doctor who thinks this way, yet I know there are many doctors who feel alone inside a system that runs on autopilot.

Doctors have voices as well.

China has a 99% vaccination uptake among children. In spite of that, they had 107,000 reported cases of measles in 2014. Vaccine "herd immunity" is not panning out well. Chinese researchers say:

*"In spite of the high measles vaccination coverage, measles incidence rates have been rising in China over the last decade. In addition, there has been a shift in peak age of measles cases from young children to adolescents and younger adults. . . Our data show that there may be **limitations in using current vaccines** in targeting infections caused by contemporary genotype H1 wild-type strains of measles virus. In addition to supplemental immunization with existing vaccines, there is also a need to consider the **development of new measles vaccines** as a surrogate strategy to achieve global measles eradication. Moreover, the 'second golden age' for measles vaccine may provide us a new insight for measles vaccine development.* [90] *"*

---

[90] Shi, J., et al., 2011 "Measles incidence rate and a phylogenetic study of contemporary genotype H1 measles strains in China: is an improved measles vaccine needed?" *Virus Genes*, Dec;43(3):319-26. PMID: 21701857

56
What Other Doctors And Nurses Say To Me

When I was working in the hospital, there were doctors who agreed with me in private. A Nigerian internist overheard me arguing that a patient I was consulted on for kidney failure, which began in the hospital, should not have had a vaccine upon admission. At that time the hospital was placing orders for flu shots to all new patients who had not been vaccinated that year. The ordering doctor was the attending physician of record, even if they didn't order it. It was hospital policy, not a perceived need by the attending doctor. The Nigerian doctor said to me "I know why the hospital places the order for the shot . . . because I would not order it." Being a new recruit and non-American, he did not want to make any waves and was not up to the task of saying anything to the administration.

Another doctor, a very fine, intelligent hospital internist, upon overhearing me lament the shutdown of yet another set of kidneys, temporally related to the vaccine, said, "But Suzanne, you are a prophet and nobody ever listens to prophets."

After doing an interview on vaccines for a magazine in Maine called *Bangor Metro*, in which my opinion was butted up against a very pro-vaccine public health doctor, a family doctor said to me, "When I read that article I cried, because I knew I was not alone."

People watched the treatment meted out to me and saw that to speak up about this issue may not be worth it.

Nurses and ward clerks often approached me in a quiet private place, and said things like 'I totally agree with you. I stopped vaccinating my kids and I won't take the flu shot ever again. I get sick every year after I take it.' One nurse said to me, "I hate those vaccines. I had to quit my job in the neonatal intensive care unit because I could not commit the crime of vaccinating new babies with hepatitis B vaccines. I watched them get sick, and it sickened me to have to do it. I totally agree with you and I applaud you."

Since *Dissolving Illusions* was published, letters have been steadily rolling in from doctors all over the world who have read my book and watched my talks on YouTube, or in person. Most of them thank me for writing the book and say they had no idea about the history, and that a lot of things make sense to them now that before were conundrums.

A US-educated doctor, working and living in Copenhagen, came up to me after a talk I gave in Aarhus to a group of doctors, on vaccine varieties and contents. This was a talk deliberately based solely on PubMed published articles and documents from the European Medicines Agency database, so there could be no hint of argument or scorn. He was mortified and said "Oh my God. I can't believe I didn't know any of this. There is so much potential for harm."

One letter from a doctor revealed something very interesting about subacute sclerosing panencephalitis (SSPE), a deadly brain disease, wrongly thought to be only associated with natural measles infections. She started with:

"I have wanted to reach out to you for several years, ever since one of my patients alerted me to your work.

"Unlike you who did it with a big bang I have silently inched my way away from mainstream medicine. I graduated from Medical School in

*1974, and have worked as pediatrician in both academia, group –
and private practice since 1981.*

*"My view of health and disease has dramatically changed. I have
become a much better physician and person in the process. However, I
have worked quietly, in my own practice, still maintaining my
privileges at* [redacted] *hospital.*

*"Following the measles craze and the witch hunt against the
unvaccinated with new legislation being passed left and right I can no
longer stay quiet. I have gone to Sacramento to protest, stated my
opposition to mass vaccination and medical dictatorship to senators
and assemblymen, but to no avail I'm afraid. However, you have
inspired me to not give up.*

*"Your book reads like a mystery novel, and I recommend it to all my
patients, along with your online presentations.*

"With gratitude,
[Name redacted], *M.D."*

I decided to ask this doctor what her experiences were with the
normal childhood diseases, since she was of an age to have seen the
course of secondary infections and death before vaccines, in
Europe.

This was her reply:

*"Yes, I have been in whooping cough and measles as well as mumps
outbreaks in Hungary between 1975 and 1979. I was working in a
pulmonary institute where chronically ill pediatric patients were
hospitalized.*

*"Not one of them died of any of those diseases during any of those
outbreaks, nor were there any complications.*

"The only case of SSPE I've seen in my entire career was at LA County USC medical center.

"The biopsy/culture revealed that it was caused by the measles vaccine virus.

"Growing up in [redacted], I had whooping cough, measles, mumps, rubella, and chickenpox, along with my two siblings. None of us had any complications, including my brother who was a hemophiliac. I've never been revaccinated and know I have lifelong immunity since I am constantly exposed to all of these illnesses.

"I recently saw two siblings, 11 and 16 years old, who had received their sixth booster shot for pertussis. Within three weeks both of them came down with a severe case of pertussis, laboratory proven. Not only did the shot not protect them, it increased their susceptibility to pertussis.

"There goes your herd immunity."

I was intrigued and wrote her the following:

About the SSPE case, was it written up? Are you sure they serotyped it and found vaccine virus? That is huge because according to the medical literature, that has never ever been reported.

To which she replied:

"All I remember about the SSPE case is that it struck me because it was vaccine related. And that the child did not have a history of ever having had the measles. I don't know if it ever got written up. In those days I wasn't enlightened about vaccines."

An emergency room doctor wrote this:

"Hi Dr. Humphries...

"So much to share – but essentially we have a lot in common.

"I am a dual boarded and dual trained emergency medicine /internal medicine grad from LIJ (Long Island Jewish).

"I stayed very academic – among one of my areas of teaching residents in IM and EM was the epistemology of medical dogma and diagnostic reasoning.

"Pretty much in med school I realized that most of what was passed off as science was hardly that – and that doctors were becoming cogs in the medical industry – whether it was a facility that was ripping the public off, insurance companies, or the biggest one – the pharmaceuticals. Promoting faulty paradigms of disease is widespread – be it blaming things on a magical virus, or taking credit for flimsy and dubious therapies.

"So we had official quackery, and of course, for disillusioned patients – we have the usual quackery that awaits them when they are rightfully turned off from conventional medical approaches.

"I do have an [redacted] background, so I have always known that allopathic curricula and approach to disease states are horribly incomplete in terms of even understanding normal.

"I tell folks that conventional medicine shines in the acute care, critical care, and tech based care areas . . . but its approach to chronic disease is smoke and mirrors.

"Last, I have to say that I admire you very much, and when I heard that you were a physics major, on top of being a nephrologist . . . it spoke volumes to me about your intelligence . . . the last few areas of study that teach young folks how to think.

"You are a brilliant and inspiring woman.

"[Name redacted], MD
FACEP FAAEM FACP
Executive VP - Physician Development"

I cannot put, in here, the numerous letters from doctors who tell me they agree with me but they are only talking to their patients in the office, not doing any public attestations to the problems with vaccines. However, one example is:

"My name is Dave [redacted]. We actually did a rotation together in Phila. Anyway, I agree with what you are doing and often counsel my patients as such. Keep up the good work."

This letter came from a RN, and it shows that 'adamant doctors' who demand compliance are just as damaging to the children of health care practitioners as lay parents:

"Thank you for all of your insight into vaccines.

"I am an RN, and from early on in my career I have felt vaccines were seriously damaging the patients that came through our pediatric

emergency department, but how could anyone prove it? (Type 1 diabetes, seizures after vaccines, peanut allergy, ear infections, autism . . .)

"It wasn't until I had my first child in 2005, that it hit close to home. I refused the hep B at birth but then I took my baby in at 2 months as a dutiful mother. I had so many questions regarding vaccines and our pediatrician was adamant that it was the right thing. I cried after the injections, not because of the needle, but because I felt like my daughter had been poisoned.

"In the year that followed, my breastfed baby had ear infections and wheezing. She developed ITP and eczema after her 18 month vaccines and is now asthmatic and allergic to almost every environmental allergen you can name. The guilt is overwhelming.

"Her younger brother had delayed vaccines and I had also omitted several, but he is also asthmatic and allergic to foods and ibuprofen.

"My youngest child is 13 months and not vaccinated. I wish I had access to all of your insightful information years ago.

"[Name Redacted], *RN"*

The situation with this RN is so common. In every country I have visited, parents tell me similar stories. They were compliant and naïve with the first child and that child wound up with serious sickness, which they were told was coincidental. So they treat the second child the same albeit against their instincts. The second child also gets sick after vaccines and the doctor says the sickness has nothing to do with any vaccination.

Then the parents think about it, research more, and develop new convictions. They have a home birth, delay the cord clamp, breastfeed, and reject vaccines and then 'coincidentally' have a most perfectly healthy child all through childhood.

I am often asked, by attorneys and pro-vaccine doctors, why there is not more than a smattering of doctors speaking out publicly, and clearly saying what I am saying. The answer is, first of all, who wants to be shafted the way I have been? Secondly, it takes a lot of time to get the type of education I have, and continue to embark on, since leaving my hospital job.

Doctors graduate medical school and residency blind to the vaccine issues apart from the idea that there is a very small group of "anti-vaccine" crazies with "low cognitive complexity in thinking patterns," which prevents them from realizing the vaccines are victims of success, and that these crazy people spread misinformation and disease, and are a danger to us all. Today, new doctors are told to refute the rumors of vaccine damage and danger that circulate due to the nutters in the "anti-vaccine movement".

The doctors who do know something more about vaccines, see how doctors like me are treated and don't want to have that kind of abuse directed at them. They send me letters of encouragement and continue their work in private.

Doctors are so scared that I have to agree to keep them behind a cloak of anonymity in order to have any meaningful conversation with them, beyond the first letter.

Parents need to realize that the medical system has progressed very little since the early days when Ignaz Semmelweis' discovery of harm (puerperal fever) and how to prevent the death of thousands of infants and mothers, was categorically ignored as quackery. The medical system considered his idea of washing hands with lime to prevent spread of disease, as the mark of a deluded doctor with low cognitive complexity and irrational thinking patterns.

Semmelweis, distraught at the continual needless deaths of women and babies, went off the rails and was tricked into confinement to a mental asylum, where he died. He's not the only pioneer who suffered the same fate. There is a cupboard full of names, which trainee doctors never get to hear about. They might be told of one, here and there, especially the ones who are well known—maybe Semmelweis, since it's good to admit something to students because that gives an illusion of full accountability.

I've taken time to study many of these people. Perhaps a hero in my eyes, because I'm American, would be Dr. Oliver Wendell Holmes, who spent many years upbraiding his arrogant American colleagues and accusing them of murdering children and mothers by spreading puerperal fever. Why is he a hero to me? Because the health and safety of his patients came before the stupid policy he was criticizing. Because he had a brilliant mind and was a fantastic medical school tutor who really understood his craft. Because he had unlimited courage and never stopped speaking out. Because he never let his murderous colleagues get him down, or stop his mouth. And because he chose to do all that while staying in the system in the hope that his colleagues would one day see sense.

In the end, however, he left the medical profession because he could see no end to the trail of deaths resulting from their stupidity and ignorance, and their refusal to listen. He resigned and lived out the rest of his life writing poetry that was nowhere near as good as his medical writings. The medical system lost a jewel in their crown and never even knew it.

He inspired me because in order to see change, we have to have courage, to speak out and be fearless, and ideally that needs to happen from inside a system. It's scary, because today it's also a system that tolerates less discussion and dissent than it did in Oliver Wendell Holmes' day.

So if you are a medical professional, and feel the same as I do, these questions are for you:

Are your convictions enough for you to be another Oliver Wendell Holmes, and try to make a difference? Or will you sit quietly on the sidelines, looking out for your own self-interests? How will you feel when you are told you need to get all of the recommended vaccines for adults? How will you feel when your children have to get all of the recommended vaccines in the childhood schedule? Will you want to exempt them from any of them? If so, you will need a qualified medical doctor to agree that your child has a condition that precludes vaccines. Will you be able to find such a medical professional, or will doctors who once were willing to sign such waivers be sitting trembling, like you, behind their own wall of silence?

Is compulsory vaccination the thin end of the wedge that also contains compulsory chemo for children with cancer? What will be next? Compulsory antibiotics? Compulsory birth control? Compulsory statins and blood pressure medication to go along with our compulsory 'health' insurance policies?

If so, that's the ultimate definition of automoron medicine, which might as well be staffed by robots. You will be out of a job anyway.

57 Do Drugs Cure?

Even though I am still a licensed MD practitioner, and rarely use prescriptions for my own patients, I ponder the value of conventional drugs.

After years of using prescription drugs on all sorts of people as my primary tool, I ask, "Do we have the ability to cure disease with drugs? What is cure?" I define cure as the reversal of pathology and attainment of a normal state of health, preferably with something that does not leave behind a trail of its own damage as it 'saves' you.

One of the reasons I moved into a specialty like nephrology was because I was dismayed at having to toss drugs and things like mammograms at otherwise healthy people. The options were so limited and toxic that I thought, "Let me go somewhere where people really need these drugs—people who are so sick, they can benefit from them." End-stage kidney patients would die without prescription drugs, dialysis, or transplantation.

Today I am back to dealing with a healthier population, and the question came back up, "Do allopathic drugs cure anything?"

If someone must remain on prescription drugs for life, they are not cured. If a prescription drug was taken that got rid of the symptom but left the person in a state they must recover from in order to be well, they were not cured by the drug. There is a difference between treatment, survival, and cure.

When I posed the question, *Do you think allopathic medicine cures anything? (As in, reverses the pathology and brings a person to higher health.) If so, what?* to a group of over 8,000 people, I got back many replies. The most common was "NO." After that came surgery, trauma, congenital defects, infections treated with antibiotics, many different sorts of surgeries including appendectomies, c-sections, sinus surgeries, and cancer treated with chemotherapy.

Then a war broke out between people who think the oncology office is a dangerous place to be, and an oncologist defending his practice, who said those who reject oncology are fringe lunatics.

A few people suggested that IV fluids for someone dehydrated, vitamin C for scorbutic people, and bloodletting for hemochromatosis, were all examples of modern medicine's fine contribution.

Why is this question pertinent to this book? Because doctors believe that what they have to offer is the best possible option for sick people. If that is true, then why do chronic disease rates continue to rise? Why are prescription drug and hospital deaths among the highest killers in the USA, with 225,000 unnecessary and preventable deaths each year?

People also often believe that the hospital or doctor's office is the safest or best place to go when they get sick, or even for 'health maintenance'.

Even though people don't necessarily like taking drugs, most still think that drugs are the best bet for getting rid of the symptom—and sometimes they are. But does that make it the best overall bet? No. If they veer outside, they may think the alternatives are better for them, but not as effective. This isn't true.

A certified physician can recertify in their particular field every 10 years. It is not necessary in order to practice medicine and become licensed, but it is the system's standard of excellence and does ensure that doctors keep up with modern recommendations and research.

There are parts of my medical education that I value deeply, because there are times when, for whatever reason, people need the medical system.

At its core, the current medical system could hold great promise if all specialties had a Dr. Charlie Swartz making sure that people understood both physiology and rationale, and taught a better understanding of the process of disease.

But the promise of 'health' for all has been perverted and twisted to become a nightmare for many patients and doctors alike. There is a large percentage of doctors who say in surveys that they feel like they are "cogs in the system"[91], pharmaceutical handmaidens, and technicians on autopilot.

There is much celebration, in medical circles, over the fact that mortality rates from cardiovascular disease have dropped. But look at the bigger picture: By 2030, according to the American Heart Association's Heart Disease and Stroke statistics, more than 40% of the USA's population is projected to have some form of CVD. This is ludicrous. We hear that people are living longer and being kept alive with chronic disease longer and that is the excuse for the pattern of rise in CVD, but the fact is that people lived well into their 90s for the past 200 years—and stayed out of hospitals. Yet today, hospitalizations for cardiovascular diseases steadily continue to

---

[91] Peckham, C., 2015 *Medscape Internist Lifestyle Report*, Jan 26, http://www.medscape.com/features/slideshow/lifestyle/2015/internal-medicine#1

rise. There were nearly six million hospital discharges for cardiovascular-related disease in 2009, with an estimated cost of 312.6 billion USD. Heart failure continues to rise in the USA with a predicated prevalence of 25% by the year 2030.

Is anyone studying the habits of people who live to be 90 or more, without any medications? Or what their vitamin C, microbiome, inflammation markers, or fatty acid profiles are?

Knowing the physiology, microbiology, and mitochondrial function, as I now do, I can't accept the dogma that the population has simply landed within a sea of lifelong drugs to stay alive and treat and prevent CVD, because we are living longer.

As doctors, we are failing our patients by lauding our sometimes puny efforts at treating all the people smashed on the rocks at the bottom of the cliff, while ignoring our duty to put a fence at the top and educate the willing who don't wish to smash the fence or fling themselves over the cliff.

Hypertension, the most common underlying cause of cardiovascular disease, is often, simplistically (with limited cognitive complexity and thinking patterns) considered to be its own disease. But hypertension is often just a symptom of other bodily pathology (like metal or chemical toxicity, mineral or vitamin deficiency, stress, obesity, prescription drugs, chemical non-food, or inflammation) that the medical system either ignores or addresses superficially. As a result, doctors know very little beyond how to adequately drug hypertension for the rest of the patient's life.

I am undertaking my board review work, and studying towards recertification exams. My enthusiasm for the best that medicine has to offer, and the increasing scientific understanding of nature's blueprints, hasn't dimmed. I'm loving the study and the work that deals with the explaining of concepts and physiology. Some things, which I have to memorize like a robot, do not thrill me because they don't actually mesh with research that exists in PubMed.

Often when we take an exam, we are given a 'rationale' that details the exam question writer's explanations of right or wrong. Ironically the rationale can be based on evidence primarily generated by the pharmaceutical industry or it can simply be based on opinions of governing bodies, which have no direct science underlying them.

Critical analyses of how medical research is conducted can be quite eye-opening to the interested reader. Joanne Embree, for instance, has some things to say regarding level A recommendations:

*"First, most of the published controlled clinical trials (level A evidence) are directly supported by the pharmaceutical industry. These are very expensive studies to do. Usually, they are conducted in relation to the development of a new therapeutic product, which the company is planning to market and from which they hope to profit financially. This is, after all, the primary goal of private industry, **and we support that goal, particularly for those of us who own stocks or mutual funds.***

"However, these studies are frequently conducted primarily to determine whether the efficacy of the new therapeutic product is similar, if not superior, to the currently used product(s). If this is found to be the case, the results of the study are usually promptly published. If the product is not found to be at least equivalent in efficacy, are the studies published as readily?

"Also, the pharmaceutical industry only rarely supports clinical trials in which old drugs are studied unless the older drugs are used in the

control groups to support the use of newer products or unless there are new diseases for which they could be used.

"Moreover, why would we expect the pharmaceutical industry to support studies designed to determine the minimum dosage of their products and, hence, reduce their profits when the current recommended dosage schedule cures or controls the patient's disease?

*"**Independent research funding to answer these questions is essentially nonexistent** because most government and private funding agencies assume that these trials can be funded by industry and direct their limited funding support toward finding the answers to more basic science or epidemiological questions. The result is that, **overall, we actually have very little independent level A quality evidence on which to base clinical practice guidelines.***

*"**If this continues, the scientific basis for the delivery of health care will be determined primarily by private industry.**"*[92]

Indeed, there has been much valid criticism in the medical literature over what is termed "evidence based medicine" and "impact factor" in journal listings[93].

Consequently, the 'rationale' is often in the eye of the beholder. Another person might disagree, because the way they see the treatment might be based on another rationale.

---

[92] Embree, J., 2000 "Writing clinical guidelines with evidence-based medicine," *Canadian Journal of Infectious Diseases*, Nov-Dec;11(6):289–290. PMID:18159301

[93] Casadevall, A., 2014 "Causes for the persistence of impact factor mania," *mBio*, Mar 18;5(2):e00064-14. PMID:24643863

My opinion has to be seen in the context of having taken five years out of the hospital system, which has enabled me to do intensive broad research relating to core concepts that are applicable to everything I once did in the system.

It also has to do with seeing patients recover much faster from illnesses after using 'unconventional means', than they do within the so-called evidence base of convention.

So where to from here, in terms of medicine?

In 2014, there were over 600 measles cases reported in the USA, most of which occurred in an Amish community. No deaths or reports of long-term issues exist. In 2015, there was widespread hysteria through the country after an outbreak that allegedly began at Disneyland in California. A total of 136 cases were confirmed in California, 18% of whom were vaccinated, and 38% had unknown vaccine status. There was a large portion of cases in under-one year olds (11%), and over 20 year olds (56%). This was unheard of in the pre-vaccine era when 95% of all children experienced measles by age 15 and had life-long immunity. In 2015, the public was told that all of those children, who had measles before age 15, were at increased risk of dying from non-measles diseases in the two years after infection and that doctors in the pre-vaccine era didn't notice that occurrence. A full explanation and breakdown of that pseudoscientific theory can be found in my video series called **Manufacturing Consent** at http://tinyurl.com/zxn2fqp

58
Light At The End Of The Tunnel

The last five years have enabled me to treat patients in ways I was not free to do within the hospital system. Repeatedly, I have seen that most people, who are committed to their recovery, can manage their health problems without the use of chemical cluster bombs.

I see a huge untapped potential within the medical system, which, were it nurtured, would make mainstream medicine something people could trust, instead of run from.

I intend to recertify with the American Board of Internal Medicine (ABIM) because I believe that for the medical system to rise from the dead, to give those they serve the best chance of life, there have to be people inside the system prepared to stand behind solid research and try to provide a form of service excellence, which the current model ignores.

Unfortunately, the system cannot be changed from outside because anyone who stays outside the system is considered a quack or a relic; the medical equivalent of a tired old, antiquated, nursing-home patient. So much for wisdom coming with time and experience . . .

Being treated with scorn and disregard in the hospital, with my friend who had a pheochromocytoma, was an eye-opening experience. Even though the diagnosis was clear to me after the cursory hospital tests were done, and I said so at every possible opportunity, the doctors around me were blindly compromised by a perceived need to avoid malpractice, and their own goals and focuses. Ironically, these blinkers of thinking could have easily been turned against them had Lazarus died and his family's attorney pin-pointed the hospital's mistakes, and sued them for medical malpractice.

The mistakes caused by conflicts of interests, limited thinking ability, and callous disregard are the sorts of things I saw all through my practice, and have to stop if the medical system wants to regain a place of trust and respect.

Throughout the world, people continue to suffer needlessly at the hands of a system that ties doctors to the monkey-see-monkey-do mantra. The results are astonishingly high annual injury and death statistics for preventable medical error and hospital-acquired infections, with resultant disillusionment from patients, and legions of frustrated, drug-addicted, deeply unhappy, and suicidal doctors.

So often what happens is that, in disgust at this trail of disappointment, treatment failure, and destruction, people leave the system and silently turn to alternative medicine, while the system fills up with bright-eyed, idealistic, naïve doctors who have no idea what they are going to be shackled to.

The system's response to patients voting with their feet is to attack and belittle the health modalities these people choose.

More recently, proponents of mandatory vaccination have gone even further and written books about how alternative health modalities are dangerous and can kill. Interestingly, the data for such assertions is missing. You can be sure that if alternative medicine killed even a thousandth of the people that conventional medicine does, we would have the PMID numbers rammed down our throats at every turn to prove it.

From where I sit, it's counterproductive and futile for the medical system to come out swinging at alternative medicine.

If we are really interested in providing a service that people eagerly seek out and trust—because it works—then the first thing we should do is heal ourselves as doctors and stop practicing the sort of Sherman-tank medicine that leads those people to walk away in the first place.

To do this, we need to rethink the medical school syllabus and system of teaching completely. We need to produce doctors who really understand the physiological, ecological, and social drivers of illness, and who are not chained to pharmaceutically driven objectives and outcomes. We need to find a better means than loading medical students with a million dollars of student loans, which duct tapes their mouths and handcuffs them into the system. That, in itself, is an additional driver behind the atrocious annual suicide toll amongst doctors who feel that they have little to offer, other than a hammer and nail inside a factory.

I still believe that it's possible for the medical system to resurrect itself; to claim the wonder and excitement of healing, and put into practice the desires and ideals that most medical students have in their heads and hearts the first day they step into the dissection lab and pull the sheet off their assigned cadaver.

Change at medical school level requires several things to come into line:

To SEE the need for a paradigm shift in the first place: to recognize that the "saber-tooth curriculum"[94] only benefits corporate concepts, and not the needs of the patient.

To give value to, and implement, some of the really good information on foundational functional health, already in PubMed, instead of ignoring it.

---

[94] Peddiwell, A. J., 1939 *The Saber-Tooth Curriculum*,:New York, London: McGraw-Hill Book Co. ASIN: B0046LZIMY

To have the conviction that what is right for patients is the core philosophy upon which all else rests.

To understand the real basis of dis-ease and dis-stress.

To commit to teaching a form of medicine that helps stop disease in its early stages, so that the person doesn't fall off the cliff and need shoveling off the rocks of the beach-head.

It could be done. Partially.

For me though, the linchpin to seeing purpose in all this mess, and renewing the hope within me that led me into medicine in the first place, has been finding God of the Fourier waves; the God who I realized created the life of the person gifted to medical school as a cadaver.

As I study in PubMed, and see so much in science that could be used God's way, to support the immune system that He made, I have hope that these scientific truths will triumph over a politico-medical system run by Wall Street-driven pharmaceutical medicine, to the detriment of humanity. If these concepts, already elaborated on in scientific literature, were woven into the minds of doctors, then medical students wouldn't have to serially watch so many patients get worse and worse, with their end point being to lose a very important organ, or be dependent on lifelong drugs.

If 'healing medicine' was what medical schools enabled doctors to practice, perhaps we wouldn't see 400 medical doctors a year committing suicide under the weight of pervasive helplessness.

> *"It has been reliably estimated that on average the United States loses as many as 400 physicians to suicide each year (the equivalent of at least one entire medical school)."*[95]

---

[95] Andrew, L. B., et al., 2015 "Physician Suicide," *Medscape*, July
http://emedicine.medscape.com/article/806779-overview

We could do so much better than that. Truly functional medicine is what my hope is.

Truly functional medicine is where doctors know enough to reverse disease, and correct systemic and gut dysbiosis in order to help the body overcome infections while fortifying the immune system. It's where doctors are able to prevent or stave off autoimmunity, where parents aren't pressured by fear, coercion, and torment, and where doctors have confidence that they can teach people the principles of fully functioning health.

This is the medicine I now try to practice. In one sense, it has the potential to make me redundant because patients aren't dependent on me for the rest of their lives. On the other hand, instead of feeling dead and helpless, every day I look forward to giving people the tools to change their focus from fear and gloom, to positive action and resultant joy.

Over the past five years, it's been a revelation to watch newly educated families gain knowledge, confidence, and peace as they successfully challenge the walking dead within the system, and rise from the dead themselves.

About The Author

Dr. Suzanne Humphries is a private medical consultant with a current American Board of Internal Medicine certification in nephrology, who practices in Maine and Virginia.

She is co-author of *Dissolving Illusions: Disease, Vaccines, and the Forgotten History*, and has lectured throughout Scandinavia, the USA and New Zealand on vaccines, holistic health, infant immunity, and vitamin C. Many of her lectures are viewable on her YouTube channel. Epigenetics, infectious diseases, and the human microbiome are other areas of interest.

Made in the USA
Columbia, SC
30 November 2018